MURDER
ON STAUNTON ROAD

The Violent Death of
Charleston Daily Mail Owner
Juliet Staunton Clark

CHARLIE RYAN & MITCH EVANS

© 2020 Charlie Ryan and Mitch Evans

All rights reserved, including the right to reproduce this book or portions thereof in any form whatsoever.

ISBN 978-0-578-72362-4

Cover design by Rinck J. Heule
Interior design by M.J. Jacobs LLC

First printing 2020
Second Printing 2020

Printed in the USA

Library of congress Cataloging in Publication Data
Names: Ryan, Charlie & Evans, Mitch
Title: Murder On Staunton Road
About the unsolved murder of Juliet Staunton Clark

For further information about this book or to order additional copies, please visit our website: **murderonstaunton.com**

MURDER
ON STAUNTON ROAD

CHARLIE RYAN & MITCH EVANS

*"They covered
up all the fingerprints and footprints and did
not leave anything that would help us solve it."*

— FANNY STAUNTON OGILVIE

Dedicated to the memory of

JULIET LYELL STAUNTON (CLAY) CLARK

and

THE FAMILIES OF STAUNTON ROAD

CONTENTS

CONTENTS	IX
PERSONALITIES	XI
FOREWORD	1
INTRODUCTION	7
—ONE— August 21, 1953	13
—TWO— Florence & Gypsy	23
—THREE— Florence & Rhuel Merrill	29
—FOUR— Walter Eli Clark	35
—FIVE— The Charleston Daily Mail Is Born	41
—SIX— Walter, Lucy & Juliet	45
—SEVEN— At This Hour	53
—EIGHT— A Pool Of Blood	59
—NINE— "Literally Beaten To A Pulp"	65
—TEN— Where Is The Baby?	77
—ELEVEN— Search The Sewers!	83
—TWELVE— Night Visitors	91
—THIRTEEN— A Rumpled Green Rug	97
—FOURTEEN— Not A Joyful Person	103
—FIFTEEN— Dr. Fred Inbau	109
—SIXTEEN— Jumpin' John Copenhaver	117
—SEVENTEEN— Arch Alexander, Jr.	125
—EIGHTEEN— A Family Gathering	135
—NINETEEN— Not A Private Murder	141
—TWENTY— I Sketch Your World Exactly As It Goes	147
—TWENTY-ONE— Slicing "Baloney" With An Axe	151
—TWENTY-TWO— Ballpeen Hammer	157
—TWENTY-THREE— A Deep Dive	165
—TWENTY-FOUR— The Quiet Of A Thousand Living Rooms	169

—TWENTY-FIVE— *Gazette* Venom	*173*
—TWENTY-SIX— The Poor Man's Mickey Spillane	*179*
—TWENTY-SEVEN— A Sneak Punch	*185*
—TWENTY-EIGHT— Frederick M. (Fred) Staunton	*191*
—TWENTY-NINE— The Father Cried	*197*
—THIRTY— A Strange Parallel Of Murder	*203*
—THIRTY-ONE— Julie Clark Alexander	*207*
—THIRTY-TWO— The Perfect Crime	*213*
—THIRTY-THREE— "Something Stinks"	*221*
—THIRTY-FOUR— The Killer Will Be Found	*229*
—THIRTY-FIVE— By Suffrage Of Copenhaver	*239*
—THIRTY-SIX— The Old Town Won't Be The Same	*245*
—THIRTY-SEVEN— 2019–A Cold Case Indeed	*253*
—THIRTY-EIGHT— Significant Questions	*261*
—THIRTY-NINE— The Final Word From City Hall	*269*
—I.— Afterword	*281*
—II.— Early Staunton History	*321*
—III.— Notes	*337*
—IV.— Acknowledgments	*351*
—V.— Bibliography	*357*
—VI.— About The Authors	*367*
—VII.— Index	*371*

PERSONALITIES

THE FAMILIES

Thomas Staunton	The first Staunton to arrive in America
Doctor Joseph Marshall Staunton and Mary Elizabeth Wilber Staunton	The first Staunton family to arrive in Virginia, later West Virginia
Sidney, Wilber and Franklin Marshall Staunton	Sons of Dr. Joseph Marshall Staunton and Mary Elizabeth Wilber Staunton
Juliet Lyell Staunton (Clay) Clark	Owner of *The Charleston Daily Mail*
Buckner Clay, Sr.	Juliet (Clay) Clark's first husband
Walter Eli Clark	Juliet (Clay) Clark's second husband, the former governor of Alaska and founder of *The Charleston Daily Mail*
Lyell Buffington Clay and Buckner Woodford Clay, Jr.	Sons of Juliet Staunton (Clay) Clark and Buckner Clay, Sr.
Florence Garland Buffington (Ma Merrill)	Mother of Juliet Staunton (Clay) Clark and Frederick M. (Fred) Staunton
Edward Wilber Staunton	Ma Merrill's first husband
Rhuel Hampton Merrill	Ma Merrill's second husband
John Buffington Merrill, Sr.	Son of Florence and Rhuel
Mary Louise Agnew Merrill	Wife of John Merrill
Buffy Merrill Wallace	Daughter of John Merrill, Sr. and Mary Louise Agnew Merrill
John Buffington Merrill, Jr.	Eldest son of John Buffington Merrill, Sr. and Mary Louise Agnew Merrill
Richard Merrill	Second son of John Merrill and Mary Louise
Juliet (Julie) Clark Alexander	Daughter of Juliet Staunton (Clay) Clark and Walter Eli Clark
Arch Alexander, Jr.	Husband of Juliet Clark Alexander
Arch Alexander III (Jay)	Son of Juliet Clark Alexander and Arch Alexander, Jr.
Shelley Cuisset	Daughter of Juliet Clark Alexander and Arch Alexander, Jr.
Antoinette Monnier	Daughter of Juliet Clark Alexander and Pierre Monnier

Milton Ferguson	Uncle of Arch Alexander, Jr.
Frederick M. (Fred) Staunton	Brother of Juliet Staunton (Clay) Clark
Fanny (Fan) Staunton Ogilvie	Daughter of Frederick M. (Fred) Staunton and Elizabeth (Dip) Brightwell
Elizabeth (Betsy) Staunton Johnson	Daughter of Frederick M. (Fred) Staunton and Elizabeth (Dip) Brightwell
Florence Fleeson	Sister of Juliet Staunton (Clay) Clark
Tom Fleeson	Husband of Florence Fleeson, brother-in-law of Juliet Staunton (Clay) Clark
Juliette Buffington Enslow	Cousin of Juliet[1] Staunton (Clay) Clark's mother, Florence Garland Buffington (Ma Merrill) and daughter of Peter Cline Buffington, first mayor of Huntington, West Virginia
Charles Baldwin	Son of Juliette Buffington Enslow

JULIET STAUNTON CLARK'S EMPLOYEES

Bessie Smith	Juliet Staunton Clark's maid
John Woodson	Juliet Staunton Clark's houseman and chauffeur
Tom Toliver	Juliet Staunton Clark's gardener

CHARLESTON AND KANAWHA COUNTY OFFICIALS

John T. Copenhaver	Mayor
Dewey Williams	Charleston Police Chief
W.W. "Red" Fisher	Detective
Joe Craft	Detective Lieutenant
Rick Westfall	Detective
Herbert W. Bryan	Kanawha County Prosecutor
Charles Walker	Assistant Prosecutor
Dave Dickens	Detective

THE REPORTERS

Frank A. Knight	*The Charleston Gazette*
Don (Seagle) Marsh	*The Charleston Gazette*
Jim Hill	*The Charleston Gazette*

---

[1] Mrs. Enslow spelled her name "Juliette", rather than "Juliet".

Harry Hoffmann	*The Charleston Gazette*
Charlie Connor	*The Charleston Daily Mail*
Bob Mellace	*The Charleston Daily Mail*
Jack Maurice	*The Charleston Daily Mail*
William A. White	*The Pittsburgh Gazette*
Ruth Reynolds	*The New York Sunday News*

THE POLYGRAPH CONSULTANTS

Dr. Fred Inbau

John E. Reid

THE ATTORNEYS

Robert H.C. Kay

Jack Savage

THE DIVERS

Harold McGuffin

Thomas McGuffin

Tom McGuffin

Jeff Meade

—FOREWORD—
BY BROOKS McCABE

Brooks McCabe serves as a member of the West Virginia Public Service Commission. He is a former State Senator and great, great grandson of the eighth governor of West Virginia, Aretas Brooks Fleming.

Charlie Ryan and Mitch Evans have written a fascinating book reexamining the circumstances and family history surrounding the many unexplained details of the most famous and historically significant murder in the city of Charleston, West Virginia. The case was never solved and many details remain, to this day, shrouded in mystery.

Murder on Staunton Road; the Violent Death of Charleston Daily Mail Owner Juliet Staunton Clark reads like a smooth blending of a classic murder mystery and the history of one of Charleston's most prominent entrepreneurial families. The political and business repercussions of the crime, the family's unanswered questions, and the resulting change in the management philosophy of *The Charleston Daily Mail* would simmer for years within the city.

In recent decades this crime and its impact on Charleston have been largely relegated to a historical footnote in what many believe was the distant past when Charleston was reaching its heights as the center for much of the commerce and business development within West Virginia.

—FOREWORD—

The Staunton family[2] was one of the drivers of this new economy, and they congregated in a small subdivision of isolated houses in one of the early residential developments on the front side of South Hills, located just across the Kanawha River from downtown. The murder occurred on August 21, 1953 at Mrs. Clark's Staunton Road residence, in what everyone presumed was a safe, pristine, park-like setting.

In the early 1950s Charleston had reached the apex of its growth and development and had become the largest and most prosperous city in the state. *The Charleston Daily Mail* was the state's leading business newspaper and the publisher was Juliet Staunton Clark, widow of Walter Eli Clark, who was responsible for the building of the newspaper to its dominance. She was a powerful businesswoman known and respected by all.

Prosperity in Charleston during the 1950s was the product of half a century of concerted effort on the part of key business leaders. The Stauntons were in the middle of this dynamic business and civic community. Members of the Staunton family were business leaders in banking, insurance, interurban railways and bus lines, coal, land development, and a host of other businesses. Much of Charleston had their fingerprints on its development. Kanawha City, South Charleston, and Patrick Street were all locations of significant industrial development, driven, in part, by Staunton leadership.

Given this expertise in land development, it was no surprise in 1915 when the Stauntons decided to develop Staunton Road. By 1953, most of the Staunton family resided there. It was an ideal location, assumed to be as perfect as any residential neighborhood could be. All the residents were family or close friends. What could go wrong?

One summer evening in August 1953 would change everything.

---

[2] The surname Staunton was adopted by those who originated in the county of Nottingham—traced from the time of William the Conqueror. The Staunton name was later recorded in Virginia legal documents as both "Staunton" and "Stanton". Staunton decedents in West Virginia would spell the name as "Staunton", but pronounced it as "Stanton."

The murder sent shock waves through the city. The residents of Staunton Road were in utter disbelief and initially feared for their own safety. Local, state, and national press covered the ensuing investigations with all the flare and drama demanded from a fascinated readership. Here were the makings of a headline-grabbing story—power, wealth, and murder mixed with healthy doses of political drama.

Charleston Mayor John T. Copenhaver jumped into the fray immediately by taking control of the investigation. The Mayor and *The Charleston Gazette*, the state's leading Democratic newspaper, did not see eye to eye on most things. The handling of the murder investigation was to become a major bone of contention between their two opposing perspectives.

Complicating the situation was the high profile of the case, the lack of substantive leads, and the glaring eye of the national press. Months passed with little progress, and then a year passed with no arrests. As time went on, there were still no definitive conclusions or identification of the murderer. The case became cold, and investigation records were misplaced, lost or destroyed.

Murder on Staunton Road puts a renewed focus on this unsolved murder and on the personal tragedy suffered by the Staunton family. Sixty plus years later, the cold case has yet to be solved. Perhaps if lost records could be found and new forensic techniques applied, answers would be forthcoming. In the meantime, *Murder on Staunton Road* provides the best summary of the facts as they were developed. It also puts the Staunton family's business and civic contributions to the city of Charleston and the state of West Virginia into historical context.

The book fills a void and helps explain a difficult and emotional time in the city's history. All of this is done through rigorous historical research, including dozens of personal interviews with those who were present at the time and whose memories can still recall the events as if they were yesterday.

Murder on Staunton Road provides a glimpse of Charleston at a time of its greatest development but also shows the violent underbelly that all cities, to varying degrees, experience. Charlie Ryan and Mitch Evans should be congratulated for a job well done.

Brooks McCabe
Staunton Road
Charleston, West Virginia

I remember a sycamore tree I always pointed to as a kid climbing up Staunton Road. I kept looking at that sycamore—lightning striking it, catching on fire at one time—losing its limbs like the people on the hill. It was like a symbol of, my God—you know? This is what happens in life. It is so sad. The sycamore died and I said, "Yes, this is the symbol of Staunton Road."

—BETSY STAUNTON JOHNSON, DAUGHTER OF FRED STAUNTON, PUBLISHER OF *THE CHARLESTON DAILY MAIL*

—INTRODUCTION—

Murder On Staunton Road is the story of a homicide that occurred more than sixty years ago. Although decades old, it remains an open case within the Charleston, West Virginia, police department. Official police files of the brutal beating and subsequent death of Juliet Lyell Staunton Clay Clark, owner of *The Charleston Daily Mail*, are said to be missing, or could have been misplaced or intentionally removed.

Strange, because the Clark murder files were stored on the fourth floor of Charleston's City Hall, viewed often throughout the years by city detectives who were fascinated by the celebrated and unsolved slaying of so many years ago.

Juliet Clark, socialite owner of Charleston's afternoon newspaper, was brutally murdered in her home on a warm summer night in 1953. National and local newspapers chased the story at every turn. Colorful reporting and dramatic commentary centered on the murder, the antics of Charleston Mayor John T. Copenhaver, and the complex history of prominent families on fashionable Staunton Road—where Juliet Clark was beaten to death.

Mayor Copenhaver's management style was to fight sin and corruption—breaking down doors of illegal gin joints and leading police raids on houses of prostitution. The murder of one of Charleston's most prominent citizens upped the ante for the crime-busting mayor.

—INTRODUCTION—

Copenhaver faced a challenge that became increasingly complex as he sought to prove he could solve a hideous murder while protecting the reputations of prominent Charlestonians who were questioned in the aftermath of what one relative of the dead woman called, "this horrible event".

The Charleston Daily Mail, The Charleston Gazette, The Pittsburgh Gazette, New York Sunday News, the Associated Press and United Press of the 1950s covered Copenhaver and the Clark murder with great enthusiasm. Dialogue quoted in this book is from those newspaper accounts and personal interviews.

It is said that journalism is instant history that is ruled by deadlines. Reporters of the 1950s, who took delight in referring to themselves as "ink-stained wretches", lacked today's computer-generated grammar checks. Many of the news columns and editorials referenced in this account contain grammatical error. We present the reports verbatim, choosing not to alter them in any way.

The Charleston Daily Mail stepped gingerly through some of its reporting on the Clark murder, at times waiting for *The Charleston Gazette* to break sensitive news about its slain owner. Meantime, the *Gazette* seemed to suspect manipulation and cover-up in the investigation that touched the lives of some of Charleston's elite families. Among those were the descendants of Juliet Clark who would eventually become immensely wealthy.

The Charleston Gazette despised the city's Mayor Copenhaver, but he was impossible to ignore, especially when reporting the Clark murder investigation. The newspaper's wall-to-wall coverage of Copenhaver seemed to further empower him, even as the *Gazette* disparaged his actions. During the Clark investigation, reporters waited in hallways at the city's police department and outside the mayor's office as the controversial mayor placed himself in total control of perhaps the biggest crime ever committed in Charleston.

In the 1950s the competition between Charleston's two newspapers, the *Gazette* and *Daily Mail,* was fierce. Each publication rushed multiple editions to the streets during the day and evening. The morning newspaper often waited for the final run of the evening *Daily Mail,* holding breaking news the *Gazette* had uncovered before blasting away with its "Blue Streak" press run later in the afternoon or evening.

Gazette editor and columnist Frank Knight and political columnist Harry Hoffmann were constant arrows in Mayor Copenhaver's side throughout his time as the city's chief executive. Copenhaver withstood their blistering assaults and won three terms as mayor. He was exceedingly popular throughout the state and twice sought the governor's office.

The mayor's boldness in usurping the case from veteran police investigators added to the *Gazette's* ongoing criticism of His Honor, evident in its editorials, some on its front page. Mayor Copenhaver, no shrinking violet, vigorously responded to the *Gazette*, calling it, "vile."

In 1953 the papers that landed on the porches of the nation were the primary source of news, competing only with radio—television news was born at the turn of the decade, but it was nascent in its 1953 presence. Newspaper profit margins of the era easily accommodated generous allocations of newsprint and ink, allowing for extensive advertising content and loquacious reporters who wrote reams of material.

"Hard" reporting of the time centered on crime, scandal, politics, government, business, and weather. "Feature" coverage extended to colorful personalities, historic families, entertainment, women's clubs, service clubs, travel, beauty, animals, and religion. Extensive editorial pages provided unbridled opinion and political columns—the plethora of information was topped off with an impressive array of comic strips.

The *Charleston Daily Mail* was proud of its extraordinary history and, between 1963 and the present, the story of the *Mail* and

—INTRODUCTION—

its founder, Walter Clark, has been printed in Charleston newspapers several times. However, those histories do not mention the murder of Clark's widow, Mrs. Juliet Staunton Clark. The brutal slaying also seemed to be a subject rarely discussed in the *Daily Mail* newsroom.

When the authors asked the knowledgeable and remarkably informed former *Daily Mail* business editor George Hohmann if he had memories of comments by older *Daily Mail* staffers about the Clark murder, he replied that he knew all about the former governor of Alaska, Walter Clark, but had never known his widow, Juliet Clark was murdered.

George Hohmann
-Charleston Daily Mail

Jim Reader, a distinguished former broadcast journalist in Charleston, said his wife Kay, who passed away in 2014, had researched the Clark murder for a number of years.

Reader said Kay, a veteran reporter of many years at both *The Charleston Daily Mail* and *The Charleston Gazette*, would be pleased to know that the Clark case has been re-visited. Reader said Kay had done superb work in researching and writing about several murder cases, including that of Charleston banker LaRoy Gorman. Her stories were well received by the *Daily Mail* and readers of the afternoon newspaper.

However, when she began researching the Clark murder, Reader said Kay was told to stop her research—there would be no story.

When Kay left the *Mail* and joined the *Gazette*, Reader said, she asked management if the *Gazette* would be interested in the Clark story she had researched. The answer was yes, and Kay began working once more toward publication of her story. Shortly thereafter, Reader said, she was told the *Gazette* had decided it would not publish the story.

Kay Michael Reader
–Charleston Gazette

"Kay was passionate about the stories she worked on, was thorough and accurate. She put people in jail. While we almost never discussed stories, this stood out because she was frustrated. She felt it was important to revisit the events," Reader said.

This, it is hoped, is the "revisit" that a remarkable journalist, Kay Reader, felt was so important—here are the events and aftershocks of late August 1953 in Charleston, West Virginia—when a heinous murder of a prominent newspaper owner and the actions of a zealous mayor set in motion intrigue, fascination and wonder in Charleston and the nation.

—ONE—
AUGUST 21, 1953

High above the city of Charleston, West Virginia, on a winding path beneath overhanging rocks, a road was built that hugged the hillside as it wound upward to the very top of an expanse that became home to pioneer families descended from notables in England, Ireland and Wales. Families that lived and died on Staunton Road boasted histories of love, ambition, service to their fellow man—and a heinous murder.

August 21, 1953, a Friday morning, and 59 year-old Juliet Staunton Clay Clark, owner of *The Charleston Daily Mail*, was back in town from one of her many travels. She lived on Staunton Road in a home she had built in 1952 following the death of her second husband, Walter Eli Clark. The choice piece of property on which she would build her home was a gift from her mother, Florence Garland Buffington Staunton Merrill, who wanted her nearby.

Juliet awakened early, put on her dressing gown, and went to her kitchen. There, she retrieved a can of drip grind coffee from the cupboard, poured tap water into a pot, and carefully counted out five tablespoons of ground coffee. Placing them in her percolator, she began her morning brew.

Juliet then moved to a nearby bedroom to check on her grandson Jay, who had spent the night with her. Jay's father had asked his mother-in-law to keep the three-year-old as he dealt with the death of one of the twin girls born to him and his wife just days before. Juliet felt a deep loss as she looked at her sleeping grandson and thought of the granddaughter she would never know.

She softly closed the door to Jay's room and walked to her front door. There, she reached down onto the small stoop of the home and retrieved the morning newspaper, *The Charleston Gazette*. She returned to the kitchen, poured her coffee, and with the *Gazette* under her arm, went to her breakfast room.

She placed the coffee on a side table, sat down, and opened the paper, glancing at a headline that said, "France Exiles Sultan In Moroccan Upheaval." To the left and above the newspaper front-page fold was a picture of "globe-trotting" Adlai Stevenson, who was quoted as saying the U.S. was winning the Cold War.

Juliet turned to the editorial page where the *Gazette* was endorsing United States Supreme Court Justice Felix Frankfurter's refusal to resign, thus preventing a Republican administration's replacement of him. A second opinion warned readers that there were severe consequences if one did not timely report income to the IRS, and a third dwelt on the importance of baseball—Charleston was baseball crazy, Juliet knew. The *Toledo Mud Hens* had, in 1952, abandoned financially troubled Toledo, Ohio, relocating in Charleston[3], where, on April 21, 1953, they took the field at Watt Powell Park as a Triple-A minor-league team affiliated with the Chicago White Sox. They were the *Charleston Senators*.

Juliet returned to the *Gazette* front page and carefully read a story below the fold that detailed the eagerly anticipated results of Dr. Alfred Kinsey's research on sex. The report had broken on *Daily Mail* time and her interest was the result of intense debate at the *Daily Mail* the prior afternoon on whether to publish the *Kinsey Report*—it was highly controversial.

The *Mail* publisher and editorial staff decided to print Kinsey's

---

[3] Source: Charleston Senators, Charleston Wheelers History, Major League Baseball.

research, but with a disclaimer that said, "*The Daily Mail*, in deciding to publish the findings of Dr. Kinsey's Report, realizes that the necessary frankness of statement in the article may offend some readers. But it is felt that the importance of the 15-year study outweighs its possibly objectionable features, and that the findings should be published as a public service."

Juliet's male-dominated *Daily Mail* staff was prudent in its disclaimer, but could not resist headlining the story, "Dr. Kinsey's Findings On Female Sexual Behavior Bared." The newspaper pointed out that the study had determined that "the only basic difference between men and women in sex is mental."

The *Mail* editorial page commented on that, saying, "Despite the study of numerous scientists, the mystery of Woman (sic) remains. It is the opinion of this department, which certainly is no expert on femininity, that neither Dr. Kinsey, nor anyone else, will ever dispel it entirely."

Juliet must have grimaced at her employees' efforts to handle the *Kinsey Report* prudently, while not being able to fully restrain themselves. She moved on, reading for almost an hour, looking up from the paper only when she heard the back door, never locked, swing open into the kitchen.

A lyrical voice cheerfully called a good morning and Juliet responded to her housemaid, Bessie Smith, who had just walked up Staunton Road from her bus stop on Louden[4] Heights Road. Bessie knew of the death of Mrs. Clark's granddaughter and, walking into the breakfast room, she gave condolences to her employer, as she had the morning prior.

Bessie then returned to the kitchen and prepared a light breakfast for Mrs. Clark. She carried it to the breakfast room, placing a small plate with buttered toast and jam on the side table. She retrieved Juliet's empty coffee cup and carried it to the kitchen.

---

[4] Louden Heights Road has been spelled at different times as "Louden" and "Loudon".

Juliet Staunton Clay Clark
Charleston Daily Mail –
circa 1950.

There, she refilled the cup, and walked back to the breakfast room, setting fresh coffee beside Juliet, asking if she needed anything else.

The sound of an approaching automobile told Juliet her houseman and chauffeur, John Woodson, had arrived. She picked up the coffee cup, walked to her bedroom, and dressed for the day in her usual attire—a tailored suit of conservative taste that subtly suggested status and power. She placed on her head a crown cap hat[5] with a net veil and ribbon. Juliet, a strikingly beautiful woman years before, had, at 59, taken on a matronly look with demure dress and style.

Walter Eli Clark, Juliet Clark's second husband–Circa 1914.
–Charleston Daily Mail

Juliet gave Bessie instructions on the care of Jay during the day and turned to John Woodson who waited to drive her to her office at the *Daily Mail*. Woodson escorted his employer to her automobile and opened the door to the back seat. Juliet sat in comfort as Woodson backed the automobile out of the driveway of the home and began his ascent to the apex of Staunton Road, topping the hill and starting down toward the intersection of Staunton and Lower Ridgeway Road, driving past a large sycamore tree.

The owner of the largest afternoon newspaper in West Virginia gazed down at the valley below as Woodson turned onto Louden Heights Road, skillfully maneuvering the twists and turns toward the South Side Bridge and the downtown business district on the north side of the Kanawha River.

---

[5] The type hat Mrs. Clark wore could also be called a "Juliette" hat, a popular style of the day. She may have whimsically chosen the style "Juliette" as a nod to her name, even though she was christened "Juliet".

AUGUST 21, 1953

A smile appeared on Juliet's face as she looked downward toward the steel, brick and Indiana limestone gray building that housed *The Charleston Daily Mail*. Her late husband, Walter Eli Clark, had, in 1927[6], built the impressive structure.

Juliet knew that Clark's optimism for the future of the Charleston market and his newspaper was prescient. Great economic growth had come to the capital city since that day in 1927 when her husband had invested heavily in a modern newspaper plant.

Buckner Clay, Sr. Juliet Clark's first husband —Circa 1903.
—Courtesy of Spilman Thomas & Battle's History of Service, The First 150

Now, in 1953, the city's population had grown to 73,000 residents, almost twice the size of Lexington, Kentucky, chasing Charlotte, North Carolina's expansion. Juliet, and most everyone in West Virginia, *knew* Charleston was destined to be one of the great cities of the South—fueled by coal, petrochemicals, and state government, employing thousands.

Hundreds of well-paid clerks worked on Capitol Street where shoppers flocked to Frankenbergers Men's Store, Embees, Palmer's Shoe Store and many other retail outlets. *The Daily Mail* employed a cadre of salesmen in its business offices. Monday through Friday, they fanned out into the bustling business sectors to sell newspaper advertising space, a commodity that banks,

---

[6] The building was completed April 17, 1927. The Mail then moved from what is now the location of the West Virginia Career College. Source: Our History, *The Charleston Daily Mail*.

automobile dealerships and retailers, large and small, could not do without.

At Christmas, Charleston's major department stores, The Diamond, Stone & Thomas and Coyle & Richardson, purchased multiple full-page newspaper ads targeting holiday shoppers. Exquisite window decorations attracted hundreds, curious to view what were always scenes of extraordinary creativity. The Diamond's holiday lights—thousands of them—illuminated the intersection crosswalk to the Daniel Boone Hotel where 465 guest rooms awaited weary shoppers from around the tri-state.

Packages deposited in their rooms, travelers spent the evening at the "Boone" in upscale dining, served by waiters in formal dress who delivered thick steaks and fresh seafood to tables draped in white linen. Meals were topped off with sumptuous desserts— finger bowls adorned the tables—roving minstrels toured the hotel, singing of holiday cheer. Charleston was a delightful city in which to live and offered cosmopolitan amenities to its residents and visitors.

Juliet Clark's *Charleston Daily Mail* chronicled every aspect of the opulence of the metropolitan area. Her husband had created a newspaper that easily and aggressively melded with the needs of a flourishing city and state, earning remarkable financial gain through a strong subscriber base and hundreds of businesses eager to grow through print advertising.

Walter Clark seldom left Juliet's mind. He had arrived in Charleston in 1914 when she was 20 years old. Two years later Juliet would marry prominent Charleston attorney, Buckner Clay.

The Clays and Clarks became social acquaintances, chatting at Edgewood Country Club and public events. Juliet and Buckner were impressed with Clark's political and journalistic credentials and the Clays quickly became good friends with Walter and his wife Lucy.

AUGUST 21, 1953

Neither Juliet nor Walter knew their lives would be forever entwined.

Juliet was widowed when 45 year-old Buckner Clay died in 1923. Among her husband's pallbearers were Juliet's brother Fred Staunton, Clay's law partner R.S. Spilman, Charles K. Payne—and Walter Eli Clark.

In 1928, five years after Buckner Clay's death, Walter Clark's wife Lucy died. Fifteen months following Lucy's death, Walter married Juliet Clay on August 13, 1929. Theirs was a whirlwind romance. Walter, at 60 years of age, was 25 years older than 35-year-old Juliet. She had no problem with their age difference and he was unconcerned that Juliet had two sons by her first marriage.

Soon, a child was born to the Clarks, a daughter who was called "Julie". It was a storybook life with three children in their home and Juliet and Walter were wonderfully happy. Then, in 1950, after 21 years of his second marriage, Walter Clark died of a heart attack.

Juliet was devastated but remained regal in stature, carrying herself with great dignity and poise. However, she was lonely in a large home on the corner of Virginia Street, East and Elizabeth Street—where the presence of Walter Clark was felt in every room.

Juliet's children, Lyell Buffington, Buckner Woodford, Jr., and Juliet Staunton, had become of age and had left the nest. Fulfilling a desire to be closer to her sons, daughter and relatives who lived in South Hills, she sold her downtown

The home of Walter Eli Clark and Juliet Clark at 1598 Virginia Street, East, Charleston. −Mitch Evans

home to prominent Charleston attorney Charles Love and built a new, smaller residence on Staunton Road. She continued to live alone, however, with servants John Woodson and Bessie Smith present during daylight hours.

With the move, Juliet regularly had dinner with her sons and daughter and often spent Sunday evenings visiting her relatives the Merrills, Stauntons, and Fleesons on Staunton Road.

Family ties were strong, but there remained a void with Walter Clark gone. Juliet refused to let depression make a claim. At Walter's death she became owner of the newspaper her husband had built to great heights, and she took command, visiting her office at the *Charleston Daily Mail* each day she was in town. Those days became fewer, however, as she began to travel widely.

Her thoughts were interrupted as her driver turned right off the South Side Bridge, coming to a stop in front of the offices of the *Daily Mail* at 1001 Virginia Street, East. John Woodson got out of the car and opened the rear passenger door for Mrs. Clark, taking her hand to assist her exit from the vehicle. Juliet thanked him as he followed her to the front door of the newspaper, opened it for her, tipped his hat, and bade her good morning.

Those in the business offices on the first floor of the afternoon newspaper greeted her as she strode toward the elevator that took her to the second floor. There, news reporters at their typewriters and editors composing opinion waved hello and smiled as the aristocratic owner entered her office and removed her hat.

She sat at her desk and began to look at correspondence as a secretary inquired if she wanted coffee. She thought her older son, Buckner Clay, Jr., who worked at the *Mail*, might drop by. However, Buckner, known by one and all as "Buck", had a busy day and did not visit his mother's office that Friday. He would always regret it.

Juliet spent the day in the usual manner, with friends and employees. She was an imposing figure to all and she acted as an owner, but she left the day-to-day operations of the newspaper to her brother, Fred Staunton, whom she had named publisher when her husband died.

She returned home that afternoon and quickly checked on her grandson Jay. Then she said goodbye for the day to Bessie Smith and John Woodson.

She would never see them again.

For Juliet Staunton Clark, August 21, 1953, would end in horror.

—TWO—
FLORENCE & GYPSY

Juliet Staunton Clark's mother, Florence Garland Buffington, was born in Huntington, West Virginia, June 25, 1872, daughter of Dr. John Buffington and his second wife, Julia Lyell Garland[7], of Sharps Wharf, Virginia. Dr. Buffington's first wife, Maria Thompson, of Culpepper, Virginia, had died. Florence was raised in Huntington, attended Marshall Academy[8], and later, Mary Baldwin[9], a school for young women in Staunton, Virginia. She then furthered her education at the Cincinnati Conservatory of Music, where she studied voice.

In 1890, Florence was eighteen and about to transition to higher education at Marshall Academy. The college crowd and the young people it attracted would bring new faces to Huntington—and forge for Florence a fresh and exciting new friendship with a girl from Fairmont, West Virginia—Caroline Fleming.

Caroline's father was the new Governor of West Virginia, Aretas Brooks Fleming[10]. In 1890 Fleming was preparing to move from Fairmont to Charleston to take office as the eighth governor of

---

[7] Cited by W. Sydney Laidley, second cousin to and in response to a letter from Florence Garland Buffington Staunton Merrill.

[8] Now Marshall University.

[9] Now Mary Baldwin University.

[10] Fleming served only a three-year term from 1890-1893 because of a dispute over the 1888 gubernatorial election.

the state. He, his wife, the former Carrie Watson, and their teenage daughter, Caroline, were busily packing their belongings to begin the journey to the seat of government. Caroline was leaving childhood friends and a life she knew and loved. She would need to adjust to a new and very public environment.

It was not easy, but the governor's daughter, known in Fairmont for her love of a good time, quickly began to seek social events upon moving into the Governor's Mansion. There was a college town 50 miles from Charleston, and Caroline, probably to the chagrin of her parents, began to regularly travel to Huntington to attend parties. There she met a young and vivacious girl, Florence Garland Buffington. The girls were four years apart in age and they quickly bonded—so much so that Florence took Caroline to her home where she met Florence's mother, Julia, and her stepfather, Frank Enslow[11].

June, 1892-Gypsy Ward, sitting on the side of a chair in which her father, Governor Aretas Brooks Fleming sits.
–Brooks McCabe collection

Florence and her friends were enthralled with Caroline and began to call her "Gypsy" because of her dark complexion and black hair—she was lovely. She *looked* like a gypsy and turned a lot of heads among the young collegians around Marshall Academy and the town of Huntington—"She was so attractive and created such a fluttering of hearts among young men[12]."

Florence and Gypsy "danced with the best of them[13], floating

---

[11] Florence's father, Dr. Buffington, died in 1878 after being thrown from a horse. Her mother then married Frank Enslow. Julia and Frank Enslow moved to Charleston, where Florence met and later married Edward Wilber Staunton on her 20th birthday, June 25, 1892 at St. John's Episcopal Church.

[12] The Herald Dispatch, June 25, 1959. This article begs the question of how Gypsy would have traveled to and from Huntington for the club dances. It was most probably by the C&O Railroad.

[13] *The Charleston Gazette* feature by Sandy Wells.

Gypsy Ward
–Brooks McCabe collection
circa 1900

around the third ballroom floor of Michael's Hall on the Marshall Academy Campus—listening to the music of Frank Leroy's orchestra playing 'After the Ball'."

The two girls became wildly popular at town and college parties. In 1889 the young men of the area decided to form a dance club. Club membership would be male and by invitation only. The men were to bring lady guests with them.

Out-of-town guests, male or female, were permitted, providing they resided more than 25 miles from Huntington. That allowed Gypsy Fleming to come aboard. The 25-mile stipulation may have been premeditated because the dancing males had decided as they formed the club that they would name their effort the "Gypsy Club" in honor of the governor's daughter. It would become the oldest elite dance club in the state, and was still active 130 years later.

The sole object was to dance the night away. Drinking of liquor was not allowed and propriety was uppermost in the club's bylaws. It was considered totally improper for a young girl to journey home in the dark in a cab or "hack" with a young man.

Usually, several couples would drive to and from the club in the same conveyance. Family-owned double rigs or phaetons[14] were pressed into service and young men and women living near dance venues were walked home, quite often in a group.

Gypsy and Florence enjoyed the company of each other throughout Governor Fleming's term, becoming best friends. The apple of the governor's eye had a flair about her that delighted all she encountered. Gypsy was electrifying and outgoing, with dignity, elegance, and gentility. She also was—*different*—those who met her would never forget her.

Within a short time, Florence's parents moved from Huntington

---

[14] A light, open, four wheeled, horse-drawn carriage.

to Charleston. It was a serendipitous move for Florence—she would be in the same town as her best friend Gypsy. They would remain there for the rest of their lives.

Gypsy met, fell in love with, and married Charles Edwin Ward, who owned Charleston's Ward Engineering Works. Ward was on his way to substantial wealth, and Gypsy and he purchased several sizable lots on Staunton Road and built a large home they named "Stoneleigh[15]" on what would become Lower Ridgeway Road in Charleston's South Hills.

Gypsy and her foremost friend, Florence, would eventually live as close neighbors—it was fortuitous because Florence sorely needed the loving companionship of Gypsy when her husband, Edward Wilber Staunton, died unexpectedly in 1904 at age 40. His death left Florence a widow with five children—a sixth child had died at birth.

Gypsy rushed to give Florence emotional support, sitting with her through days of despair, accompanying her to social events, providing constant encouragement— slowly bringing gaiety and humor back to Florence's life, erasing some of the anguish of losing a husband who died at such an early age.

Years passed, and Gypsy was elated when Florence was attracted to a Presbyterian minister who had come to town. The Reverend Rhuel Hampton Merrill would marry Florence and eventually build a home for his new wife on Staunton Road. It was just a short walk from Gypsy and Charles Edwin Ward's Stoneleigh residence on Lower Ridgeway Road.

---

[15] In 1916 the Wards would build the first permanent home on Staunton Road as a wedding present to their daughter, Margaret Fleming Ward and Robert E. McCabe. It was christened as "Dalgain". The home later became vacant for over fifteen years and fell into disrepair. The Ward's great grandson, Brooks Fleming McCabe, Jr., and his wife Barbara Given McCabe then acquired Dalgain and fully restored it. The home is listed on the National Register of Historic places. It is an American Four Square design with Italianate influences, featuring a white stucco exterior and a green tiled shingled roof. H. Russ Warne designed the home. His firm still exists in Charleston as Silling Associates.

FLORENCE & GYPSY

"Gypsy was a real heart-breaker, pretty and petite with soft dark hair and flirty eyes...reared amid the grandeur of the coal market[16] at the turn of the century...she built a mansion on the hill, Stoneleigh. She had beautiful clothes, several servants, a yacht, a bountiful flower and vegetable garden[17]."

Gypsy never lost her flair. She danced, partied, and hid bootleg whiskey in the attic of Stoneleigh[18]. "She liked a certain brand of Scotch, Teacher's Highland Cream. Miss Gypsy was quite a girl."

"She was a delightful, intelligent and handsome lady," Charleston insurance executive Ruffner Payne said. Buffy Merrill Wallace[19] said Gypsy was very fond of Payne and wanted him to purchase Stoneleigh when she died.

He did[20].

---

[16] Gypsy's mother, Caroline Watson Fleming, was the oldest daughter of James Otis Watson, who was the founder of what became the Fairmont Coal Company, the predecessor to the Consolidated Coal Company.

[17] Source: *The Charleston Gazette* column by Sandy Wells.

[18] Recalled by Miss Gypsy's great grandson, Brooks Fleming McCabe, Jr.

[19] Mary Louise Merrill, daughter of John Merrill, Sr., owed her nickname "Buffy" to Gypsy. Buffy said, "My parents were calling me Molly and Miss Gypsy looked at me and said, 'That's not a Molly. That's a baby Buffy.' And I've been Buffy ever since."

[20] Ruffner Payne was married to Dorothy McCabe, who was the younger sister of Margaret Fleming Ward's husband, Robert E. McCabe.

—THREE—
FLORENCE & RHUEL MERRILL

Gypsy Ward was not alone in watching over and caring for the young widow Florence Garland Buffington Staunton. Following her husband Wilber's death, his brothers Sidney and Frederick Marshall Staunton hovered over Florence and her family—providing any assistance wherever needed. With their support, she continued to live in Charleston with her five young children, Juliet Lyell, Florence Buffington (Houncie), Edward Wilber, Jr., Katherine Brewster, and Frederick Marshall.

Florence and the children faithfully attended the Kanawha Presbyterian Church[21] where her family had worshipped for many years. She was a striking beauty and the new minister at Kanawha Presbyterian, Rhuel Merrill, may have fought back thoughts of pursuing the widow Staunton even as he presided at the funeral of her deceased husband.

As time passed and the Reverend Merrill preached his sermon each Sunday morning, he became totally smitten, looking down on his congregation, his gaze dwelling on a young woman with five children.

---

[21] Isaac Noyes purchased the land for the Kanawha Presbyterian Church following his wife's recovery from a grave illness. –*1876 History of Kanawha County*, by George Atkinson.

FLORENCE & RHUEL MERRILL

Florence was from one of Charleston's most prominent families. Pursuing her would be complicated—but he was the son of a Dutch couple—stubborn and determined, believing in the axiom, "Faint heart ne'er won fair lady."

Rhuel was born in 1867 in Vienna, New Jersey, a suburb of Hackettstown. He attended Wyoming Seminary, a private school in Wilkes-Barre, Pennsylvania, where he was valedictorian. He was given an appointment to West Point, which he was unable to accept, because he was deaf in one ear.

After teaching school for two years Rhuel won a scholarship to and graduated from Rutgers University. He attended Center College of Kentucky where he took his pre-ministerial training. He then went on to Auburn Theological Seminary in Auburn, New York, completing his divinity degree. His first church was the Second Presbyterian Church in Binghamton, New York.

In 1897 the Reverend Merrill was called to lead the Kanawha Presbyterian Church. There, his courtship of Florence Garland Staunton began.

She and the bachelor minister fell in love and married, with Rhuel bravely taking on the responsibility of helping to rear the five Staunton children.[22] Florence and Rhuel's marriage soon learned the good news that the new Mrs. Merrill was pregnant. A daughter was born to the couple, but died at birth.

Grieving for the lost child, the Merrills moved to Pittsburgh where Rhuel was called to minister the Craf-

Florence Buffington Staunton Merrill (Ma Merrill), 1872-1952.
– *Brewster King's Journal*

[22] Florence (called "Houncie"), Juliet Lyell, Edward Wilber, Jr., Katharine (called "Kay"), and Frederick Marshall.

ton Presbyterian Church. Florence became pregnant once more and John Buffington Merrill was born in Pittsburgh on December 21, 1910. As an adult he would wed Mary Louise Agnew of Charleston.

During the time the Merrills lived in Pittsburgh they often visited family in Charleston, braving rudimentary secondary roads. The frequent sojourns enabled their children to keep their ties with their West Virginia cousins. During one such visit, their daughter Katharine Brewster Staunton met Lewis Newton Thomas, son of a prominent Charleston family. Katharine and Lewis were married December 10, 1924.

In yet another visit back to Charleston, the Staunton daughter Juliet met young lawyer Buckner Woodford Clay, her husband-to-be. Clay was a handsome attorney and member of a growing law firm, *Price, Smith & Spilman*.[23]

The Merrill family moved back to Charleston in the summer of 1919 when Rhuel retired from the ministry. They lived on Kanawha Boulevard until 1921 when they moved to Grosscup Road. They later built "Briarwood"[24] at 1240 Staunton Road, moving there on October 24, 1924. Later, the Reverend Merrill built a carriage house that included a library.

Rhuel was said to be a lovely man, kind, courteous, devoted to his wife and six youngsters—never showing any deference to the child of his and Florence's to the detriment of his five step-children. At family dinners the Reverend carved the meat for the family and, with numerous mouths to feed, found his children asking for servings of seconds by the time he sat down. A relative, Brewster Buffington King, said Rhuel exercised by "rolling around on his stomach, hoping, I guess, to wear it down a little."

---

[23] *Spilman, Thomas & Battle's History Of Service, The First 150 Years*, 2014, page 35, by Elizabeth Jill Wilson.

[24] The English Tudor style house is found on the National Register of Historic Places.

FLORENCE & RHUEL MERRILL

In conservative Charleston the match of Florence and Rhuel had been the subject of much conversation—Buffy Merrill Wallace remembered that the courtship caused eyebrows to be raised—and that the soubriquet "Ma" Merrill was given to Florence Garland somewhere along the way. Buffy reminisced:

Miss Sadie Barber, a young girl at the time, said it was the talk of the church when the Reverend Merrill started courting the widow Staunton. After their marriage, he was called to Crafton Heights Church in Pittsburgh. It was there that my father, John, was born in 1910.

Ma Merrill and Grandfather Rhuel Merrill, who had been given a doctorate by Grove City College in Pittsburgh, retired back here. They ended up buying 23 acres in South Hills. Grandfather Merrill hired an English architect who designed their house, which they called "Briarwood".

When my parents[25] got married Ma Merrill and Daddy Merrill were elderly. Daddy Merrill died in 1942, my parents were living with them and continued to stay with them to assist Ma Merrill. My mother, Mary Louise Agnew, went to work with my father at Merrill Photo. My grandmother Merrill helped raise my brother John and me in their big house.

Brewster Buffington[26] King contrasted Ma Merrill's first husband, Will Staunton, to Rhuel, writing, "I imagine that living with a dynamo...who also had periods of sinking to the danger point of weakness, must have been very difficult for Ma Merrill and I'm sure the contrast with the nice, even, Daddy Merrill was a delight to her and that she looked back on her life with Will as being

---

[25] John Buffington Merrill, Sr., and Mary Louise Agnew Merrill.

[26] The Staunton family had impressive lineage that dated to the Mayflower and Elder William Brewster of Scrooby, Nottinghamshire, who was a senior member of the Mayflower Colony and one of the founders of New Plymouth, Massachusetts. The Brewsters and Stauntons came together in the eighth generation of Brewsters when Sally Brewster married John Warren Staunton. The union begat Joseph Marshall Staunton who married Mary Elizabeth Wilber–their son Edward Wilber married Florence Buffington and she married Gordon Coltart King. They had three children, Gordon Coltart, King, Jr., Morris Larimer King, and Brewster Buffington King.

somewhat more difficult."

Ma Merrill—Florence Buffington—was indeed fortunate that Rhuel Merrill came into her life. She and her children were heartbroken when Rhuel died October 30, 1942. Ma Merrill would die ten years later on September 5, 1952. Her great friend Gypsy Ward died two years later, in 1954, of a heart attack. She was in Florida, visiting her daughter Margaret Fleming Ward and son-in-law, Robert E. McCabe.

Florence was remembered as a quiet, warm, and intelligent person who loved not only to dance, but was fond of canaries. Florence was meticulous. In her later life she kept day clothing neatly folded on one chair so that if she became ill during the night she could easily dress before the doctor arrived.

Florence's grandchildren had close and loving relationships with her. Granddaughter Buffy Merrill Wallace said, "My grandmother is buried between Mr. Staunton (the first husband) and Rhuel Merrill (the second husband). When Wally (Buffy's husband) and I got married he said, 'I can't imagine this woman buried between two husbands!' I said, 'Well, my gosh, I'm sure Will Staunton was eternally grateful that Doctor Merrill came along and raised his five children who would have been fatherless."

"The year my grandmother died, in September of '52, I was probably in the seventh grade and went to Thomas Jefferson Junior High. My parents were always so thankful that Ma Merrill died before this horrible event happened to her eldest daughter."

John Buffington Merrill, Jr., whose father rode his horse "Flashlight" through the pastures of South Hills, also had fond memories of his time with his grandmother at Briarwood:

My grandmother built the house in the 1920s. It had six bedrooms—big. We used to laugh—everyone had a different bedroom. If I came home late and someone was in my bedroom, I'd go to another bedroom. Ma Merrill, to a degree, raised us right there

FLORENCE & RHUEL MERRILL

At Briarwood, the Merrill home on Staunton Road. John Buffington Merrill, Sr.'s friend Ben Grosscup is on the left; 9-year-old John is to the right on his horse "Flashlight".
–Merrill family
circa 1919

in that house. She lived in nice style. She had a fulltime cook, yardman, and housemaid.

She was in her late 60s when I was born and I always considered her an elderly lady. She was diabetic and took insulin. When I was six years old I would go in mornings and crawl up in bed with her. She would rub my back.

When she died, I found her body. She was a dear lady.

—FOUR—
WALTER ELI CLARK

In 1914, a young entrepreneur arrived in Charleston, West Virginia. His name was Walter Eli Clark, and he had impressive credentials. He was born January 7, 1869[27] to Oren Andrus and Jeanette (Jones) Clark in Ashford, Connecticut. He attended local public schools and then graduated from the Connecticut State Normal School.

Upon graduation, at age 19, Clark taught school at Waterville, Connecticut and then became Principal at a Manchester, Connecticut grade school. In 1891 he enrolled at Williston Seminary and upon graduation entered Wesleyan University, graduating with a Bachelor of Philosophy in 1895.

Following Wesleyan, Clark entered journalism. He worked for the *Hartford Post* as a reporter, staying there only a short time until moving to Washington, D.C. where he landed a job as telegraph editor for

Young Walter Eli Clark, circa 1900
–Wikipedia

---
[27] Some publications listed the date of birth as 1866.

the *Washington Times* and Capitol correspondent for the *New York Commercial Advertiser*.

In Washington, Clark met Lucy Harrison Norvell, originally from Lynchburg, Virginia, the daughter of Captain Edward Norvell. Walter and Lucy were married August 13, 1898.[28] She soon learned that her new husband was a man of many facets—their marriage would take many turns. Nevertheless, it was a good match of grace, harmony and, finally, financial resources of large measure.

Always intent on advancing his career, Clark moved to the *New York Sun's* Washington bureau, where he remained for 12 years, except for two leaves of absence in 1900 and 1906 when he visited the wilds of Alaska. There, he displayed his adventurous nature, prospecting and mining for gold near Nome—then he visited all parts of the District of Alaska in search of his fortune.

Clark's gold digging proved disappointing and he soon returned to Washington and journalism. His credentials as one who knew Alaska enabled him to add to his *Sun* employment correspondence for the *Seattle Post-Intelligencer*, a large illustrated newspaper that covered the mining, fishing, and other industries common to Alaska. Soon there were additional assignments from the *Toronto Globe* and the *New York Commercial Advertiser*.

In Washington, Clark came to know and become politically intimate with many notables—his journalistic credentials and moxie enabled him to meet and engage in dialogue with President Theodore Roosevelt and Senator Philander C. Knox of Pennsylvania.

President William Taft succeeded Roosevelt, and soon he and his Secretary of the Interior Richard Ballinger knew of Clark's experiences in Alaska. The president and secretary were looking for someone to appoint as the first governor of what would become the nation's 49th state.

---

[28] Some publications list the marriage date as June 15, 1898.

Many Alaskans, hearing of Taft's consideration of Clark, expressed indignation, tagging Clark a carpetbagger, strenuously resisting his possible appointment. Then, *The New York Times* said editorially that Clark was "unusually well-informed on Alaskan affairs." That was good enough for the 340-pound Taft, who, with a stroke of his pen, appointed Clark as governor of the District of Alaska. The ink dried on May 18, 1909. Clark had finally found his Alaskan gold—in the statehouse—where he oversaw the founding of the state's first legislature.

Clark could be distant. But, when they were around him for some time, Alaskans found that Clark's wit, gregarious curiosity and rock solid integrity could easily win over naysayers and opponents.

Utilizing his considerable talents, Clark sought to bring Alaskan political factions to harmony. It was a tough job. Clark, short in stature, was a hale fellow well met, but he firmly held his own opinions on divisive issues that affected Alaskans. His views were often quite different from the thoughts and prejudices of natives. Territorial status was the paramount divisive issue—most Alaskans wanted the District of Alaska to be named a territory. Clark adamantly opposed the idea.

But, in Washington, D.C, there was different thinking. In 1912, the U.S. House of Representatives, newly controlled by Democrats as a result of the 1910 election, pushed through a vote to give the Alaska district its new status as a territory.

Clark was then named territory governor and he deftly brought about creation of agencies to regulate environmental and business workings, implemented compulsory education, juvenile courts, eight-hour workdays, and women's suffrage, and then shepherded through the legislature a tax on the canning of salmon that delivered huge revenue to the territory's coffers.

On November 15, 1912, Democrat Woodrow Wilson unseated President William Taft, and Clark embraced the political belief of, "live by the sword, die by the sword"—he resigned as the first territory governor of Alaska on May 21, 1913. Alaska was not admitted as the 49th state of the United States until 1959, but Clark would be referenced for the rest of his life as the "first governor" of Alaska.

Clark left Alaska and scoured the United States to find his next adventure. Seeking a warmer climate and itching to return to journalism, he found an opportunity in Charleston, West Virginia where the tiny *News Mail* was in financial crisis. Clark did due diligence and decided he liked the odds of building the *News Mail* into a major enterprise in the capital city.

The origins of the small West Virginia newspaper Clark purchased April 6, 1914 dated to the 1880s, the beginning of change and exchange for newspapers in Charleston. At one time there were three daily and six weekly papers in the capital city. Among them were *The Evening Call, The State Tribune, The Evening Mail,* and the *Star Tribune.* Many of the papers were simply political mouthpieces for politicians who populated the town.

A writer of the time called the Kanawha Valley, "the graveyard of newspapers." In an April 4, 2014 *Charleston Daily Mail* article about those rip-roaring times, "Life" editor Zack Harold wrote, under the headline, *Daily Mail Founder was Committed to Fairness,* "Publications popped up and disappeared almost as quickly as their daily editions."

The newspaper merry-go-round was mind-boggling. F.R. Swann and George Warren established *The Evening Call* in June 1881. The first Charleston publication to use the *Mail* name was *The Evening Mail,* which Swann began publishing in 1893. *The Evening Mail* became a morning newspaper in 1894 after Warren sold his interest to John B. Floyd and John W. Jarrett. Jarrett changed the name of the new morning newspaper to *The Charleston Mail.*[29]

---

[29] Floyd and Jarrett explained to readers that morning trains offered faster service throughout the state, enabling more timely news coverage.

The *Mail* name disappeared altogether in 1896 because of yet another purchase and some consolidation. The name was back again in 1899 when Moses Donnally, owner of *The Charleston Gazette*, purchased the *Star-Tribune* newspaper and named it the *Charleston Mail*.

Donnally hired five Republican politicians as editors while he handled the business side of the newspaper. It was not a good decision; the five politicos spent their days arguing as to what the newspaper should and should not say, endorsing a candidate one day, only to change their minds the next day, giving their backing to the fellow's opponent. Readers, understandably, scoffed at the editorial page.

Donnally published the *Mail* as a morning newspaper and *The Gazette* as an afternoon paper. In 1900, he sold *The Gazette*, and a year later, he returned the *Mail* to afternoon publishing as the *News Mail*. It appeared consistently until 1910, when it was sold because of dire financial difficulty.

On April 2, 1914, the *News Mail* was again put on the auction block. Four days later, 45-year-old Walter Eli Clark purchased it for $10,000[30] and never looked back.

---

[30] Estimated as equivalent to $258,000 in 2019.

—FIVE—
THE CHARLESTON DAILY MAIL IS BORN

Charleston's *News Mail* was small in size and the number of employees reflected it—Walter Clark and his managing editor Grady Damron constituted the entire editorial staff. But, with hard work and perseverance, the paper began to grow. Clark announced that Charleston was to be his permanent home and that his whole interest would be in bettering conditions in the state, county and city.

Readers were quick to warm to Clark's straightforward manner and his pledge that his newspaper would be operated for the good of the "whole" people. Clark said any one individual, even the owner, would not control his newspaper. Clark was a registered Republican and the *Mail* was most certainly a Republican paper, but Clark supported candidates of that party only when he thought they deserved support, and repudiated them when he believed that such repudiation was serving the interests of better government.

Clark changed the name of the *News Mail* to *The Charleston Daily Mail*, emphasizing and capitalizing on the *Mail's* location in the state's largest city, stating capital city prominence. Clark exhibited a talent to lead and grow. He built a staff of energetic, intellectual reporters and editors and told them their experience would be different at the *Daily Mail*. He put his money where his mouth was, paying good wages. He often repeated his promise

THE CHARLESTON DAILY MAIL IS BORN

that the *Mail* would always strive for accuracy in its reporting and practice fair play.

On April 4, 1920, Clark inaugurated a Sunday edition of the *Daily Mail* and by April 17 of 1927 he was in the money—the paper was doing well enough that he moved his production plant and news and editorial offices to a state-of-the-art steel, brick and Indiana limestone building at 1001 Virginia Street, East. It was the most modern newspaper plant in the state, publishing three editions at 11 a.m., 2 p.m. and 4 p.m.

Walter Clark's loyalty to his staff of professional journalists was strong, but warm, causing conservative editor Jack Maurice to think of the *Daily Mail* as a family. Clark may have been cordial, but he never let "family" deter him from forceful leadership.

On one occasion when first in the editorial chair, Maurice, uncharacteristically, wrote a humorous commentary. In short order he received a telegram from the traveling Walter Clark that said, "*Daily Mail* editorials are always about serious subject matter."

The Western Union "Stop" that followed each sentence in telegrams of the day seemed to emphasize Clark's critique. Maurice did not need the Western Union admonition—the directive from Governor Clark was all that was required. Maurice's editorials after that might contain wry wit, but they were absent of any attempt to make readers laugh. What they *were* full of was astute observation on the most critical issues of the day.

Daily Mail columnist Adrian Gwinn was an energetic and peripatetic young reporter whom Clark admired. One day, the publisher called Gwinn to his office. This had never happened to the cub reporter. Gwinn nervously knocked on the owner's office door and heard the word, "Come." He entered the sanctuary and Clark looked up at him from behind his publisher's desk. "Sit down, sir!" the former governor of Alaska ordered.

Clark handed the perspiring young Gwinn a three-paragraph story Gwinn had written for a previous *Mail* edition, asking him if he wrote it. Gwinn answered that he had. It was a story concerning the arrest of an intoxicated person, complete with the drunk's address. Gwinn had copied it from an official police report. As it turned out, the intoxicated fellow had listed someone else's address.

Clark looked at Gwinn and said, "Mr. Gwinn, the family at the address has notified us that they will sue the newspaper and the writer of the article for a million dollars.[31]"

Then, Clark said, "I just want you to know, Mr. Gwinn, that the newspaper will stand behind you 100 percent, regardless of what happens."

The story, unearthed by Zack Harold from Gwinn's long-running column, quoted Gwinn as saying, "no suit was ever filed." Gwinn said of his publisher, "He was courteous, crafty, industrious, gentlemanly, hard shelled, soft hearted, aspiring, considerate and willing to give more than he demanded."

Walter Clark, circa 1920
History of West Virginia, Old and New
- The American Historical Society, 1923.

There was no doubt the staff of the *Daily Mail* was captivated by the man from Connecticut. The word was out, the governor of Alaska had come to town, and he was a mover and shaker. The city and state was abuzz about the dashing and handsome Walter Clark and his bride, Lucy.

---

[31] Estimated as equivalent to $10 million in 2019.

—SIX—
WALTER, LUCY & JULIET

Walter Eli Clark brought with him to Charleston a love of roses. He and his new bride Lucy founded the Charleston Rose Society in 1922, pledging to make it the "Rose City of the East." Thousands responded, planting rosebushes. Amateur rose growers eagerly flocked to Clark's desire to create the Rose Society, electing him their first president. Pursuing his avocation in earnest, Clark was eventually elected national President of the American Rose Society in 1928, serving through 1929 when he acted as a judge at the International Rose Show.

He was a member of the Congregational Church, affiliated with the Chi Psi college fraternity, and editor of its magazine during his early career in Washington. He had membership in the Metropolitan and Chevy Chase Clubs of Washington, the Arctic Club of Seattle and Edgewood Country Club in Charleston.[32]

Walter spread his and Lucy's social activities and largesse across Charleston society, ingratiating them to the populace as they cultivated electoral bodies and businesses, giving generously to charitable groups. Clark was a busy man, dynamic and sympathetic for causes of public good. He was a founder and ardent supporter of Charleston's Community Fund, predecessor of the United Way. He gave extraordinary support to the Boy

---

[32] *History of West Virginia, Old and New,* the American Historical Society, Inc., 1923.

WALTER, LUCY & JULIET

Scouts, eventually becoming president of what was then called the Kanawha Boy Scout Council.

He helped establish the capital city as a place where business owners came to regard public service as obligatory, a legacy that endured for decades. Clark rejected overtures to run for public office, feeling his professional and charitable services far outreached that which he could accomplish as a West Virginia governor or United States senator.

Walter and Lucy assimilated in fast fashion and were firmly ingrained in the fabric of established leaders of the city and state. Lucy was so proud of the man who had entered her life, engaging her in days and years of excitement and accomplishments. As for Walter Clark, he was infatuated with Lucy.

And then, May 1928, thirty years into their marriage, Lucy Clark died unexpectedly.

Walter Clark was devastated. The light of his life had been extinguished. Lucy was gone. The couple had been childless and Clark spent his days and nights alone, diving deeply into the business of running his newspaper. He was despondent for months, but slowly recovered. Clark loved people and soon emerged from a deep sorrow to making his rounds of the acquaintances he had formed with Lucy.

In his circle of friends was an attractive young widow, Juliet Staunton Clay, born January 1, 1894. She was the daughter of Edward Wilber Staunton and Florence Garland Buffington, the family going back to early Kanawha Valley settlers. Clark knew that her father was a former Charleston mayor, a long-time Republican leader in Kanawha County, and a pioneer in the street railway system that later became the Charleston Interurban Transit Company.

A graduate of Smith College in 1916, she had married Charleston attorney Buckner Woodford Clay that same year. Buckner, born in 1877 near Paris, Kentucky, joined the Charleston law firm of *Price, Smith & Spilman* in 1903.[33] Robert S. Spilman, Sr., had met Clay in law school at the University of Virginia and recruited him.[34] The name of the firm was then changed to *Price, Smith, Spilman & Clay*. Clay was given credit for being a key organizer of the firm.[35]

Clay, 20 years after coming to Charleston, became ill and died at the age of 45 on November 26, 1923.[36] The firm's records revealed that he was under consideration for a judgeship at the time of his death. He left Juliet with one child, Buckner Woodford, Jr., and pregnant with another, the soon-to-be-born Lyell Buffington. Juliet's two boys would favor their strikingly handsome father.

Buckner, Jr., born May 23, 1919, was four years old when his father died. Lyell, four years Buckner's junior, was born in Baltimore, Maryland on December 15[37], 1923, 20 days after his father's death, leaving Lyell with no memory of him. Juliet and Buckner Clay were married just seven years. Six years after Buckner's death, Juliet married Walter Clark.

Walter's life was further blessed when Juliet became pregnant with a baby girl, also to be named Juliet and called "Julie". Walter, childless in his first marriage, a stepfather in his second, was ecstatic with yet another child in his life.

Wanting the best for their daughter, the family employed a woman by the name of Helen Slade as governess for Julie. Miss Slade was treated as a member of the family. She was diligent—to an extent that some saw her dedication as overbearing. She doted

---

[33] *Spilman, Thomas & Battle History of Service, The First 150 Years*, by Elizabeth Jill Wilson.

[34] Ibid.

[35] Ibid.

[36] Ibid.

[37] Susan Augusta Staunton's genealogical sketch cites Lyell's birth as February 15, 1923. However, most references list December as the month in which he was born.

on Julie as a child and was dominant in governing her into her teen years. When Julie went to prep school, Miss Slade departed.

Juliet Clark was extremely proud of her sons, daughters-in-law and young Julie. The children were certainly among those born with the proverbial silver spoon. Early on, their parents owned a home on the Connecticut coast next door to the famed actress Kathryn Hepburn. Buck and Lyell, as young men, were enamored of Hepburn. Buck often recounted the scene of Howard Hughes flying in on a seaplane, landing on the water, disembarking, and escorting Hepburn onto his plane, flying out with panache.

His parents enrolled Lyell in the exclusive Lawrenceville School in Lawrenceville, New Jersey. Lawrenceville graduates were considered as the upper tier of candidates to find success at the top of their chosen fields, prepared by a superior education to go out and face the world. The school had been in existence for over 100 years.

Lyell's demeanor later in life may well have reflected the homogenous atmosphere at Lawrenceville. He was regal in nature, thoughtful, intellectual, and driven to succeed. The school proudly stated, "Lawrenceville graduates have gone on to success in their chosen fields, prepared by their education for the changing world around them."

That line certainly applied to Lyell Clay.

From Lawrenceville, Lyell entered Williams College in Williamstown, Massachusetts, graduating in 1944. He joined the U.S. Marine Corps the final year of World War II. Two years later he was enrolled at the University of Virginia Law School where his father had completed his formal education. Lyell graduated UVA Law in 1948.

One year later, December 3, 1949, he married Patricia Kennedy in New York City. The 1949 marriage was spread across a full section page of the *New York Sun*, with large pictures of Lyell and his new bride. The caption under the newlyweds read, "Lyell Clay leaves the Fifth Ave. Presbyterian Church with his bride, the former Patricia Kennedy."

As they left the church, the new Mrs. Clay wore a bridal veil and a long coat that covered her wedding dress. She was holding a corsage and smiling broadly. Lyell wore a double-breasted tuxedo with a four-in-hand tie; the lapel of the tuxedo featured a boutonnière. He carried a felt hat in his hand. He smiled at the camera.

Lyell and "Pat" honeymooned abroad and then made their home in Charleston where Lyell joined the law firm of *Spilman, Thomas, Battle and Klostermeyer*—his father had practiced law with the firm and had been a partner at the time of his death in 1923.

Lyell's older brother, Buckner Woodford Clay, Jr., eschewed the limelight and seemed almost shy in nature. Buckner, known to one and all as "Buck", gladly gave his articulate brother the front seat in their interactions in both social and business settings. Buck was tall, lean, and angular with an engaging smile.

While Buck was seldom, if ever, in the public spotlight, his wife Toni was mentioned repeatedly in Charleston newspapers for her charity work and love of golf. The June 13, 1956 *Charleston Gazette* reported that Toni Clay tied with Mrs. Charles Twichell in the 27th Annual Women's Golf Tournament at Berry Hills Country Club. It must have been small solace for her as Mrs. Clay was defeated in tournament play by Mrs. D.H. Huffman, 6 and 5.

The Buckner Clays were social, regularly playing bridge with socialite friends. Toni Clay was active in the White Cross and Junior League. At Fernbank Elementary School she helped construct a thatched cottage for a production of *Rumpelstiltskin* in which her children performed.

Juliet Clark also was proud of her energetic husband Walter, and his enterprise, *The Charleston Daily Mail*. Walter's journalistic endeavor had swiftly become the leading afternoon paper in a growing state with a good economy and hefty *Daily Mail* profit margins—times were good and the Clarks lived well.

The Clark home on Virginia Street was luxurious with big rooms, high ceilings and a grand staircase to the second floor. Relatives visited regularly. It was always a learning experience.

"We would go down there often for dinner," Buffy Merrill Wallace said. "I remember the first time I ever saw a finger bowl was at the table at 1598 Virginia Street. The maid brought in these finger bowls—Johnny Merrill and I had no earthly idea what they were—Aunt Julie told us what they were."

John Merrill, Jr., and Buffy Merrill Wallace who often visited the Clark home on Virginia Street; their mother's elbow can be seen under the stool as she supported the children as their picture was taken.
–Merrill Family
–circa 1942

The Merrill children played in a large side yard that extended to Elizabeth Street. Often, they encountered the Clark's houseman and gardener, John Woodson. "I still have a bench that Aunt Julie gave to my mother, made by a company from Maine called *Weatherbeater*. That bench sets outside my mother's little carriage house now. I have a picture of my father sitting on that bench when he was probably 13 or 14. That bench is almost 100 years old.[38]"

---

[38] Interview with Buffy Merrill Wallace, January 18, 2019.

For Walter and Juliet all was good for sixteen years—until one day in 1945 when they were returning to Charleston following a ceremony in Connecticut where the former governor was acknowledged for his accomplishments by his alma mater, Wesleyan University.

There, in his native state, Wesleyan proudly conferred upon its prominent graduate an honorary Doctor of Letters. From that time on, Walter Clark's grandchildren, nieces and nephews, referred to him as "Doc".

Wesleyan's president said of Clark, "He has spent 50 years in using his pen in service of his community, his state and his country. His editorials in his *Charleston Daily Mail* have been written with striking courage and independence."

It was a delightful day and Clark accepted the honor with brief remarks that reflected his love of the university and the state of Connecticut. Then, Walter and Juliet departed by train for Charleston. During the trip, the governor began to complain of chest pains. He sought medical attention when arriving home, but to little avail. Shortly thereafter, he suffered his first heart attack.

John Buffington Merrill, Sr.
–Merrill-Wallace Family
-circa 1924

For the next five years the respected newspaper owner experienced a series of such attacks and his health steadily declined. As his heart faltered, he began to lose his exuberant energy. Doctors were consulted regularly during those five years.

—SEVEN—
AT THIS HOUR

Despite his numerous heart attacks, Walter Clark continued to write. For the most part, however, he limited his prose to his widely-read editorial column on page one titled, *At This Hour*. He seemed at times to have returned to his old self. Yes, he was now a senior citizen, heavier and balding, but employees and friends remarked that he was doing well.

Although his main focus was on his column, he found one day he could not resist penning for the paper's news columns a story about his favorite subject—plans for the annual Charleston Rose Show staged each spring in the capital city.

It was the last story he would ever write.

Charleston and the state were shocked by the Sunday morning, February 5, 1950, headline in the *Charleston Daily Mail*:

WALTER E. CLARK, PUBLISHER, SUCCUMBS

How could it be? Clark had been at his *Daily Mail* offices adjoining the newsroom on the second floor of the newspaper at 1001 Virginia Street, East at least two hours every day, sometimes more. He had made his last visit to the office shortly before noon

Friday, February 3. So far as is known, staffers found no indication that their publisher was in any distress.

The *Daily Mail* report said Walter Eli Clark, its beloved owner and former governor of Alaska, died February 4, 1950, following a heart attack at his home at 1598 Virginia Street, East. The 81-year-old publisher succumbed in a Charleston hospital at 1:27 p.m., just two hours after the attack. The article noted that the governor and Juliet Staunton had been married since 1929.

At his death, Clark's estate appraisement of 18,700 shares of stock in *The Charleston Daily Mail* was valued at $327,250.[39] He had purchased the paper in 1914 for $10,000.[40]

The *Mail* obituary of its owner said that Clark's transformation of the tiny newspaper he had purchased attracted new readers every day, and that each day there was an improvement in the product. "Thus," the obituary read, "the present *Daily Mail* began to exert its influence upon the community."

The community certainly took notice of Clark's death. A visitation at Simpson Funeral Home attracted hundreds, revealing the status of the man. His funeral at Kanawha Presbyterian Church, with the Rev. Bernard E. Venderbeek officiating, drew admirers from around the state, and beyond.

When the Clark casket was moved to the church, the pallbearers were *Daily Mail* editor Jack Maurice; city editor Vint Jennings; sports editor Dick Hudson; and staffers J.B. Martin, Howard Wolfe, Robert Thompson, Clyde Jenkins, Southall Burke, Arthur McQueen and Frank Polk.

At Mountain View cemetery a grieving widow said goodbye to a giant of a husband whom she had loved dearly. The title of

---

[39] Estimated as equivalent to $9,500,000 in 2019.

[40] Estimated as equivalent to $258,000 in 2019; source, Ancestry.com, Walter Eli Clark estate appraisement.

Walter Clark's column, *At This Hour*, hung heavily in the air. Walter Clark, believing always that the institution is greater than the man, had insisted that, when he died, his newspaper was to give his death only a brief mention. "A few words at the top of the editorial column" was his dictum, "and that's all."

But, *Daily Mail* editorial writer Jack Maurice refused the final wish of his publisher. Maurice, who would become West Virginia's first Pulitzer Prize recipient, wrote two poignant goodbyes:

It is one measure of the man that those who knew him and worked for him now break that stern commandment, confident that he would have granted them his final indulgence. It would be an injustice—to let him go without a word of the appreciation and esteem he so richly deserved.

He was, in a saying once familiar, a man of parts—teacher, gold prospector, reporter, public official, editor and publisher. These, the index cards to his long career, are developed at great length in his obituary. To his old friends they cannot tell of what he was and grew to be or why he was loved and honored quite apart from his accomplishments.

Although he had lived in West Virginia for nearly 40 years, something of the New England birth and heritage lingered in the man. There was a gentlemanly reticence, often mistaken for austerity, a strong disinclination to trade upon his personality, often mistaken for a lack of warmth and personal feelings. These were merely the shell of his life. As acquaintance broadened into friendship, a deeper insight became possible.

There was a keen wit there, a student's understanding of history, a joy in companionship, and above all, his grace and talents, a deep and abiding concern for what he felt to be right and proper. If one word can suffice to characterize him it is integrity—both personal in his life and publicly in his conduct of a newspaper.

His life was a rare life, a long and useful one, marked by a qual-

ity and a humanity which lend its closing a special sadness. The world is not so filled with good and just men that it can suffer the departure of another without a pang of deep sorrow and a sense of great loss.

In a second farewell, Maurice wrote that Clark had the utmost integrity— and the editor defined the word "integrity":

That word was implicit in his declaration when he took over this newspaper in 1914: "Under the new ownership this newspaper will serve no interests except the interests of the whole people—the legitimate concern of those who believe, as we do, that a law-abiding community is the only community worth living in, and that there is no true democracy without equality under the law. The Mail will be a Republican newspaper—mighty positively so—but not a factional opponent; and with no disposition to quarrel, but only to protest occasionally with those excellent citizens who happen to belong to some other party. It will be a political or personal organ of no individual—not even the owner. But it will strive for accuracy in reporting the news, and it will espouse and practice most incessantly the doctrine of fair play."

It was an exciting credo, and Mr. Clark did not deviate from it. The same staunch purpose which led him into the publishing business 36 years ago sustained him throughout his life. He fought many a hard campaign, and he did not relax in his determination.

Juliet Clark, her son Buckner Clay, Jr. and her brother, Fred Staunton would each play a role at the *Daily Mail* after Walter Clark's death. Juliet created an office for herself at the newspaper and met with her brother, Fred Staunton, appointing him publisher of the *Daily Mail.* Buckner Clay, Jr. continued to work in the *Mail's* circulation department.

Juliet went to her office each day she was in town, but her approach to ownership was hands off in deference to her brother. She did not impose editorial, reportorial or management restrictions—her only insistence was a dedication to honesty and continued excellent wages for employees. The *Daily Mail* staff appreciated that she did not assume management or editorial control and they looked forward to her presence. At times she would make carefully worded comments and suggestions, but never as directives.

A newsroom associate said, "Mrs. Clark was a great lady who took an interest in the young kids in the newsroom. She hosted meals for *Daily Mail* staff on various occasions and there are pictures of the newspaper owner, and editor Jack Maurice, laughing along with those kid reporters of the day as they relished a table filled with chafing dishes chock full of goodies, the kids eating far better than they ordinarily did."

For the *Daily Mail* "kids" and veterans, those good times were near an end.

—EIGHT—
A POOL OF BLOOD

On August 22, 1953, the sun baked Charleston and the temperature would climb into the 90s by day's end. Bessie Smith's alarm rang true and harsh at 6:00 that Saturday morning. Bessie worked six days a week and was thankful to do so—thankful for employment with one of Charleston's most prominent residents, Mrs. Walter E. Clark.

Bessie methodically dressed and prepared for the day—due at Staunton Road in the city's fashionable Louden Heights neighborhood at 9:00 a.m. She would return home on the city bus at around 4:00 in the afternoon.

Bessie chose a plain white dress, carefully tying the pretty bow at the front. She placed a black and white belt around her waist, inserted her earrings, and donned black-framed glasses. She slipped on sturdy shoes and clambered into the kitchen, patiently beginning the process of brewing her morning coffee, glancing out the window, squinting at the sunrise, possibly humming a few bars of the Mills Brothers' hit of the day, "Glow Little Glow Worm".

Each day except Sunday Bessie Smith joined other domestic workers boarding a Charleston Transit bus to travel to the homes of their employers who lived in the city's South Hills, just across the Kanawha River from downtown and the state capitol. The bus would eventually take Bessie to Staunton Road.

Bessie Smith, Juliet Clark's maid.
–Charleston Daily Mail

Bessie knew her bus driver, seeing him every morning for many years. Transit buses were a home away from home for drivers and they characteristically shouted cheerful welcome to their riders as they maneuvered from stop to stop.

Her driver accessed Virginia Street, then turned right onto the South Side Bridge leading to Louden Heights Road, where he began a twisting, hilly climb that seemed to defy gravity. Passengers sitting up high on the bus looked directly down to the rocks and trees far below.

Most folks, in their first ride up Louden Heights, were somewhat taken aback, and for good reason. It was quite an experience—many hands perspired just a little as the diesel engine under the passenger's feet groaned through switchbacks that clung to the side of the hill.

After the first few trips, those aboard relaxed, and some even looked forward to the mobile roller coaster ride. Veterans of the daily climb could put themselves in a blessed place—in harmony with nature and the day. It was, after all, a great view, even when rain pelted the river and lightning threatened on the horizon.

Bessie's first stop on the Louden Heights bus line was at Grosscup Road, where she watched her fellow workers begin to stir, moving to the front of the bus and disembarking—waving goodbye as the driver shifted to low gear and headed for Staunton Road, where Bessie moved forward as the bus lumbered to a halt.

A smile and a wish for a good day from the driver—Bessie responding with thanks and a returned smile as her shoes touched the road named for an historic family name—Staunton.

Then, her upward trek began.

Charleston Transit was always timely and her stop was scheduled at 8:55—giving Bessie time to walk up Staunton Road, past the McCabe residence, the driveway leading to the Bannerot

A POOL OF BLOOD

home, and a stately sycamore tree. It was an exclusive and private neighborhood.

At the top of Staunton, Bessie began her descent to the Clark residence. She passed heavily canopied trees, extreme underbrush, and huge rhododendron. The lush greenery created a splendor of privacy for Staunton Road residents—so much so that those living on the "front of the hill" could barely see their neighbor's houses.

Juliet Clark's home came into Bessie's view at 9:00 a.m. Below the Clark residence was the home of Juliet Clark's sister Florence and her husband Tom. Nearby was the home of Juliet's half-brother John Merrill, Sr. and the home of her brother and *Daily Mail* publisher Fred Staunton.

The Clark home was not large, but it was impressive in detail. The roof was made of slate and the walkway into the home featured large and separate sections of stone. The walk extended to a small front stoop with one step onto the front porch. An ancillary walkway of stone veered to the right around the house, leading to a back door.

The front door opened to a hall that led to a stairway that climbed to a maid's room. Inside the home were a kitchen, dining room and three modest-sized bedrooms. A breezeway connected the house to a stone garage, even though the house was made of brick.

Arriving at the Clark house at about the same time as Bessie was Mrs. Clark's houseman and chauffeur, John Woodson. Both Bessie and John noticed that the porch light and the lights inside the house were still on, even though the sun was now burning bright. Bessie walked around the house to the back door as Woodson crossed the stone walkway, stepped onto the small porch, and approached the front door.

It was strange—the main door to the house was slightly ajar and it swung open at Woodson's touch. Woodson knew those who lived on Staunton Road seldom locked their doors, but they never left them standing open. Woodson also knew that Mrs. Clark's three-year-old grandson was staying with her, making an open door even more unusual.

Woodson moved on to the breakfast room where Mrs. Clark, on weekdays, ate her morning meal and read the *Charleston Gazette* before departing for her office at the *Charleston Daily Mail*. Today was Saturday, and Woodson assumed Mrs. Clark would be at home. But the breakfast room had not been accessed. It was as he had left it the night before.

Approaching the back door of the house, Bessie found it also was ajar. Concerned, she pushed the door fully open and entered the kitchen, calling out. There was no response. Strange. Her employer was always an early riser and was in the habit of brewing a pot of coffee and retiring to the breakfast room.

Bessie removed her hat and went looking, stepping from the kitchen into the reception hall, almost bumping into John Woodson—an open purse lay on the floor of the hallway, its contents strewn about, envelopes, receipts, and two pair of glasses nearby.

Tension mounting, Bessie and Woodson entered the living room. A half-smoked cigarette was near an overturned ashtray on a coffee table in front of a couch in the room—Bessie looked beyond the couch, to a far corner of the room. She walked across the Oriental rug, braced herself, and looked down.

She let loose a terrible scream, staring at a mangled body, horribly sprawled in a pool of blood that spread across a rumpled green rug.

A POOL OF BLOOD

Hallway of Clark home as Bessie Smith found it.
–Charleston Daily Mail

—NINE—
"LITERALLY BEATEN TO A PULP"

Staunton Road in Charleston's South Hills was the epitome of terror the morning of August 22 as a horrendous scene unfolded in waves of anguish.

Bessie Smith, standing in a corner of the killing room, half bent, screaming hysterically, pointing to a body on the floor—her employer, Juliet Staunton Clark—blood everywhere.

John Woodson going to Bessie, cradling her in his arms, trying to soothe her—gently pulling her from the living room, down the hall and into the kitchen, drawing up a chair for her to sit on—easing to the door, looking back at Bessie—holding his right arm out toward her, hand palm down, moving it slowly up and down—indicating she should calm down, backing away—going to the telephone to call for help.

Media reports of the events that morning said John Woodson's call went to Mrs. Clark's half-brother, John Merrill, Sr., who lived just 75 yards away. Merrill was the owner of a Charleston photo supply store on Hale Street downtown, located a few doors from *The Charleston Gazette.*

The *Gazette*, in its first reports of the murder, said Merrill listened to the frantic Woodson, hardly believing what Mrs. Clark's houseman was telling him. The newspaper report said Merrill

"LITERALLY BEATEN TO A PULP"

hung up on Woodson and called the city police.

Stories differ, 66 years later, as to what happened next.

Newspaper accounts say that Woodson, whose nerves must have been badly jangled, dashed onto Staunton Road and began yelling at a man in a car coming up the road toward the Clark residence. The driver was the next-door neighbor, Mrs. Clark's brother-in-law, Tom Fleeson, who sold sporting goods to retail stores. Fleeson was on his way to his office on Saturday morning.

Fleeson rolled down his driver's side window and asked Woodson what was going on. The houseman quickly conveyed that Mrs. Clark was dead. Fleeson jumped from his car, ran the short distance to his sister-in-law's home and burst through the front door where he heard Bessie weeping in the kitchen. He went there first.

Finding Bessie hysterical, not able to respond, Fleeson quickly moved on. Entering the living room he came to a lurching stop, taking in a scene he would never forget—looking down on the tortured body of Juliet Clark—the stale smell of a half-smoked cigarette on a nearby coffee table attacking his nostrils.

He knew immediately that his sister-in-law was dead.

Fleeson fought down his emotions, gathered himself, moved to the hallway and, not knowing that neighbor John Merrill had already called the police, looked for a phone. He dialed the operator and shouted, "Get me the police. There's been a murder."

Murder on Staunton Road—the second call—it came into the Charleston Police Department at around 9:35 a.m. that morning of August 22, 1953. The desk sergeant who had received the initial call from John Merrill again scribbled notes from this second frantic person, this one identifying himself as a Tom Fleeson.

Second caller, name of Fleeson...dead woman...says it's murder,

MURDER ON STAUNTON ROAD

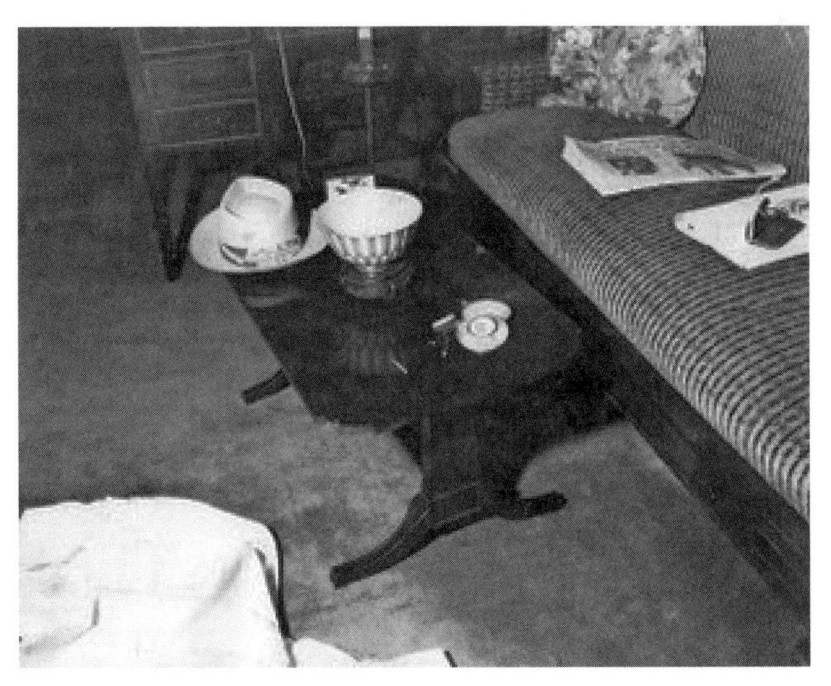

Living room of Clark home, cigarette on coffee table, overturned ashtray and a man's straw hat*
—*Charleston Daily Mail*

*Research failed to find any mention whatsoever of the straw hat. One explanation might be that a detective left his hat on the table and the photographer did not remove it.

"LITERALLY BEATEN TO A PULP"

South Hills, Staunton Road...crying in background...Daily Mail mentioned...urgent request to hurry...told him on our way...advised caller to remain at residence until police arrive...

Fleeson hung up the phone. Only then did he hear soft sobs. It was not Bessie.

Fleeson looked at houseman Woodson with a question on his face. Woodson pointed to a small bedroom adjacent to the living room. There, Fleeson found the three-year-old grandson of Mrs. Clark, Arch Alexander III, called by his parents, "Jay".

Fleeson gently lifted Jay from his bed and comforted him. Soon, Fleeson's shock was penetrated by the sound of two police cruisers, their flashing red lights and wailing sirens cutting through the morning humidity, heading toward South Hills and Staunton Road.

The day would be a scorcher[41] in Charleston, the temperature climbing as investigators spilled out of their cruisers, quickly labeling the home a crime scene, possibly a burglary gone awry. Prominent woman dead—mutilated.

Mayor John T. Copenhaver and his top brass were alerted and the police radio went into overdrive, summoning Charleston Police Chief Dewey Williams, Detective Sergeant W. W. "Red" Fisher, and Lieutenant Joe Craft. The city police contacted the state police and soon the master technologist and chief chemist for the state's criminal identification bureau, Sgt. K.V. Shanholtzer, arrived at the Clark home, along with Kanawha County Prosecuting Attorney Herbert W. Bryan and County Coroner Goff P. Lilly.

Charleston Gazette journalist Jim Hill, Charleston's ace crime reporter, had sources throughout city, county and state law enforcement. It was only natural and entirely anticipated that he would

---

[41] Charleston experienced a heat wave in August of 1953 that persisted for weeks, threatening the city's water supply.

be the first newsman to rush to South Hills, racing his car across the South Side Bridge, swerving onto and up Louden Heights Road, then on to Staunton Road, where he was briefly stopped by a patrolman whose car blocked the top of the roadway.

The officer recognized Hill from the reporter's many rounds at City Hall and waved him around his cruiser. Hill rolled down his driver side window, asking questions as he slowly motored by. The policeman readily informed Hill that a woman had been murdered—the owner of the *Daily Mail.*

Hill's blood surely surged through his veins as he grasped the enormity of the event on Staunton Road. He was the first reporter on the scene, but he realized he would get beat on the story. The gruesome discovery of Juliet Clark's body was breaking on *Charleston Daily Mail* time—the *Mail's* Saturday afternoon edition would scoop Hill.

But, Hill was an exceptional reporter and he was confident his skills would enable him to bring added detail to the *Gazette* Sunday morning edition. He drove down the road to the front of the Clark residence, got out of his car, and walked to the front of the house where a swarm of investigators was coming and going.

The *Daily Mail* was not far behind. Its reporter was faced with the enormous task of covering what was believed to be a shooting that killed his newspaper's principal owner—the powers at the newspaper were immediately looking over his reportorial shoulder. The *Daily Mail* edition the afternoon of August 22, 1953 did not carry a byline. The headline, however, was large:

"LITERALLY BEATEN TO A PULP"

MRS. W.E. CLARK DISCOVERED DEAD

BULLET WOUND IN HEAD FATAL

Mrs. Walter E. Clark, 59, the principal owner of The Charleston Daily Mail, was found dead on the living room floor of her Louden Heights home today and police said she had apparently been murdered.

She had been slain by a pistol shot wound through the right eye. The left eye was blackened and discolored.

Chief of Police Dewey Williams said tersely that, "it looks like murder."

Williams said that a final official verdict would await an autopsy at Charleston General Hospital by Dr. Walter Putschar.

DISCOVERED BY MAID

The body was discovered at 9 a.m. by Mrs. Bessie Smith, a maid of Mrs. Clark, and John Woodson, houseman and chauffeur.

When they approached the home they noticed that all lights were burning and that the front door was partially open.

None of Mrs. Clarks' personal possessions, including valuable diamond rings, were missing.

Her grandson, Arch J. Alexander, III, 3 years old, was found sleeping in a small bedroom just off the large living room. He had not been disturbed and was still in pajamas.

Dr. Goff P. Lilly was checking the head for fractures. Police said it appeared that Mrs. Clark had been beaten before she was shot.

LYING FACE DOWNWARD

Mrs. Clark's body was sprawled on a disarranged rug and was face downward. The body was not overturned until the arrival of Chief of Police Williams, Dr. Lilly, Lt. of Detectives Joe Craft and Sgt. Karl V. Shanholtzer, head of the criminal investigation division of the state police.

There was no gun beneath the body of Mrs. Clark and none was found nearby on the premises.

The bullet that killed the highly prominent social and civic leader has not been found.

Williams said there is a wound on the back of the head through which the bullet may have emerged. This has not been established as fact.

Williams said it appeared certain that Mrs. Clark had been beaten in the front of the face.

The nearest residence to the home of Mrs. Clark…is some 300 to 400 feet away and police said that it would be unlikely that neighbors would hear any outcry or disturbance there.

Gazette reporter Jim Hill's notebook was full of additional and sometimes different observations than those that appeared in the *Mail*. His report in the *Gazette's* Sunday edition of August 23, 1953 featured a large picture of the Clark home, photos of Mrs. Clark and Bessie Smith, investigators at the scene, and a headline in large type. Hill's story revealed Mrs. Clark had not been shot.

POLICE SCOUR AREA FOR CLARK SLAYER

WOMAN FOUND BADLY BEATEN IN HER HOME
Officials Seek Motive In Brutal Bludgeoning;
$2,500 Reward Posted
By James A. Hill
(Staff Writer for The Gazette)

The Charleston Gazette

The State Newspaper—Where You Read or See the Big Four—AP, INS, UP, Acme

Established 1873. Nine Cents Plus Tax.   Charleston, West Virginia, Sunday Morning, August 23, 1953   78 Pages—7 Sections

Police Scour Area For Clark Slayer

Woman Found Badly Beaten In Her Home

Officials Seek Motive In Brutal Bludgeoning; $2,500 Reward Posted

By James A. Hill
(Staff Writer for The Gazette)

Armed city and state police plunged into a full scale hunt yesterday for a suspect and a motive in the bludgeon death of Mrs. Juliet Staunton Clark, a socially prominent Charleston newspaper executive.

The blood-spattered body of the 59-year-old woman was discovered on the front room floor of her residence at 1234 Staunton Rd., about 9 a. m. by a maid and a executive.

A $2,500 reward immediately was offered by the Charleston Daily Mail Assn. for the arrest and conviction of the guilty person or persons.

Police blamed her death on an unidentified attacker here in the last generation.

Mother of City Solicitor

Mrs. Clark, mother of City Solicitor Levitt B. Clay, was the widow of Walter E. Clark, former owner and publisher of the Charleston Daily Mail.

At the death of her husband, former Governor of Alaska, she remained as principal stockholder in the evening publication.

A preliminary autopsy, performed by pathologists at Charleston General Hospital, listed the cause of death as multiple fractures of the front part of the skull.

Police Chief Dewey Williams, who heads the investigation, quoted an unidentified source that her skull had been "literally battered to a pulp."

The murder weapon was tentatively identified as a blunt instrument of an unknown type. A preliminary search of the grounds and house failed to disclose any weapon of the type described by doctors.

Later last night Chief Williams said at least three persons were called into police headquarters for questioning.

He said none of the three were actually suspects, but added he was merely attempting to find a motive.

One "lead" being followed was a report that about a week ago a photographer was noted taking pictures of the Clark residence.

Two persons reported seeing the photographer, but neither could identify him or describe his approach to his taking the pictures.

Fragment of Oak Found

Williams said practically the only clue discovered in the scene of the crime was a varnished fragment

(Please Turn to Page 6 Col. 7)

Allies Frown On Red Offer

Kremlin Wants Single Air Corridor to Berlin

BERLIN, Aug. 22—(AP)—The Western Allies are bowing down Russia's request to put but let one air corridor into Russian-made trucks and let out a volley of curses.

In a message of greeting to the peacelink, President Eisenhower said that "no real security exists in a second Soviet Air Force." He said such sentiments are as true today as when he first expressed them in a talk to the newsmen in 1957.

In his speech, Talbott observed that the nation's first heavy air bomber, the Boeing B52, has "surpassed expectations in flight covering more than 700 hours of continuous testing."

Only two B52s, the X and Y models, have been announced. A third exchange of Korean war prisoners was...

Talbott told the association that the Air Force has some 62 models which it has in development, but are expected to be produced and operate.

"To insure the minimum expenditure of our Air Force funds, we..."

(Please Turn to Page 6 Col. 3)

Socialite Pair Thwart Kidnaper With Fast Talk

CHICAGO, Aug. 22—(AP)—Fast thinking socialite thwarted the abduction of herself and a young woman rescue singer early Saturday by braving the grand jaws and talking away to the cop who stopped him.

The muse delivered a gun-toting passway on the lot into police custody and notched the kidnaping of Reston Sykes, 36, of Chicago and Ellsburg, Wis., and his girl friend, Miss Carol Plumstarr, 21.

Police identified their would-be abductor as Richard Brantley, 25, reportedly an ex-convict and kidnaper wanted for six recent holdups.

Sykes is the son of Aubrey Sykes, head of the Sykes Sheet Metal Co. of Chicago. Miss Plumstarr's father, Alfred, is president of the Jefferson...

(Please Turn to Page 6 Col. 5)

Man Balances 14 Floors Up

Thousand Watch Vet Threatening Suicide

NEW YORK, Aug. 22—(AP)—A Navy veteran balanced precariously on a 14th-floor hospital ledge tonight as some of his frightened family members looked on.

Fireman laid a desperate plan to prevent him from toppling off the marathon suicide threat.

Since 1 p.m., Sidney Herman, 25, had stood on the ledge at Fort Hamilton Veterans Hospital for more than a thousand persons gazed in horrified fascination.

At 10:10 p.m., New York time, Herman carefully took off his shoes and socks and laid them on the ledge.

"It won't be long now," he told frustrated rescuers, who stood at open windows along the 14-foot ledge.

Clergymen, members of his family, nurses and physicians have been rebuffed during the afternoon.

Two attempts by firemen to drop nets over the youth had been frustrated when he ran down the ledge, which exceeds 100 feet.

(Please Turn to Page 6 Col. 2)

Stassen Urges Collective Action In Bomb Threat

DENVER, Aug. 22—(AP)—And Chief Harold E. Stassen said after a conference with President Eisenhower today that Russia's declared possession of the hydrogen bomb underscores the importance of free world collective security.

At the conference, Stassen gave the President a report showing the speeding up of U. S. deliveries of military equipment to friendly countries all over the world. Stassen reported that in recent months of the Eisenhower administration. It showed that from January through June the United States delivered $2,583,000,000 worth of military equipment compared with that sent in the last six months of the Truman administration.

(Please Turn to Page 6 Col. 2)

Reds Blocking Atomic Control

United States Favors International Curbs

WASHINGTON, Aug. 22—The State Department believes that prospects for international control of atomic energy are "dim" because of Russia's uncompromising stand.

Nevertheless, it says the United States still favors international control and will co-operate with any proposals that the United Nations on any effective plan.

These statements came from Gen. Walter Bedell Smith, acting Secretary of State, in the form of confirmation here that the Soviets were succeeded in exploding some kind of hydrogen device.

Smith's report was made public today by the office of Sen. H. Alexander Smith (R-N. J.) chairman of the Senate Foreign Relations Committee, who is in New York attending the U. N. Assembly.

Miller had asked for comment from the State Department on the "full impact" of purchasing atomic programs in adequately reflected in our current military and diplomatic plans and policies.

In his reply, Smith recommended a greater exchange of atomic

(Please Turn to Page 2 Col. 2)

SIX WEST VIRGINIANS, freed from Communist POW camps in the Panmunjom prisoner exchange, await the ship will that will carry them home from Korea. The Mountain State men are: (front, left to right) Sgt. John A. Kirk, Malden; Sgt. Homer M. Dahlin, Charleston; Pfc. Billie J. King, McComas; (standing, left to right) Pfc. William R. Burke, Taylorville; Pfc. Estle L. Cooper, Wimfrede; and Sgt. James Flowers, Charleston. The group is shown at a replacement company in Inchon.

(UP Telephoto).

'Friendship and Brotherhood'
Shah of Iran Greeted By Worshipping Throng

TEHRAN, Iran, Aug. 22—(AP)—Shah Mohammed Reza Pahlevi returned in triumph today to his troop-guarded capital and the tearful adulation of royalists who overthrew a government that had wanted to dump him. They kissed his boots and kissed his hand.

"I cannot contain my immense joy," the 33-year-old monarch said, and tears glinted in his own eyes. Officials in formal coats and pin-striped pants flung themselves to the ground in welcoming the Shah at Mehrabad Airport while special royal guards looked on slant-faced, cradling their light machineguns. Top hats rolled away unnoticed. Shouts of "Long live the Shah" filled the air. One man cried "At home where his followers surrounded Premier Mohammed Mossadegh Wednesday by an uprising that left 300 dead, he was in fighting garb when he expertly landed his private plane on Iranian soil.

He wore a brilliant uniform as he stepped out of the plane. The uniform was shipped to him at Baghdad, where he made an overnight stop on the way home. He had not looked big while there.

"As you know, sometimes it can't be the truth, I can tell you that in the future...

(Please Turn to Page 6 Col. 3)

Reds Release 150 Yanks In Latest PW Exchange

PANMUNJOM, Sunday, Aug. 23—(AP)—American soldiers freed from Communist prison camps today whooped, cowboy yells, shouted and laughed as they regained freedom. But fellow South Korean repatriates shook their fists and cursed at Red Korean officers in an angry demonstration.

South Korean Red Cross workers told the Republic of Korean troops demanded that the Reds release all of the ROK soldiers being held in the North.

Earlier accounts said thousands of South Koreans were being held back to do forced labor far the Reds, including building airfields and rehabilitating war wrecked buildings and railroads.

Today's repatriation movement involved 150 Americans—many of them Puerto Ricans—and 250 South Koreans.

The 29th day of Operation Big Switch got under way promptly at 9 a. m. (7 p.m. Saturday, EST) in a light drizzle. It did not dampen the spirits of the returning Americans.

"Let me out of here, I've been waiting a long, long time," yelled one impatient American from the indoor of the truck.

"Look at them," whooped another, pointing to a raggedly dressed GI decked out in white helmet, white feet and white combvers.

The good spirits of the American contrasted sharply with the turning anger of the ROK veterans.

Three shook their fists at Red Koreans as they dismounted from Russian-made trucks and let out a volley of curses.

(Please Turn to Page 6 Col. 8)

Air Force Chief Says Reds Able To A-Bomb U.S.

WASHINGTON, Aug. 22—Air Force Secretary Harold E. Talbott said tonight that Russia has a powerful air force capable of immediate attack on any point in Europe and any point in the United States.

"If a nation has enough air power, the destruction it can inflict upon another nation is limited only by imagination," Talbott told the Air Force Assn., in a prepared address.

The association, composed of present or former members of the Air Force, is holding a convention here. Earlier in the day it voted on the administration for a "clearcut" approach to air power which unequivocally maintains "air supremacy."

"Look at them," whooped another, pointing to a raggedly dressed GI decked out in white helmet, white...

(Please Turn to Page 6 Col. 1)

Enemy Releases Ten State POWs

The 150 Americans released by the Communists last night included 10 West Virginians, the largest group of Mountain State soldiers freed at one time since the prisoner exchanges began.

Passing through the "Freedom Gate" at Panmunjom last night in the 28th exchange of Korean war prisoners were:

Cpl. Lowell D. Fisher, son of Mr. and Mrs. Lewis G. Foster of RFD 4, Box 297, Charleston.

Pfc. Willard L. Caplinger, husband of Mrs. Marjie A. Caplinger of Porgertown.

Cpl. John J. Coberly, son of...

(Please Turn to Page 6 Col. 1)

MURDER SCENE (top) is surveyed by the Kanawha County Coroner, Dr. Goff P. Lilly (in shirt sleeves) and City Detective Sgt. A. L. Chapman shortly after the bludgeoned body of Mrs. Juliet Staunton Clark was discovered on the front room floor of her plush South Hills residence. The front room door, directly to the right of Sgt. Chapman, was found open when the blood-caked body was discovered by a maid. Shown arriving to open the investigation into the cause of death are (left to right) Sgt. Chapman, Coroner Lilly, Police Chief Dewey Williams, State Police Sgt. K. V. Shanholtzer, and Detective Lt. Joe Craft. A widespread search of the house and grounds has so far failed to divulge any clues. At bottom left is the victim, Mrs. Clark, and (right) the maid, Mrs. Bessie Smith, who discovered the body. (Top photos for The Gazette by E. T. DuMetz).

Sunday Specials!

It's always fair weather in the home of the Gazette reader. No matter what the weather, New West Virginia can stand with the best of them in the matter of facts. To start off the annual fair season, the State Fair at Lewisburg will open tomorrow at the school which will provide master entertainment and regional buzz throughout the Mountain State. The Gazette has a story and feature story of the first fair in Ronceverte...

If your child looks tired, run-down and despondent these days, he's probably thinking about the return of the school buses and bells. As usual, The Gazette has prepared a special Back to School section to help you in preparing your children to go back to school. In addition to many news stories of interest to parents, the section contains lots of special features to help the youngsters. Turn to Page 17C.

Another Gazette Promotion

Fair at Dunbar to Feature Selection of Beauty Queen

Who will be crowned "Miss 1953 Southern West Virginia Fair Beauty Queen?"

How will she be selected?

When? Where? and Why?

Where and Friend.

The Gazette, in cooperation with the Southern West Virginia Agricultural and Industrial Fair which will be held in Dunbar at the 4-H Grounds Sept. 4-12, will select a new beauty queen for 1953 prior to the close of the Fair-going period.

Each individual holds a distinction at the Fair will nominate a queen of his choice. The nominee may be...

(Please Turn to Page 8 Col. 1)

Italy Senate Okays Pella's Premier Bid

ROME, Aug. 22—(INS)—Italian Premier-designate Giuseppe Pella passed the first hurdle today toward recognition as premier when the Senate voted 138 to 50 to approve his government.

The ministry abstained from vote and left-wing members voted on the basis of La Della Croce.

Debate on Pella's moderate government then began in the chamber of deputies. It is expected to last until Monday or Tuesday when the confidence vote decided. Observers say Pella has a better chance than did the previous government since Premier Alcide De Gasperi resigned June 29.

Suspect in Many Killings Nabbed

LOGANSPORT, Ind., Aug. 22—FBI agents tonight announced the arrest of a Kansas City priest, in the shooting of a soldier in the recent Pennsylvania Turnpike slayings.

Agents seized William J. Tauseros here just 10 minutes after he arrived at Lagansport, where they had been alerted.

Missouri authorities issued a pickup order for Tauseros Wednesday. They quoted Mrs. Cara Louise Nunn, 32, as naming in confession of slaying the Rev. Robert Hodges.

The priest was found dead about a week ago on lonely Kansas City road near Kansas City.

Lt. Chester Oliver of the Missouri State Highway Patrol said Tauseros is a Navy deserter and a pickup order was out for him anywhere. Mrs. Nunn, a waitress discovered a few days ago on the morning road, is said by court authorities he had had his mother and couldn't help her.

He gave his name as Roy Edwards and claimed an automobile accident killed his mother. He said sleepless nights in the city jail he was...

(Please Turn to Page 6 Col. 8)

'Glad They Found I'm Phony'

AWOL Paratrooper Admits He's Not Poor, Lost Orphan

OKLAHOMA CITY, Aug. 22—"I'm glad they found out I'm a bushel shot at his high school and but said he was kicked out."

The stripling 15-year-old said he was a bushel shot at his high school and but said he was kicked out."

Dragon youth said today after it was discovered his story of being alone in the world was a hoax.

Dozens of Oklahoma City families offered Milton Mowdy of Oregon, Mo., a home after he told buey, Ore., a home after he told a courtroom sojourn. He said he had lost his mother and couldn't help her.

He gave his name as Roy Edwards and claimed an automobile accident killed his mother. He said sleepless nights in the city jail he was...

(Please Turn to Page 6 Col. 2)

Charleston Senators

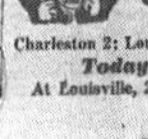

Last Night's Game

Charleston 2; Louisville 0.

Today At Louisville, 2 p. m.

Aroused city and state police plunged into a full-scale hunt yesterday for a suspect and a motive in the bludgeon death of Mrs. Juliet Staunton Clark, a socially prominent Charleston newspaper executive.

The blood-splattered body of the 58 year-old woman was discovered on the front room floor of her residence about 9 a.m. by a maid and a caretaker.

A $2,500[42] reward immediately was offered by the Charleston Daily Mail Assoc. for the arrest and conviction of the guilty person or persons.

Police termed her death the most sensational murder here in the last generation.

MOTHER OF CITY SOLICITOR

Mrs. Clark, mother of city solicitor Lyell B. Clay, was the widow of Walter E. Clark, former owner and publisher of the Charleston Daily Mail.

At the death of her husband, a former Governor of Alaska, she remained as principal stockholder in the evening publication.

A preliminary autopsy, performed by pathologists at Charleston General Hospital, listed the cause of death as multiple fractures of the front part of the skull.

Police Chief Dewey Williams, who heads the investigation, quoted an unidentified surgeon that her skull had been "literally beaten to a pulp."

The *Charleston Daily Mail* of the same day, Sunday, August 23, announced a $2,500 reward for information "furnished to Dewey E. Williams, Chief of Police of the City of Charleston, leading to

---

[42] Estimated as equivalent to $23,500 in 2019 dollars.

"LITERALLY BEATEN TO A PULP"

the apprehension and conviction of the person or persons guilty of the murder of Mrs. Walter E. Clark..."

The report gave additional information:

> **Chief Williams said one clue revolved around the identity of a photographer who reportedly took several pictures of Mrs. Clark's home a week before the murder. He said at least two persons gave a description of the man, who held a small camera in front of him as he took a snap of the front of the Clark home. Neither witness knew that the other observed the picture taking, Chief Williams said.**

Charleston Gazette staff writer Don Seagle[43] added scenes to the event in a February 14, 1954, *Gazette* retrospective that Seagle wrote:

> **That day was one that Chief Dewey Williams, Lt. Joe Craft and Det. Sgt. W.W. Fisher, will not soon forget.**
> **When the three officers who've been closest to the investigation reached Mrs. Clark's house on Staunton Rd. here's what they found:**
> **A nearly hysterical maid, a badly shaken handyman and the brutally beaten body of Mrs. Juliet Staunton Clark lying on her front room floor.**
> **The Maid, Mrs. Bessie Smith, had come to work around 9 a.m. on Saturday, Aug. 22, and found both the kitchen and front doors standing slightly ajar.**
> **Walking slowly into the home she saw the body and ran screaming for the handyman, John Woodson. He took one look and knew his employer was dead.**

---

[43] Seagle later wrote under the surname of his adoptive parents, "Marsh".

The Weather
CITY—Fair and warm (88) Sunday; late showers. Mon. fair.
STATE—Mostly fair, little temperature change today, Mon.

The Charleston Daily Mail

"Today's News Today"

6 Sections
General, Sports, Society, Classified, Comics, and Television

VOL. 121—NO. 54 | ASSOCIATED PRESS UNITED PRESS CENTRAL PRESS AP SPORTS WIRE | CHARLESTON, WEST VIRGINIA, SUNDAY MORNING, AUGUST 23, 1953 | ASSOCIATED PRESS WIREPHOTOS NEA-KING FEATURES PICTURES | NINE CENTS Plus Tax

Intruder Slays Mrs. W. E. Clark; Daily Mail's Owner Bludgeoned

U.S., Britain Split On Note For Moscow

Scope Of Big-Four Discussion Agenda Brings About Rift

WASHINGTON, Aug. 22 (AP)—The United States and Britain were reported divided today over whether to agree to discuss general international tensions with Russia at a proposed Big Four meeting on Germany.

Diplomatic officials report that Britain favors such an agreement and the United States does not.

Malenkov Sees War

LONDON (AP) — Soviet Premier Georgi Malenkov told East German Communist leaders Sunday that West German Chancellor Konrad Adenauer is "leading Germany towards a new war."

Malenkov's bitter propaganda attack on the West German leader came in a Moscow address to the East German Communist delegation called to Moscow last week for talks in the Kremlin.

He made a new call for a quick German peace conference.

France was described as tending to support the United States view.

The division has developed at the very outset of 3-power talks at Paris on a new note to Moscow regarding a Big Four session. The situation reflects the same basic difference between London and Washington over how to deal with the Communist bloc which has

See ANGLO-U. S. SPLIT (Page 6, Column 7)

Rabat Hails New Sultan

RABAT, Morocco (UP)—The new pro-French Sultan of Morocco Sidi Mohammed Ben Arafa was welcomed to his new capital Saturday by cheering crowds bearing the traditional gift of milk and dates.

But the sultan's nationalist opponents and followers of deposed sultan Sidi Mohammed Ben Youssef again warned France they in-

See RABAT HAILS (Page 6, Column 7)

★ ★ ★

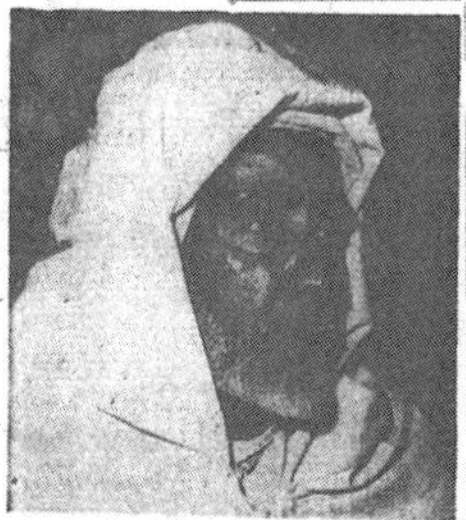

Cousin Gets Morocco Sultan's Job

Sultan Moulay Mohammed Ben Arafa, above, newly-named Moslem leader of Morocco by virtue of French authorities, posed for this portrait after the proclamation which led to the dethronement and exile of his cousin and predecessor, former Sultan Sidi Mohammed Ben Youssef. Tribesmen gathered in Rabat Saturday for installation ceremonies of the new sultan today while the former ruler, Ben Youssef, languished in exile in Corsica. (AP Wirephoto).

Trucker Killer?

WILLIAM TOWNSEND

Pastor's Son Seized In Pa. Pike Killings

Murder Of Priest Also Laid To Young Prison Fugitive

LOGANSPORT, Ind. (AP) — FBI agents Saturday seized a man who they said is wanted for the killing of a Kansas City Catholic priest and as a suspect in recent truck driver slayings on the Pennsylvania Turnpike.

Agents identified the man as William Townsend, 23. Townsend had escaped from the Indiana Reformatory at Pendleton, Ind., where he was serving a 2-to-21-year term for rape given him at Huntington, Ind., in 1949.

Agents sought him in Logansport as this is the home of his father, the Rev. Shelby Townsend, a Pentecostal church minister.

The Missouri State Highway Patrol announced Friday it was seeking young Townsend for questioning in the slaying of the Kansas City priest, the Rev. Robert A. Hodges. The priest was found shot to death last month on a bank of Little Blue River near Kansas City.

State police who aided in Townsend's arrest said he also is wanted for the shooting of a soldier in Kansas City.

Officers said they found young

See PASTOR'S SON (Page 6, Column 8)

Crime Motive Baffles Police

A savage killer wielding a blunt instrument bludgeoned Mrs. Juliet Staunton Clark to death late Friday night in her fashionable Loudon Heights home, touching off one of the state's most intensive murder investigations in more than a decade.

Mrs. Clark, 59, was the widow of Walter Eli Clark, owner and editor of the Daily Mail from the time he acquired the property on April 1, 1914, to his death on Feb. 4, 1950. Since his death she has been the principal stockholder in the property.

REWARD

The Charleston Mail Assn. will pay a reward of $2,500 for information furnished to Dewey E. Williams, Chief of Police of the City of Charleston, leading to the apprehension and conviction of the person or persons guilty of the murder of Mrs. Walter E. Clark at her home at 1234 Staunton Rd., in the City of Charleston, during the night of Friday, August 21, 1953.

The Charleston Mail Assn.

By F. M. Staunton, President

Police Saturday night said they had made no arrests in the case. They said no clear motive, other than robbery, had been established. However, a search of the spacious Clark home revealed nothing missing.

Chief of Police Dewey Williams said the only clue discovered at the murder scene was a varnished fragment of oak wood that lay in a pool of blood, just to the right of Mrs Clark's head.

He explained this could have broken off the murder weapon.

SNEAK SNAPSHOT PROVIDES CLUE

Chief Williams said one clue revolved about the identity of a photographer who reportedly took several pictures of Mrs. Clark's home a week before her murder. He said at least two persons gave a description of the man, who held a small camera in front of him as he took a snap of the front of the Clark home. Neither witness knew that the other observed the picture-taking, Chief Williams said.

Lt. Joe Craft, head of the Charleston police department detective division, last night added:

"We're just up against a blank wall. This is one of the most vicious murders this department has ever been called upon to investigate."

His statement came after state and city police searched the hillside surrounding the grounds of the Clark residence for evidence of a murder weapon.

Craft said 30 officers have joined in the search. He said the investigation would continue around the clock.

SERVANTS DISCOVER BODY FACE DOWN

The body of Mrs. Clark, a woman widely known for her gentility and graciousness, was found face down on the living room floor of her home at 1234 Staunton Rd. yesterday at 9 a. m. by a maid, Mrs. Bessie Smith, and her houseman and chauffeur, John Woodson.

State, city and county police immediately set in motion one of the most widespread investigations in the city's history. They admitted that there was little significant evidence on which to proceed.

It was first reported by police that the socially prominent Mrs. Clark, first president of the Charleston Junior League, had been killed by a pistol wound over the right eye.

The penetrating wound had caused police to believe that she had been shot.

An autopsy performed by Dr. Walter Putschar, chief pathologist at Charleston General hospital, revealed however that Mrs. Clark had been savagely beaten to death.

MULTIPLE SKULL FRACTURES FOUND

Mrs. Clark suffered five wounds on the forehead and on the back of the head which caused three massive skull fractures.

Dr. Putschar told Robert S. Spilman, Sr., Mrs. Clark's attorney and a trustee of The Charleston Mail Assn., that "it has been found conclusively that death was caused by a blunt instrument."

Asst. Pros. Atty. Herbert Bryan, in a separate announcement, said that the autopsy had disclosed that "Mrs. Clark's death was due to multiple fractures of the skull with resultant hemorrhages caused by the blows."

Dr. Goff P. Lilly, Kanawha county coroner, said his examination prompted him to place the time of death between 11 p. m. and midnight Friday.

Arch J. Alexander, Jr., son-in-law of Mrs. Clark, is the last person known to have seen her alive. He called at the home to bring his son, Arch III, 2 years old, to spend the night, and talked with Mrs. Clark for some time.

See MRS. W. E. CLARK (Page 6, Column 1)

Charleston Social Leader Victim Of Shocking Crime

Mrs. Juliet Staunton Clark, 59, bottom picture, widow of Walter E. Clark, owner-editor of The Charleston Daily Mail, was found bludgeoned to death Saturday at her home in the fashionable Loudon Heights section. No motive was established immediately for the vicious slaying. Mrs. Clark's home is pictured at the top. She lived alone.

On Ledge 11 Hours, Man Delays Leap

NEW YORK, Aug. 22 (AP)—A Navy veteran balanced precariously on a 14th floor hospital ledge tonight as firemen laid a desperate plan to prevent him from carrying out a marathon suicide threat.

From noon (EST) to past 11 p.m. Sidney Herman, 23, stood on the ledge at Fort Hamilton Veterans hospital as more than a thousand persons gazed in horrified fascination.

At 9:30 p. m. (EST) Herman carefully took off his shoes and socks and laid them on the ledge.

"It won't be long now," he told frustrated rescuers who stood at open windows along the four-foot ledge.

Clergymen, members of his family, nurses and physicians had been rebuffed during the afternoon.

Two attempts by firemen to drop nets over the youth had been frustrated when he ran down the ledge, which extends for 100 feet along the side of the building, to elude the trap.

But as he indicated he was preparing to jump they readied another attempt, waiting for the approval of Dr. Harvey Kay, a hospital psychiatrist.

A net 35 feet long and 25 feet deep was held concealed from the veteran's view on the 13th floor.

See LEDGE-SITTER (Page 6, Column 6)

Bulletins

HAMBURG, N. Y. (UP) — Eleven persons were injured, two critically, when a dynamite bomb, used to eject a Hell-Driver's car from a cannon, exploded prematurely at the Erie County fair here Saturday night.

PHILADELPHIA (UP) — Nathan G. Goodman, 54, a widely-known historian and authority on Benjamin Franklin, plunged to his death from a 185-foot bridge Saturday, police said.

Shah Returns; Boots Kissed

Late Bulletin

NICE, France, Aug. 22 (AP)—Princess Ashraf, twin sister of the Shah of Iran, returning today to the French Riviera from Rome, said she hopes to accompany Queen Soraya back to Iran in about a month.

TEHRAN, Iran, Aug. 22 (AP)—Shah Mohammed Reza Pahlevi returned in triumph today to his troop-guarded capital and the tearful adulation of royalists who overthrew a government that had wanted to hang him. They kissed his boots and kissed his hands.

"I cannot contain my immense joy," the 33-year-old monarch said, and tears glinted in his own eyes.

Officials in formal coats and pin-striped pants flung themselves to the ground in welcoming the Shah at Mehrabad Airport while special royal guards looked on stony-faced, cradling their light machineguns. Tophats rolled away unnoticed.

Though the Shah was a royal refugee in Rome when his followers unseated Premier Mohammed Mossadegh Wednesday by an uprising that left 300 dead, he was in

See SHAH RETURNS (Page 6, Column 3)

Red Purge Widens

MOSCOW, Aug. 22 (AP) — Newspapers arriving here today from the Soviet Republic of Azerbaijan — adjoining Iran — showed that the purge of officials there has widened.

The papers said U. D. T. Sumbatov has been removed as deputy chairman of the republic's council of ministers. No reason was given for the action. Sumbatov was for many years a member of the republic's Communist party central committee.

The reports also showed that the Supreme Soviet confirmed a shakeup in the Azerbaijan Internal Ministry and put Anatoly Gukov in charge, replacing Maj. Gen. Stephan Emolyanov.

Chinese Pass Middle Point In Yank List

150 GIs Included In Men Released Sunday By Reds

PANMUNJOM, Sunday, Aug. 23 (AP)—The Communists released 150 shouting and laughing Americans from Red prison camps today and told the United Nations Command another 150 would be sent home tomorrow.

An additional 250 South Koreans also will be repatriated tomorrow.

While the Americans exchanged today generally were in high spirits Republic of Korea troops coming back from the Red northland were burning mad.

See CHINESE PASS (Page 6, Column 4)

Strip Mining Mars Famed W. Va. Hills

By BOB MELLACE
Of The Daily Mail Staff

RICHWOOD, Aug. 22—Priceless forest lands and three of West Virginia's few remaining pure stream systems will be ruined if strip mining desecration is permitted to spread into the great Monongahela National Forest, on the southern edge of which this community is located.

Twenty miles away as the crow flies northeast, 4,000 feet up on Gauley Mountain, gigantic mining operations are cutting into the rich Sewell Seam of coal. They are moving away from the headwaters of the Gauley River, which is already polluted, and are within a few hundred yards of the headwaters of Tea Creek.

Once they move into that stream

See STRIP MINING (Page 4, Column 1)

British Warn Of Awesome C-Bomb Depopulating Earth

LONDON (UP) — British nuclear scientists warned the world today to watch out for the C-bomb that might wipe out the human race at one shot.

The bomb would be a deadly refinement of the hydrogen bomb, which the Russians have learned to produce along with the United States.

Now that the atomic method of destruction appears to have struck a balance on both sides of the Iron Curtain, some physicists have quietly put aside their data on the A-bomb and H-bomb. They have started, instead, a new docket under the initial "C" for cobalt, according to the scientists who asked not to be identified.

The cobalt bomb, as far as can be ascertained, is still only an idea. But the scientists said its operation would depend on "simple and well-established" principles which leave little doubt as to its feasibility.

The idea is to make a bomb big enough and powerful enough to release a radioactive dust that would contaminate most of the world and stay active for a year or more.

The scientists said the bomb would be made from cobalt, which costs about $2,000 a ton.

According to the informants, the C-bomb could be made in three parts beginning with an ordinary A-bomb in the center. This would act as a detonator for a hydrogen bomb.

The whole contraption would then be packed in a thick shell of cobalt, which would be blasted into a fine dust giving a "penetrating radiation lasting for at least a year."

'No Closer to Solution Than at Start'
Six Months Work Fails to Find Answer To Question: 'Who Killed Mrs. Clark?'

By Don Seagle
(Staff Writer for The Gazette)

Who killed Mrs. Clark?

The answer to that question has baffled the best minds in the Charleston police department for six months—months of work and worry for the investigators.

And, at the end of those six months, they say unofficially, they're almost as far from providing the answer as they were when they started.

The biggest stumbling block in Charleston's most publicized murder of all time, is lack of a motive.

Who wanted to kill the socially prominent newspaper owner whose life was a model of gentility and gracious living?

If police know, they're not saying but chances are they're not sure themselves.

Officers have done a lot of work, as much as they've ever done on any other case, in the Clark death. But despite that, Fred Staunton, the dead woman's brother and president of the Charleston Daily Mail, had this to say a few days ago when he increased the reward for apprehension of her killer from $2,500 to $15,000:

"While scores of tips and rumors about the murder have been run down, the investigation into the slaying of Mrs. Clark has dragged along for weeks and her murder is no nearer solution today than the day it occurred."

That day was Aug. 21, 1953, one that Chief Dewey Williams, Lt. Joe Craft and Det. Sgt. W. W. Fisher will not soon forget.

When the three officers who've been closest to the investigation reached Mrs. Clark's home at 1234 Staunton Rd., here's what they found:

A nearly hysterical maid, a badly shaken handyman and the brutally beaten body of Mrs. Juliet Staunton Clark lying on her front room floor.

The maid, Mrs. Bessie Smith, had come to work about 9 a. m. Saturday, Aug. 22, and found both the kitchen and front doors standing slightly ajar.

Walking slowly into the house, she saw the body and ran screaming for the handyman, John Woodson. He took one look and knew his employer was dead.

Juliet Staunton Clark

(Please Turn to Page 6 Col. 2)

Charleston Gazette

—TEN—
WHERE IS THE BABY?

Jim Hill and Don Marsh were great reporters, but Buffy Merrill Wallace and her brother John Merrill had different memories of the events of the day Mrs. Clark's body was discovered. Buffy was thirteen years old that day, and sixty-six years later, at age 79, she possessed remarkable acuity and recollection:

On the morning that this happened, I remember being in our kitchen—the kitchen side of the big old home place is the side of the house that faces down the hill where Aunt Julie lived. My father looked out the window and he saw a man who had been in the employ of Aunt Julie's at the newspaper, and also her personal attendant, named John Woodson. He was a wonderful black man—he helped young Julie (Juliet Clark's daughter) with her horses—he just was like a member of the family.

John Woodson walked up here and Daddy met him at the back door and said, "John? Do you need to borrow some eggs?" Something like that. You know, he made some casual comment. And John Woodson said, 'Mr. John, come quick, Miss Julie is sick."

So, my father, I think he probably had on his pajamas, walked down the hill and he said the minute he saw her he knew

WHERE IS THE BABY?

she wasn't sick, he knew she was dead. So, I'm sure that was horrible, to walk in and see his older sister dead on the floor of that house.

And the first thing he said was, "John, where is the baby? The baby is in this house!" And they ran back to the bedroom and there was little Jay. He was probably two or two and a half, I'm not exactly sure, and he was there in the crib, and they, of course, grabbed him and got him out of there.

From then, it was just a nightmare of policemen and everybody trying to be sure they were finding out the right things. The night that this happened (the night of the murder), I had had a teenage party and there were probably 20 or 25 teenage kids running around the yard playing "Hide & Go Seek", or "Sardines", the kinds of things kids do in the eighth grade.

So, there was a lot of noise outside that night, including two young men, who were good friends of mine, who had small motor scooters and they had ridden them over here, so there was a lot going on outside in the neighborhood that night. If she yelled, or something, we probably would never have heard it because there is a little bit of a distance, maybe 100 yards down the hill to Aunt Julie's house.

Buffy Merrill Wallace's older brother, John Merrill Jr., had yet another memory of the Saturday morning when Mrs. Clark's body was found:

Dad came into my bedroom and said, "You need to come with me. John Woodson just walked up the hill and he says Aunt Julie has been murdered!" I walked down to the house with Dad, but I did not go into the house. Dad said it looked like she had been beaten to death.

After Mrs. Clark's son Lyell Clay learned of his mother's death, John Merrill, Jr. remembered that Lyell came to the home demonstrably upset:

I remember Lyell coming up to the house and I remember him crying out remorsefully about his mother. I remember people coming around the house all day, oh, my God, very upset!

Buffy's younger brother Richard Merrill, who was close with Juliet Clark's grandson Buckner Clay, III, has little memory of the day his bludgeoned aunt's body was found. But, he recalled that there was a "certain amount of fear" after the murder, and he and his brother John had total recollection of John Woodson attempting to clean the rug on which Juliet Clark's body had been found:

I walked over to Aunt Julie's after the murder and John Woodson had taken the rug out of the living room. He was in front of the garage with a garden hose, washing out the rug. I vividly remember the blood coming out of the rug and going down the drain.

—Richard Merrill

Buffy Merrill Wallace remembered two men who seemed strange to her. She wondered, could they have killed her aunt?

At the time when I was growing up, there were two rather strange men that you would see walking up and down Louden Heights Road. And they would stop—you know the funny steps that go up off Louden Heights Road? They are called the "Stone Steps" that go nowhere—they kind of were right underneath where Phil Bond built his house up there on Grosscup.

These two funny men... they were two kind of "rounders"...I think some people suspected that one of them could have been involved and I'm sure the police probably interrogated them. They were probably very harmless. But, if you were a young person, these two kind of weird men walking up the hill and sitting—I just remember we'd drive up and they'd be sitting on those steps... parents told their children to stay away from them.

WHERE IS THE BABY?

Fanny Staunton Ogilvie,[44] daughter of *Daily Mail* publisher Fred Staunton and Juliet Clark's niece, remembered numerous details surrounding the slaying of her aunt, Juliet Staunton Clark:

Edward Wilber Staunton was Juliet Clark's father. "Will" Staunton, was mayor of Charleston at 35 years of age. He was an intense person; the Stauntons were always intense people, strong and ambitious.

Aunt Julie owned the Daily Mail newspaper and a lot of other media outlets that came to her with her husband's death. She was a rich woman, the Katharine Graham of Charleston. My father had stock in the Daily Mail but he was never a principal owner.

My father and our family were in Nags Head that August for a month's long vacation. I was nine years old. My father learned of Aunt Julie's death through a phone call while we were at the beach.

Uncle John Merrill said my father had to decide whether to use it (the Clark murder investigation) *in the newspaper. He did allow it to go to print. There was a headline years later in the March 9, 1958 New York Sun, titled, "The Murder Of The Woman On The Green Rug".*

There was a lot of suspicion about Arch Alexander, Jr. Uncle John (Merrill) *said he did not believe the murder was committed by Arch. My dad felt the same.*

I called Uncle John years after the murder and had a long conversation with him. We just started talking. He recognized my voice and said, "Fanny, I know it's you!" I said, "Yes, Uncle John!"

---
[44] Fanny Staunton Ogilvie married Donald Gordon Ogilvie in June of 1966. Ogilvie was the son of Mrs. Elmer R. Stephens of Ridgeville, Connecticut, and Dr. John Black Ogilvie of Darien, Connecticut. The groom graduated cum laude in 1965 from Yale University and became a life-long member of the Yale Club of New York. He worked in London with the International Publishing Company, Ltd. The bride graduated in June 1966 from Smith College with an A.B. degree. She went on to a career as an accomplished author of both poetry and prose. She was featured in numerous newspapers and magazines and named a Poet Laureate of Martha's Vineyard.

I told him, "I am still so bothered by this unsolved murder of my aunt. What is your opinion?"

Uncle John said, "Fanny, I think it was the monkey on the wall."

"What?" I said.

Uncle John said there was a funny guy who worked for Mrs. Clark. He said he walked by this fellow many times, sitting on a stone wall from where he could look at the Merrill and Clark homes on Staunton. "He did not look like he had all his marbles," my uncle said.

When you have a murder not solved and no way to get the truth, it does not sit well. I still want the truth. I want a videotape of who did what that evening, even though it would be horrible. They covered up all the fingerprints and footprints and did not leave anything that would help us solve it.

My father worked for the Daily Mail his entire life. He left Princeton after one year and came back to Charleston and married my mother. He wanted to get on with his life. Grandmother gave him the land. She was alive at the time and living in Uncle John's Tudor house.

The aftermath of the murder changed the casual lack of concern about security on Staunton Road and in much of South Hills. Doors were locked, curtains pulled. A police presence around the clock did little to ease fears.

The day of shock and horror that began with the discovery of Juliet Clark's beaten body finally came to an end with Buffy Merrill and her brothers John and Richard bedding down on the floor of their parent's bedroom. Caring parents placed a thick comforter on the floor and draped soft white sheets over them. Buffy could not sleep—she was distracted by the sight of her father's loaded shotgun that leaned against the nightstand, near his fingertips.

WHERE IS THE BABY?

Five-year-old Richard lay to her right, her older brother John, soon off to prep school, was to her left. Sleep would prove difficult for the three children and their parents—police cruisers came and went through the night, shining their searchlights through the woods, sweeping by the windows on the front of the Merrill home, awaking the family again and again.

—ELEVEN—
SEARCH THE SEWERS!

As the city tried to come to grips with a horrible murder in the midst of its silk stocking district, the *Charleston Daily Mail* of August 23, 1953, paid tribute to its owner in the following editorial by editor Jack Maurice:

MRS. WALTER E. CLARK
1894-1953

Few of us here at the Daily Mail ever worked for Mrs. Clark. We worked with her. She was, as we all knew, its principal proprietor and, after the death of Gov. Clark, its greatest power, but it was a role she chose to play lightly. She delegated the active management of the paper to others. For herself she reserved the part of housemother, presiding over the establishment with a maternal grace, ever watchful, sometimes critical, always indulgent and forever dedicated.

She married into the newspaper business, but like all of her attachments—to her family, to her church, to her community—it was for life with all of her abounding energy, her keen intelligence and her loving care. She would have nothing of quick successes and easy triumphs. She was concerned with the institution, with its reputation for veracity, its adherence to the highest standards of journalism, and its enduring influence upon a better city and a better state. And while she spoke of the problems of putting out a paper, it was always on these themes: Is it right? Is it just? Is it wise? Is it helpful?

They were the same themes that ran through her long and productive life. At an age when most women would have been content to slip into retirement, Mrs. Clark was still busy at work. She traveled. She read. She lent her hand and her inspiration wherever there was a need for leadership, and the catalog of her civic interests is something like a history of Charleston over the past generation. Characteristically, she was the chairman of the 1953 rose show, long one of her enthusiasms, and it was like her that she was here at her desk on Friday morning, full of vitality and interest, sharing with her newspaper family the confidence and zeal she had for living and growing.

These qualities, we like to think, survive her tragic death as they triumphed over more than her share of personal loss and bereavement. Mrs. Clark was a rare and gracious spirit, gentle by inheritance and strengthened by self-discipline, whose life was a record of devotion to a circle of friends and interests lying far beyond herself. They and we will miss her as men and institutions miss one of the underlying sources of their understanding and strength.

The painful and bewildering tragedy of her death will rob us of her generous presence. It will also serve to preserve the memory of a great and gentle person.

Police Chief Dewey Williams, Detectives Joe Craft and W.W. "Red" Fisher, under the observant eye of Mayor John T. Copenhaver, went about the methodology of investigating a homicide. County Coroner Dr. Goff P. Lilly did his work, declaring that Mrs. Clark died "about 10 or 12 hours before the body was found," which would have put the death between 9 and 11 p.m. Friday, August 21st. The time of the death was determined, Lilly said, by the undigested food found in Mrs. Clark's system.

Authorities photographed the scene and the living room where the body was found. The body would not be removed for seven hours, a delay that was later questioned. On the floor, encrusted in blood and several human hairs, was a small polished chip of oak wood that authorities thought might have come from the murder weapon. It was the most important piece of evidence to be found in the home. The chip was sent to a West Virginia State Police criminal lab for inspection.

Chief Williams told reporters that a pathologist said Mrs. Clark's skull had been, "crushed by a blunt instrument of an unknown type." There appeared to be no forced entry of doors or windows, causing investigators to believe that the assailant had been given entrance or that the doors to the house were unlocked.

Handyman John Woodson had told police that his employer had been shot through the right eye. That proved not to be the case. When Mrs. Clark's body was finally moved, seven hours after it was discovered, investigators found no exit wound at the back of her skull. She had simply been hit so hard that her eye socket was obliterated.

Dr. Walter Putschar, chief pathologist at Charleston General Hospital, said Mrs. Clark died of multiple skull fractures and bleeding by blows on the head. The autopsy showed at least seven fractures in the skull.

A savage attack—but, by whom? Who could have assaulted her in such a murderous way? What had been said or occurred that could have so enraged her attacker?

SEARCH THE SEWERS!

One media account quoted police as saying the only sign of a struggle was the disarrangement of three small rugs in the living room, perhaps caused when Mrs. Clark's body, falling to the floor, skidded across the room. Her body was lying on one of the rugs, described as a "rumpled green rug."

Yet another newspaper article quoted police as saying evidence indicated Mrs. Clark had resisted her attacker. The report said Mrs. Clark's clothing was in disarray, but an autopsy showed no indication of a sexual attack.

The half-burned cigarette found on the coffee table next to the body was identified as a Camel cigarette—a package of Chesterfield cigarettes also was found in the room. Mrs. Clark's son Buckner Clay told police he could not say if the half-burned cigarette was his mother's. He said she did not have a preferred brand.

And, what about the child? Arch Alexander III—Jay? What did he hear? Why was he in the house?

His father, Arch Alexander Jr., 28, had left the small boy with his grandmother while his wife, Mrs. Clark's daughter, also named Juliet, was recuperating in Kanawha Valley Hospital from childbirth just days before Mrs. Clark's murder. She had been, a newspaper account reported, "confined to a hospital where she gave birth last week to twin girls, one of whom died."

Gentle questions were asked of the grandson, who was calm by the time police arrived at the home. The boy was confused by all the excitement around him and, obviously, could supply no information on what happened that hot summer night on Staunton Road.

Police initially labeled the motive, tentatively, as robbery. But that was quickly dropped because a $2,500[45] diamond studded wristwatch on the arm of the victim was not taken. The watch

---
[45] Estimated as equivalent to $23,500 in 2019 dollars.

was frozen at 11:40 but police said it could not be determined if the watch stopped at the time of death or had simply run down. The watch was not shattered.

Juliet Clark was fond of expensive jewelry. In addition to her valuable wristwatch, she wore five diamond rings that were still on her fingers. One ring featured a diamond flanked by two pearls. Additional rings and jewelry were found in the home. Any robber would have had a field day. Yet, nothing had been taken.

Family members and neighbors arrived at the Clark home one after the other as they learned of the death of Juliet, not believing what had happened. A blanket of grief covered their comings and goings as police worked to keep the crime scene undisturbed.

"Where is her billfold?" one relative asked. Had Mrs. Clark's red leather billfold, which she always kept in her purse, been located? The answer was no, the red billfold was nowhere to be found. A thorough search began through the house and nearby woods. The efforts failed to produce the wallet.

Chief Williams moved on, saying the motive in the Clark murder certainly was not robbery.

The murder was a sensation in Charleston. Word quickly spread that Mrs. Walter Clark had been killed. The Associated Press picked up *Gazette* reporter Jim Hill's prose and said in national coverage, "The alarm spread by the two servants touched off Charleston's most sensational murder investigation in a generation."

Shortly after the murder, a close family friend, "Q" Giltinan[46] (Zon and David Giltinan's mother) wrote to her daughter[47] in Pittsburgh, saying, "About eleven oclock (sic) Julia Coyle said, "someone wants you on the phone, Mrs. Giltinan."

---

[46] The Giltinans, Smiths, and Stauntons were all in various businesses together.

[47] From Buffy Wallace's files.

SEARCH THE SEWERS!

"This is Dittie, I hate to call you but they found Juliet Clark dead this morning...I'll send the evening paper account but this morning doesn't tell much more except they are sure it was murder. Mr. Spilman and Lyell were there yesterday when Unk (sic) and I stopped at Julie's house.

"We had first been up to see Carrie who was baking her knee as she had just come home from there, still not knowing, but said there had been a man prowling around that John Merrill had seen and he said he was hunting blackberries...

"It is all too awful. You read about things like this in Pittsburg (sic) and New York papers but never before in Charleston to people you love."

Among the clippings "Q" Giltinan[48] sent her daughter was the August 22, 1953 *Daily Mail* front page story that said, "Mrs. W.E. Clark Discovered Dead", with a subhead that read, "Bullet Wound In Head Fatal".

Reporters continued to converge on the scene for days and more than twenty police officers were dispatched to cover all angles. Trained foresters were ordered to search the brush and nearby woods in a systematic effort to find the murder weapon, but to no avail.

"Search the sewers," Mayor Copenhaver ordered. City workers began to remove manholes in the area, climbing down the sewer ladders, flash-lighting their way beneath South Hills streets, finding no trace of anything that might be thought of as a murder weapon.

On Staunton Road, Juliet Clark's mutilated body, wrapped in a shroud, was removed from her home as photographers recorded the event. Three men pushed a gurney along the stone walkway.

---

[48] Zon Giltinan did not move on to Staunton Road until much later. "Q" Giltinan lived in Harrison B. Smith's previous home on Quarrier Street. Harrison B. Smith built "Bougemont" on Bougemont Road and was the business partner of Frederick M. Staunton.

Juliet Clark's body is carried from her home.
–*Charleston Daily Mail*

SEARCH THE SEWERS!

Framing the scene were several large bushes that hugged the front of the residence and a single small tree that cast a shadow on the coroner who stood silently, watching the procession with respect.

Apartment owners in South Hills advertised in Charleston newspapers that "the South Hills" was a haven, being "naturally air conditioned." Casement windows of the Clark home attested to the claim—the windows were fully rolled out on a hot August day—there was no air conditioning in the house.

Several onlookers gathered and watched as Juliet Clark left her home for the final time. As the hearse that carried her body wound down Staunton Road, it passed a large sycamore tree, its branches reaching skyward.

—TWELVE—
NIGHT VISITORS

"For days, we all slept on the floor of my parents' bedroom—house locked up tight as a drum. The police would drive up here like every hour, all night, and shine a spotlight through the woods. Staunton Road is woodsy and down on the back hill the property goes almost to Porter Hollow Road."
—Buffy Merrill Wallace

The temperature climbed steadily toward 90 degrees the 22nd day of August 1953. Perspiring police were all over South Hills as the scramble began in the effort to find clues that might lead to an arrest and conviction of the perpetrator of the "horrible event". City workers who had slogged through sewers were reassigned to wade through the foliage on the front of South Hills, looking throughout the day for anything that would help solve the murder of Juliet Clark.

Excitement mounted the next day, August 23rd, when news surfaced that a man living a 10-minute walk from the Clark home had committed suicide shortly after the Clark murder was discovered. He had shot himself with a .32 caliber pistol—as the report surfaced, detectives still believed Mrs. Clark had been shot—the suicide report had to be checked out.

Investigators rushed to seek the slug that killed the South Hills man, hoping for a ballistics match if a bullet were found in the

Clark residence. The suicide connection was quietly abandoned when it was determined that the Clark murder was a bludgeoning, not a shooting.

Detectives then turned to a man who had been doing gardening work for Mrs. Clark. They picked up Tom Toliver who was working in a nearby field, just down Staunton Road from the Clark house. Toliver would never forget the experience:

I was working for Mrs. Clark when the murder happened. Boy, was I upset because she was really a nice lady. One of the reasons they interrogated me was Mrs. Clark paid me big money. The police came and picked me up and interviewed me.

They kept grilling me, they wanted to know if I saw anyone go in and out of Mrs. Clark's house, but I hadn't paid any attention to that. I was given a lie detector test. A man came here from Chicago; I never will forget him, his name was Inbau. He gave me the lie detector test. It went on and on. He asked me who I saw come and go, why did I have money from Mrs. Clark, things like that. He asked them in a way that was not accusatory. He did not directly ask me if I was involved in the murder.

Then, late the same day, momentum picked up once more as three men were found in the woods around the Clark home, walking directly into the police dragnet that surrounded Staunton Road.

The three were detained for questioning. What were they doing near the Clark property?

"Just drinking beer," a young David Rollins said, as the temperature neared 100 degrees.

Rollins said he and his two friends were on summer break from college and decided to "go drinking."

Rollins[49] related that he and his buddies had driven out Staunton Road, walked into the woods, and opened their cache of suds. Police at first thought they had three prime suspects, but they realized after a 45-minute grilling that they had only "three kids, home for the summer, just drinking beer."

The suicide investigation and the corralling of three young men near the home bore no fruit for police, but Chief Dewey Williams was optimistic, saying, "We have a little evidence that might help in our work, but I prefer not to mention it at this time."

Asked by reporters to again describe the manner in which Mrs. Clark was killed, Williams said, "It was a savage blow because it greatly depressed the heavy frontal bone of the skull. What must have been the second blow was equally powerful and brutal. It fractured her skull in two places, from front to rear."

Williams then said it had been definitely established that a hammer, hatchet or other similar weapon, did *not* strike Mrs. Clark. Ironically, later in the case, Mayor Copenhaver focused the investigation on a ballpeen hammer, calling a news conference to describe the hammer as possibly the murder weapon.

Meanwhile, the probe of the haute monde Staunton Road neighborhood wound through dense woods, ravines, and streams as the gritty groundwork of searching and interviewing continued in full force. Juliet Clark's neighbors were the first to be interviewed.

Detectives went to the home of Mr. and Mrs. John Merrill, Sr., parents of John, Buffy and Richard Merrill. The Merrills lived 75-100 yards away, less than a football field from the Clark home. John Merrill, Sr., investigators knew, was the half-brother of Mrs. Clark. Merrill had been questioned the day of the murder, but police were revisiting a number of neighbors who had shown up at the Clark home, asking additional questions.

---

[49] Rollins, as an adult, would head the esteemed Charleston accounting firm of *Rollins, Cleavenger & Rollins*.

NIGHT VISITORS

Investigators understood the Merrills were greatly distraught by the brutal murder of a family member, and were solicitous, trying not to step on frayed nerves. But they had a job to do, and the Merrills understood.

Terribly shaken, but eager to help in any way, the Merrills told police they had heard, the night of the murder, loud voices coming from the Clark home.

"At what time did you hear the voices, what were they saying?" Police Chief Dewey Williams asked, sitting in the Merrill living room.

John Merrill, Sr. said he and his wife had returned from the movies about 10:30 Friday night (the coroner estimated the time of death at between 9:30 and 11 p.m.). "We thought Juliet had houseguests and they were just saying goodnight. It was loud, but we couldn't make out exactly what was said."

Merrill pointed out that the Clark house was nearby, but partially secluded by trees and foliage, and they saw nothing. He said again that his wife Mary Louise and he simply thought "goodnights" were being given in a boisterous way, probably after an evening of cocktails and friendly visitation.

Police moved on to yet another South Hills home, that of Mr. and Mrs. J. Horner Davis II. Mrs. Davis, a personal friend of Juliet Clark, told Detective Red Fisher she had chatted by telephone with Mrs. Clark about 10:30 the night of the murder, the same time cited by the Merrills in remembering the loud conversation they had heard that fateful night. Mrs. Davis said Mrs. Clark gave no indication she was distressed in any way. Mrs. Clark had not mentioned visitors. Based on the interviews of the Merrills and Mrs. Davis, investigators theorized Mrs. Clark must have known the assailant who killed her.

Were there visitors to the home of Juliet Clark the night of August 21, 1953 who were known by her?

Yes, there were two...

—THIRTEEN—
A RUMPLED GREEN RUG

Juliet Clark dined the night of August 21, 1953 with her son, the recently appointed City Solicitor, Lyell Clay. Lyell was a tall, handsome and quiet young man who favored his mother. He moved with the same easy flow that many wealthy southerners shared. A full head of wavy brown hair topped his 6-1 frame. He was well-known and admired.

Lyell told investigators he left his mother's house around 8:30 the evening of August 21. Media accounts differ in regard to the visit of Mrs. Clark's son-in-law, Arch Alexander, Jr. One report said that Arch told police he visited about 9:00 PM, and another said he told authorities he visited at 10:00. Neighbors told police they heard loud voices coming from the Clark home at 10:30 that night.[50]

The afternoon of the murder, Alexander's wife Julie had returned home from Kanawha Valley Hospital where she had given birth to twin daughters, but one had died a few days earlier. Newspaper reports quoted Alexander as saying he had simply dropped by his mother-in-law's home to inquire about a practical nurse for his wife and to check on his small son who was

---

[50] The times of the visits are important, but reports vary. A New York newspaper referenced 8:00 PM as the time of Arch's evening appearance at the Clark home. Reporter Ruth Reynolds said Arch stopped by the Clark home "a second time"–it is the only reference the authors found suggesting Mrs. Clark's son-in-law visited her home twice that evening.

staying with his grandmother. He later picked up a magazine at a drugstore and said he was home, "about 10:00."

Five years later, a recap story in the March 9, 1958 *New York Sunday News* article by reporter Ruth Reynolds, famous for her reporting on sensational murders, had an expanded version of events. The tabloid newspaper had a long history of reporting lurid details of crime, scandal and violence.

Reporter Reynolds' lead paragraph recounted the finding of Mrs. Clark's body by Bessie Smith and John Woodson. Then she focused on Arch Alexander, Jr., who apparently gave her a different timeline for his visit with his mother-in-law the night of the murder. Reynolds also quoted Buck Clay and Fred Staunton.

THE BODY ON THE RUMPLED GREEN RUG

By Ruth Reynolds

In the living room, newspapers and magazines were sorted out on the sofa. A partly burned Camel cigarette was beside an overturned ash tray on the coffee table. The cigarette had eaten deep into the wood of the table before it went out. A corner of the coffee table had been dented and a leg split. Was this an old furniture wound or a new one—perhaps incurred during a fight the previous night?

While Coroner Goff P. Lilly superintended the moving of the body to the morgue at Charleston General Hospital, Police Chief Dewey Williams concerned himself with questioning relatives as they arrived.

The first was John Merrill, Mrs. Clark's half brother, who was her nearest neighbor. He said that when he and his wife came home from the movies about 11 the night before they heard Juliet talking rather loudly to someone. They thought she was just saying goodnight.

City Solicitor Lyell Clay, 30, who was one of two sons of Mrs. Clark by her first marriage, said he had a pleasant dinner with his mother at 7 o'clock and left the house "about 8."

Mrs. Clark's son-in-law, Arch Alexander, 28, told of seeing her, "about 8." He said that his wife Julie, and the surviving twin, returned from the hospital early Friday. Mrs. Clark visited them and took Jay home with her. Later, Arch stopped by to borrow a hot water bottle Julie wanted.

Arch said he chatted with his mother-in-law, saw his son put to bed down the hall from her room and departed without the hot water bottle. Mrs. Clark was cheerful and it was an amicable visit.

Buckner Clay, 28, Mrs. Clark's younger son, regretted bitterly that he hadn't seen his mother for several days before her death, hadn't even seen her at the Mail where he worked in the circulation department.

Mrs. J. Horner Davis, a friend, said she and Mrs. Clark had a lengthy telephone conversation at 10:30 P.M. Mrs. Clark spoke of having Jay with her but did not mention anybody else.

Fred Staunton said he saw his sister several times during the day before her death, but only briefly because Juliet was such a busy woman.

After listing the many civic activities of Mrs. Clark, reporter Reynolds wrote:

> Mrs. Clark's sisters, Mrs. L. Thomas Newton and Mrs. Thomas Fleeson, both of Charleston, never heard her express any fears of burglars or personal enemies. She had no gun and never kept large sums of money in the house.
>
> After looking over the house—Mrs. Clark built it in 1950 after her husband died—the sis-

A RUMPLED GREEN RUG

ters told police so far as they could tell, nothing valuable was missing—unless a missing red billfold contained a large sum of money.

Another brother, Wilbur[51] Staunton, flew in from Tule Lake, Calif., "to find out what this is all about." However, he was not able to aid in the murder investigation.

Yet, Lt. (Dewey) Craft and (Detective) Red Fisher felt that one of these relatives unwittingly held the key which could unlock the mystery.

Reynolds then wrote that Mrs. Clark's autopsy revealed that a splinter of white oak that had blood and hair sticking to it could have come from the handle of a hammer, or from a policeman's Billy club—made of white oak.

Reynolds' report said Mrs. Clark's pastor noted at her funeral that she was a gracious, useful, self-effacing woman born with wealth and prominence— regardless, the minister said, she had worked for the public good.

Reynolds wrote:

Many nodded. A Daily Mail linotype operator remembered how Mrs. Clark played with his children and bought his expectant wife a layette. A staff photographer thought of her as, "a member of our newspaper family." From apprentices and newsboys and white collar workers, Mrs. Clark's employees took her bludgeoning slaying as a personal affair.[52]

But, there was an undercurrent of talk in Charleston that beneath Mrs. Clark's gra-

---

[51] Also spelled as "Wilber".

[52] Years after the murder, when the Clark home was sold, a Staunton Road resident said the new owner dragged items from the house as it was prepared for renovation. In the basement, the resident said, was a rug that had been left behind–stained with blood. The rug was said to have been hauled away and incinerated.

ciousness lay a strong will and a violent temper. Some said she was also a snob. They scoffed at the theory that she inherited an enemy from her mild-mannered husband (Walter Clark).

Reynolds also reported that Juliet Clark disapproved of her daughter's choice of men:

> Mrs. Clark was busy, but not happy. She and her daughter quarreled frequently over Julie's choice of beaus. When the girl married Arch Alexander she was several months pregnant, yet her mother opposed the marriage.

—FOURTEEN—
NOT A JOYFUL PERSON

Memories of those who knew *Daily Mail* owner Juliet Staunton Clark differ. Her public persona, projected by her newspaper and social presence, gave every indication she was lovable and dedicated to the finer ideals in life. But there were some who thought she was unkind to her child, despised her son-in-law, and suffered from mood swings. A relative who visited evenings with Juliet for drinks and conversation returned home one evening and said, "Julie is not well." It was said she and her sister Florence would visit a sanatorium, or rest home, and then return.

Betsy Staunton Johnson, Fred Staunton's daughter and Juliet Clark's niece:

She was quite a lady—she (Mrs. Clark) was bipolar, which ran in the family, big time. She had extreme highs and extreme lows, which Dad (Fred Staunton, Juliet's brother) *also suffered from. I remember every autumn he kind of went down. I said, "Dad, it's hunting season, you know, this ought to be your favorite time." But, I think he loved growing so much. He was into gardening big time, so he kind of hated to see everything go to sleep.*

Betsy said she imagined her dad and his sister were close, because they were in the business[53] together—but something

---
[53] *The Charleston Daily Mail.*

NOT A JOYFUL PERSON

seemed to be lacking.

Aunt Julie got Dad into the Daily Mail and yet I never felt the warmth between them that Dad had for Aunt Kathy, Newt Thomas' mother, who was a younger sister. I just felt like Dad was always wondering where Julie was going to be coming from, because her moods were so swinging.

I can remember the anxious conversations, but, basically, being away at school I was sort of out of the fray. I didn't get that day-to-day thing that Fan (her sister) *and Buffy* (her cousin) *got, but they were so much younger.*

The biggest thing she (Juliet Clark) *did for me was to give me a coat. This was just out of the range of what we were going through. We lived in a wonderful house at the top of the hill, but we had chickens in the garage, turkeys in the attic and every now and again Dad would bring home frogs from gigging and put them in the bathtub. I always wondered how Mom ever got through that.*

But, Aunt Julie brought me this gorgeous camel hair coat when I went away to school. I have never forgotten it. That was just the kindest thing, because—you know, it just wasn't in the cards for us.

She was tough...she was not a very joyful person. I can imagine she probably upset a few people. But, my being a young girl, and she the older aunt—I just felt like I never saw her. I did not feel any incredible warmth. She was just sort of a staid lady to me. In those days aunts weren't all warm and fuzzy.

Her house was like "Bleak House", very formal, very dark. We went down there quite often (the Clark home on Virginia Street) *and all I remember is playing outside, running through the rose garden and the wonderful trellis that she had in the rear end of the garden.*

We all felt sorry for the daughter Julie, because she was raised by

Miss Slade, a very stereotyped—oh, my gosh, you can only think of her as an English school teacher. She was just very strict, and Julie was internally on fire. She was very sexually prone, and I know this because she told my older brother everything he ever knew and he wasn't really ready for it. But Julie, this child, was just, I'd say, lost.

When you look at the life, it was so sad. I don't feel like she ever had a mother that she could really hug. That may be very severe of me because I don't know, I really don't know, I didn't live in that house with them. My immediate family was pretty connected, pretty warm and pretty honest with each other.

Betsy Staunton Johnson continued:

Dad was very touchy-feely. He used to wash my hair, which is really weird for a father. He had ulcers and had to be on a strict diet. He had his bipolar moments and was not always the guy that was outside working with the kids like he did when he was younger. They missed what we had. It seems to me like it (the murder) *was just one of those gauche things that, you know, happened. But, because your life was so vital, going away to school, you were distanced from it. There was a lot of frustration.*

I think Aunt Julie's story is wonderful, marrying the governor of Alaska who decided to come and buy this little punkie newspaper. Why in the world he ever did that? But, I think he looked at it like a hobby.

We loved Uncle Doc (Walter Clark). *He was a darling man. We called him Uncle Doc, I don't know whether he had a doctorate or not, but he was he was joyful and kind of looked like Tom Dewey and had kind of a mustache. He was just a neat person.*

Mrs. Clark, I think he absolutely adored her and admired her because she was pretty prominent—out there, very busy. I think there was huge respect, huge respect.

NOT A JOYFUL PERSON

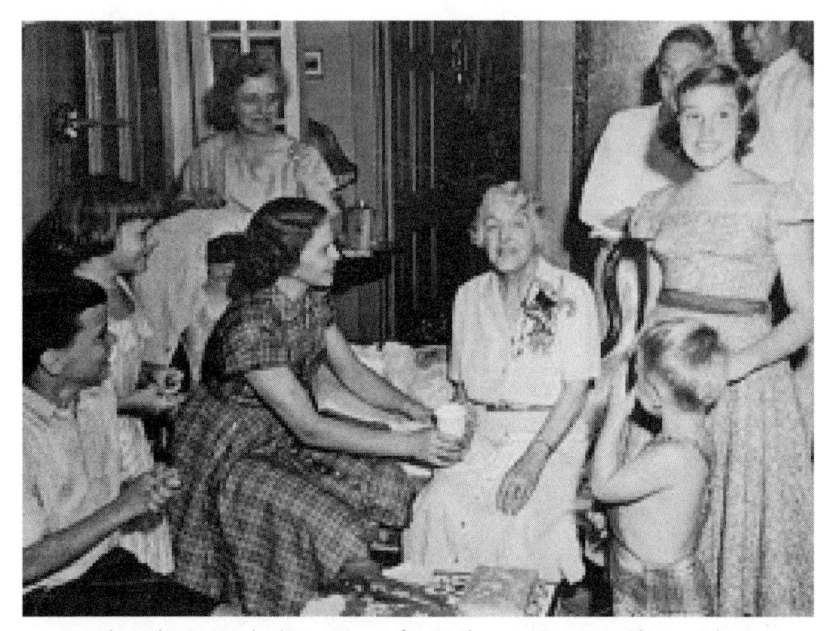

Family gathering in the living room of Aunt Florence Staunton Fleeson's home. *Left to Right:* Platt Staunton; Fan Staunton; Juliet Clark (to rear) Mary Louise Merrill; Florence Buffington Staunton Merrill (Ma Merrill-seated); John Merrill, Jr. (standing, partially hidden); Richard Merrill (small boy); Buffy Merrill; Joe Peck (far right, standing).
-Staunton-Merrill Families

Asked about Arch Alexander, Jr.'s relationship with Juliet Clark and her daughter, Julie, Betsy had mixed emotions:

I knew Arch Alexander, but I didn't know him. I think he dismissed me. I think I was too young. We were probably ten years different. I can't give you any kind of feeling about him. I always thought he was kind of sly. But, I can't give you any reason why. He just never seemed to be around.

I don't know where Julie (Arch's wife) *and Arch spent their time. I just wasn't in their scope. We had family parties, maybe weddings, funerals, he was there, but I just don't really remember if their marriage was warm and fuzzy. I don't have any feeling of seeing them together.*

When you look at this life (Juliet Clark's daughter, Julie), *it's pretty tragic.*

Some who remembered the murdered woman said they believed Arch Alexander, Jr. hated his mother-in-law because Mrs. Clark believed Alexander was not good enough for her daughter.

Betsy's response: *I'd say absolutely to that.*

Asked if she believed that Mrs. Clark was unkind to her daughter, Betsy said:

As far as not treating her daughter well? I think she just dismissed her daughter. I know you can have people take care of your kids, but Julie was a teenager and she had this woman in charge of her. I just remember being up in Julie's room and Miss Slade saying, "Juliet, it's time for this! Juliet, it's time for this!" And I just thought, "God, how does anyone live like that?" So I would say, Aunt Julie did not pass "motherhood" at all. I am so sad about it, because I think that's one of the bigger tragedies of the whole story. Julie (Mrs. Clark) *was such a lost person, and her sister Florence also—the tragedy of these women, tragedy in this part of the family.*

I think our world was very distanced from Julie and Florence (Juliet's sister) *because they had a lot of money. They were traveling and doing things, living in different places in the summer. There was a real division between the Merrills, and my family and the two sisters. I feel like they were all on another plane and we looked like objects from another world.*

Buffy Merrill Wallace remembered Juliet Clark and her sister, Florence Fleeson, with admiration for their courage:

Mrs. Clark was a small woman who had a very nice figure. I think of her as wearing suits—but it always impressed me that these two women[54] in their teens—these sisters—went off to Smith College in Northampton, Massachusetts. That was a heck of a trip

---

[54] Juliet and Florence.

NOT A JOYFUL PERSON

from Pittsburgh, Pennsylvania.[55]

Aunt Florence, who built Lyell's house[56], I remember her going back to her 50th reunion at Smith. They[57] called themselves the "Geritol Ladies". They were active, strong women. Aunt Florence was taller and probably a prettier woman than Aunt Julie.

Aunt Juliet decided, after Uncle Doc's death in 1950, that she wanted to live in a smaller home than the large residence at 1598 Virginia Street. She sold the house on Virginia Street and built her red brick house (on Staunton Road) in 1950. Her house on Staunton was nice, but modest, much more modest than the one down the hill that her sister Florence had built.

---

[55] Florence and Juliet, at the time, lived in Pittsburgh, Pennsylvania.

[56] Lyell Clay bought the Fleeson house after Mrs. Fleeson died and completely renovated it– the home was completely destroyed by fire November 22, 1997 and a Charleston physician purchased the property, building a large home there.

[57] Florence and Juliet.

—FIFTEEN—
DR. FRED INBAU

Attempting to use all resources of the day, Charleston Mayor John Copenhaver ordered his police department to retain a polygraph technician to administer lie detector tests to all persons who were in any way connected to Juliet Staunton Clark through family business or social relationships.

There was a problem, however. The two men who were polygraph specialists in southern West Virginia were not to be found; they were occupied elsewhere. Stressing expediency and choosing to raise the professional ante, Mayor Copenhaver himself contacted Dr. Fred Inbau of Northwestern University, a renowned polygraph expert. "Could Dr. Inbau travel to Charleston to assist in the investigation of this nationally known murder mystery?" Copenhaver asked.

Fees were discussed and Dr. Inbau readily agreed to take on the challenge. He packed his bags and equipment. The cost, in 1953, would be relatively high, $150 a day[58], but Inbau carried impressive credentials. He was the former director for the Chicago Police Scientific Detection Laboratory, and was *the* nationally known expert[59] regarding lie detector tests.

---

[58] Estimated as equivalent to $1,411 in today's dollars.

[59] Inbau had written several books, including, *Lie Detection and Criminal Investigation*. It was regarded as the standard work in the field.

DR. FRED INBAU

Inbau insisted that the lie detector was correct 95 percent of the time. His testament was borne out in thousands of tests. However, he pointed out that information obtained by the tests was not admissible in court evidence, and in West Virginia, the person taking the test had to do so voluntarily.

Inbau, a former member of the scientific crime detection laboratory at Northwestern, boarded a flight in Chicago and was picked up by city police at Kanawha Airport at 12:30 p.m. on September 3, 1953. He was whisked to the mayor's office as an incredibly hot summer afternoon began to creep over 100 degrees, the heat increasing as the day wore on.

Finding comfort in the cooler office of Mayor John T. Copenhaver, Inbau was handed a sandwich and soft drink and the briefing on the Clark murder case began. It was obvious that the mayor was leading the investigation. Police sat by, joining in the conversation when prompted by the mayor.

Briefing over, Inbau was again in a city car, this one the mayor's private sedan, driven by His Honor's personal driver, Lieutenant Van Brown. Copenhaver accompanied Inbau and continued to give his impressions of the case. The lie detector expert paid rapt attention but could not help but remark on the beauty of the city, peering down steep Louden Heights Road as the vehicle climbed its way to the Clark home in the city's exclusive South Hills neighborhood, on the front of the hill.

There, Inbau and Copenhaver went through the house with detectives describing the death scene. The mayor returned to City Hall, leaving Inbau to inspect the home, and nearby road access. Inbau was thorough, gaining an insight as to the lay of the killing grounds.

Later that afternoon, *Charleston Daily Mail* reporter Charlie Connor learned from sources at City Hall that Inbau had telephoned Mayor Copenhaver from the Clark home. The mayor called Chief Williams to his office, and he and Williams spoke with Inbau.

Connor wrote, "This prompted the chief to hastily summon detectives W.W. Fisher and Mayford Haynes, assigned exclusively to the case, and dispatch them hurriedly. They roared away from police headquarters in an automobile at high speed."

Connor also was going at high speed, rushing to City Hall, arriving just after Inbau had returned to join the mayor in his office. Chief Williams also was there and the three men were preparing to leave the building.

Connor cornered them, wanting to know what was so alarming about the Inbau call, a call that caused a high intensity dispatch of police.

The mayor, his chief of police and Inbau huddled a few feet from Connor and, after a brief conference, the mayor said they would decline to answer the question, saying there were many aspects of the detailed probe that could not be discussed for publication.

Connor was not pleased and unwilling to accept a "no comment".

Then, another huddle and an official statement was issued, with flowery language from the mayor, who said: "From the scientific examinations conducted by Dr. Inbau there will come to the police much help in their endeavor to build a case around the one guilty of the cruel murder." Copenhaver added that Detective Fisher had now been assigned permanently to the Clark investigation.

Connor continued to press, this time turning to Chief Williams for some explanation of the bizarre afternoon. What had Inbau learned? Williams looked at the mayor and then refused to discuss the nature of the information given by Inbau.

Inbau stayed in Charleston for two weeks and gave lie detector tests to 20 people. During that time reporters learned that an unidentified man was questioned for six hours in connection with

DR. FRED INBAU

Left to right, Mayor John Copenhaver (seated), Police Chief Dewey Williams, Detective Lieutenant Joe Craft, and Dr. Fred Inbau. –*The Charleston Gazette*

the investigation. "It was announced," Charlie Connor wrote, "a lie detector test cleared him of all suspicion in connection with guilty knowledge of the slaying."

None of Inbau's polygraph findings were ever revealed to the public. He submitted lengthy reports, not to the police chief, but to the city's mayor, John T. Copenhaver. The mayor decreed the findings were not to be revealed to anyone. Copenhaver, known by one and all in the capital city as Jumpin' John, was tightening his hold on the Clark investigation.

The mayor loomed large in all matters Juliet Clark, to the chagrin of police department veteran officers. In Copenhaver's defense, he was being assailed from all sides to quickly solve the murder and, until absolute evidence was uncovered, to protect the prominent names that were being thought of as possibly involved. One can appreciate the mayor's predicament, "damned if you do and damned if you don't."

"Why," onlookers and the media asked, "is the mayor acting as though he is police chief and prosecutor?"

Response from those in City Hall was not forthcoming—the mayor could hire and fire.

Word of "lie detector" tests leaked out in spurts. Fred Inbau believed that a "flutter" in one polygraph test, at the mention of the Kanawha River, might mean the murder weapon would be found there. Was it the break investigators needed?

It also was said that some of those who were polygraphed, "did not do too well." Reporters hounded the police for disclosure. "Go see the mayor," was the stressful reply, "he's the only one privy to Inbau's reports."

And reporters did—they had no choice. Jumpin' John's control of the Clark case increased as the *Daily Mail* front page pressure cooker gathered steam, offering a reward of $2,500[60], later raised to $15,000[61] to anyone with information leading to the arrest of the person or persons who had killed its owner.

Charleston residents who had contact with Mrs. Clark found themselves facing interrogation. *Charleston Daily Mail* publisher Fred Staunton's daughter, Betsy Staunton Johnson, recalls that the custodian at Mrs. Clark's church, Kanawha Presbyterian, faced grilling from the city's detectives:

There was a custodian at our church, Kanawha Presbyterian Church. He told me he once was working for Aunt Julie. He was in line for suspicion by the police. He said to me, "Oh, Miss Betsy, they called me into the station! I have never been an ignorant black." This man was very wise and he had worked with young kids on the west side. He was magnificent; he should have been a minister. He said, "I got in that station and I said, officer, I don't know

---

[60] Estimated as equivalent to $23,000 in 2019 dollars.

[61] Estimated as equivalent to $141,000 in 2019 dollars.

anything about anything. I'm just an ignorant black man. I just done my work, I just done anything anybody told me to do." He imitated this acute dialect. I laughed. I said, "Oh, God, how smart you were!

Betsy was referencing Tom Toliver, the gardener who had worked for Mrs. Clark. Toliver vividly remembered the game he played:

When I was facing questions from Judge Thompson, I'll be truthful, I played games with them. The judge said to me in the inquiry, "I heard you come from a good family, but you're the black sheep in that family."

I said, "No sir, judge, all the sheep in my family are black." People broke up laughing. He said, "Okay, okay, okay, I'm gonna' get you for contempt." I said, "Man, I ain't did nothin'!" I was just acting ignorant. He said, "I'm a judge, I'm not a man." And I said, "Well, a man's a judge, ain't he?" He said, "Keep runnin' that mouth of yours!"

They kept questioning me and I put my hand over my mouth, my hand over my ears and then my hands over my eyes. The judge looked over at me and said, "Well, what's all that about?" Back then, they called us Negroes, and I said, "I was told up in South Hills, that when you go to work for white people, Negroes don't say nothin', they don't see nothin' and they don't hear nothin'."

He said, "Bud, I've had enough of you."

I said, "If you want to send me to jail, send me then!"

When they picked me up I had everybody up there in South Hills behind me and, like I said, I got to be a little smart with the judge—I was just having fun with him, it intimidated him.

I'm 86 now. I worked all over South Hills from Myrtle Road to Louden Heights Road, I knew everyone there.

There were so many hush-hush stories. The case was just strange.

—*Tom Toliver*

Other elements of the Clark story were also strange. In 1953 *Air Progress* was a semi-official publication dealing with advances and progress in aviation. The September 20 edition went on sale at city newsstands the night Mrs. Clark was murdered. City police placed a notice in Charleston newspapers that asked, "Did you buy *Air Progress*?[62]"

Police said they were trying to locate those who may have bought the publication, connecting it to the Clark murder. It was ascertained that not many of the magazines were sold, but there were a few individuals that came forward with copies in their hands. There was no elaboration as to why the publication figured into the Clark case other than to, "check on already received information."

The *Mail* continued to front-page the Clark murder story every day from Saturday, August 22, 1953, through September 8 of that year. After that, it ran its reward offer for many weeks, cancelling it the day of a critical city election.

---

[62] The magazine was on sale at Trivillians Pharmacy and was said to have been on sale at what was then "Kanawha Airport".

—SIXTEEN—
JUMPIN' JOHN COPENHAVER

To understand the calamitous scene that developed around Charleston City Hall in the aftermath of the Clark murder, one has to explore the personality of Mayor John T. Copenhaver. He was highly controversial. Charlestonians opened their newspapers each day to follow the exploits of Jumpin' John, son of Ulysses Grant Copenhaver, a former Republican assessor and six-year member of the Kanawha County Court.

Copenhaver was elected Charleston's mayor in 1951, returning City Hall to Republicans. On April 17, 1951, the *Charleston Gazette* headline read, *Copenhaver wins as GOP Sweeps Major Offices in City Election.* In an accompanying *Gazette* photograph, a smiling Copenhaver shakes hands with Republican councilman-at-large John Shanklin. Copenhaver, the *Gazette* reported, had carried the bulk of the GOP ticket with him in a surprising victory over incumbent Mayor R. Carl Andrews.

Also in the photograph, congratulating the new mayor, were Republican National Committeeman Walter S. Hallanan; former Republican State Chairman Robert H.C. Kay; and victorious municipal judge, Republican Joe Thomas. Thomas had just defeated Democratic power broker Sam MacCorkle.

Charleston city council chamber was packed as interested onlookers kept vigil, watching returns roll in. The crowd supporting

Copenhaver was jubilant as they learned the news—Copenhaver and the Republicans had swept the election. Most supporters of Carl Andrews began their withdrawal from the council chambers and their power at City Hall.

Some Andrews faithful noted that returns from three city precincts were unavailable because the tally sheets had been "inadvertently" sealed with ballots not to be opened until the official canvass of the vote by council the following day. Hope remained.

But the GOP, newspaper reports said, outnumbered the Democrats in automobiles that carried the electorate to the polls. In some precincts, the *Gazette* reported, there were, "three Republican cars to two for the Democrats." The election was over and the Republicans had won going away.

Copenhaver would step into a job that paid $10,000[63] a year—it was twice the salary Carl Andrews had received. City Council had voted the increase the Saturday before Copenhaver was elected, in line with a measure passed by the 1951 West Virginia legislature. The new mayor's timing was indeed fortuitous.

Copenhaver was flushed with excitement, having received at 11:10 on election night a conceding telephone call from the defeated Carl Andrews. Andrews congratulated Copenhaver on his stunning win. The call from Andrews to Copenhaver was arranged through the *Charleston Gazette* switchboard. The call, the *Gazette* reported, was as follows:

"Who is this?"

"This is Carl Andrews. It looks like you just gave us a trimming today."

"It does seem that way, Carl. I just want you to know it was a clean fight and I want your cooperation."

---

[63] Estimated as equivalent to $94,000 in 2019.

"I will be glad to. I just want to give you my congratulations."

"We kept the punches above the belt. I'll need your help in getting started."

"All right, John, we'll give you all the help we can. Good night."

"Good night, Carl."

Copenhaver quickly told Charleston newspapers he would fulfill his campaign promises.

"It is with the deepest sense of gratitude and humility that I have received the verdict of the people of Charleston, entrusting the management of their public affairs to the Republican Party for the next four years.

"It will be my purpose, upon assuming the office of mayor, to enlist the support of all political, economic and social groups in carrying out our program for a greater Charleston. I will give the best that is in me toward the attainment of that objective."

The name "Copenhaver" dominated Charleston newspapers for eight tumultuous years and four months, as he was elected for a second time in 1955 and a third time in 1959. There is little doubt that he was the city's most colorful chief executive ever. Media coverage gratified him and he never missed the opportunity to speak to a reporter or pose for a camera.

He was so peripatetic he was tagged as "Jumpin' John" early in his first term. The moniker was pinned on him by *Gazette* political columnist Harry Hoffmann. The soubriquet stuck.

Copenhaver painted himself as a law and order man and claimed the city he had taken over was rife with crime. Following his re-election to a second term, he once again reminded voters of his commitment to wipe out vice in the city.

John T. "Jumpin' John" Copenhaver chats with young admirers
in a Charleston mayoralty campaign.
–*Charleston Daily Mail*

"I look upon this victory for the preservation of the moral fiber of our city. I shall do my utmost to continue the progressive community program in the next four years that was started four years ago," the mayor said.

Copenhaver was referencing his first term in office that began early one Friday morning just after he took the reins at City Hall. That morning was to be long remembered as he summoned top city officials and the entire city police force to council chambers on the second floor of City Hall.

And, oh yes, he also called all media outlets in town and invited reporters to the gathering.

Standing at the mayor's podium overlooking council seats that were occupied by city hall workers who answered to him, and reporters who were hanging on his every word, Copenhaver charged his police department with dereliction of duty and ordered a general cleanup of city "vice dens". Film and audiotape rolled and pencils scribbled, recording every word that the man the *Charleston Gazette* referred to as "always having his own halo around his head", spoke.

"Charleston abounds in gambling, bootlegging and prostitution," the mayor warned. He said it was not a new situation, but had gone on for some time, and he was going to bring it to a halt. He ordered acting police chief Bernard Simms to swing into action within 24 hours "to rescue our city from these evils." He added, with emphasis, "Anyone who fails to undertake to carry out the order will be fired." Those in council chambers who were there through political patronage felt both admiration for Copenhaver, and no small amount of fear of him.

It was the beginning of years of Jumpin' John following his police phalanx—sledgehammers in hand, breaking down the doors of such institutions as Momma' Nanny's, Edna's Tourist Home, the Zanzibar Club, and the A and D Grill.

JUMPIN' JOHN COPENHAVER

Raids occurred often, hundreds of arrests were made for illegal possession and sale of liquor. Startled visitors of houses of prostitution were harshly interrupted by Copenhaver's cops, and hookers stopping cars near the intersection of Dryden and Egan streets discovered their targeted customers had badges.

The mayor, the sledgehammers, and Copenhaver's Stetson hat were irresistible fodder for West Virginia's first television station, WSAZ-TV, owned by the *Huntington Herald Dispatch*. "Dispatch" WSAZ did, sending news crews to Charleston, 50 miles away, to film the crusading mayor for its 6:00 and 11:00 nightly newscasts—people wanted to see the crusader.

Jumpin' John was elated—he was *made* for TV.

Copenhaver's war on houses of gambling and prostitution that had come, he said, "dangerously close," to City Hall, emptied *Gazette* and *Daily Mail* vending machines that were located on most every corner of the capital city's downtown.

Both newspapers made three runs daily, replenishing the vending outlets each time, selling multiple editions on the city's streets with newsboys yelling headlines that zeroed in on Mayor Copenhaver's crime busting. "Copenhaver targets back end of town!" they shouted, referring to Summers Street, and environs thereof, where the action was.

Ironically, one of Copenhaver's favorite detectives, dispatched to clean up the capital city, was Bob Crouse, whom many referred to as the "Mayor of Summers Street." Even as Copenhaver pledged an end to vice in his city, one of the mayor's favorite cops was suspected of taking payoffs from illicit actors in the back end of town.

Crouse regularly patrolled Summers Street, standing in the entranceway to stores and bars thought to house illegal activity. Crouse was a tall, imposing figure who displayed a baby face that belied his dominant and, some said, brutal manner with those who crossed him. He had his supporters. Stories abound about his soft side—taking errant youths to their parents for punishment rather than arresting them.

In 1974, Crouse was indicted, following a federal investigation, and was found guilty of obstruction of justice charges.[64] He was sentenced to a minimum of three years in prison for "attempting to intimidate a witness cooperating in an FBI grand jury investigation into alleged police corruption.[65]"

Meantime, across town, at the Army-Navy and Charleston Press Clubs on Capitol Street and Kanawha Boulevard, whiskey was casually being sold in violation of a law that said only state-owned stores could sell liquor. The club's members happily enjoying bootleg booze were attorneys, judges, and the city's elite.

Those clubs did indeed experience a few police raids, but the constabulary was dutiful in calling ahead, advising club management to hide their liquor supply. Army-Navy and Press Club raids featured not a sledgehammer through the door, but a gentle knock, politely announcing the arrival of the law. It was usually determined a mistake had been made—no liquor was to be found.

---

[64] *Charleston Gazette*, March 15, 1974.

[65] Ibid.

—SEVENTEEN—
ARCH ALEXANDER, JR.

Two days after the murder of Juliet Clark, Mayor John Copenhaver issued a loquacious statement, saying, "The vile wickedness of the crime that took the life of Mrs. Clark prevents respite until its solution. The sullen mystery must surely fade before the searchings of the law and an outraged citizenry. The victim's prominence and honored standing make it clear that no one is safe from the foul hands of the criminal. The efforts of the criminal division of the Charleston Police Department are pledged to a timely solution to this awful murder."

Those efforts almost immediately centered on one of the men who had last seen Juliet Clark the night of her murder.

Arch Alexander, Jr., whose father was a former West Virginia State Mines Chief, became the son-in-law of *Daily Mail* owner Juliet Staunton Clark when he married her daughter, Julie, September 29, 1950, nine months after the bride's father, Walter Clark, had died.

A Washington and Lee Law graduate, Arch Alexander Jr. was employed in the legal department of United Fuel Gas Company, located on

Arch Alexander, Jr.
–The Charleston Gazette

ARCH ALEXANDER, JR.

Quarrier Street in the heart of the city. He and his wife and children lived on Clark Road in South Hills.

City police had originally questioned Alexander shortly after the murder of his mother-in-law. As the last person to see Mrs. Clark alive, he was asked to undergo another interrogation.

Ruth Reynolds, in her story, *The Body on the Rumpled Green Rug*, wrote, "Arch...said that he arrived at his mother-in-law's house 'about 8 o'clock,' but didn't see Lyell (Clay), who said he departed 'about 8.' This, and the hostility that existed between Arch and Mrs. Clark, at one time, apparently made his activities the day of the murder a matter for intensive probing."

Reynolds then cleared up the importance of *Air Progress* magazine:

Alexander said that after work in the legal department at the gas company (United Fuel on Quarrier Street), *he stopped at a stable to look at some horses he and Julie owned. He went home and ate, then returned to look at the horse again. Next, he went over to Mrs. Clark's to borrow the hot water bottle which, incidentally, he didn't get. He stopped at a drug store to buy a copy of the magazine annual, Air Progress, and reached home about 11:20[66] p.m.*

Reynolds then asked:

What time did he buy that magazine? Where did he buy it? Who sold it to him? Where was the magazine now?

Detectives pressed this point in an effort to break down the young husband's alibi. The proprietor of the drug store, Trevillians[67], received his order of the aviation annual on Friday, August 2. One

---

[66] The time quoted raises the question of whether a small pharmacy would be open at near midnight in 1953.

[67] Reynolds misspelled the name "Trivillians".

copy had been sold, but none of the store employees could remember when or to whom.

Police asked anyone who had bought a copy of Air Progress *in Charleston to come forward. Several people responded. But none said he bought his copy at Trevillians.*[68] *That left the situation right where it had been.*

Arch Alexander drove himself to Charleston City Hall August 27, 1953, at the invitation of Charleston police chief Dewey Williams. He arrived between 10 and 11 in the morning and readily agreed to be questioned by police for the second time. Detectives Red Fisher and Joe Craft grilled Alexander for more than 13 hours as he sat in the police chief's office. Assistant County Prosecutor Charles Walker and Mayor Copenhaver participated in most of the session.

As evening approached in the marathon questioning, sandwiches and drinks were ordered for a famished Alexander and his equally tired questioners. Reporters stood outside the interrogation door and shouted questions at Alexander as food arrived.

Alexander, newspaper reports said, "looked fresher than his interrogators." The composed young attorney repeatedly refused to reply to questions from reporters, except to ask that he not be photographed. He repeated the same phrase over and over, "No comment. I do not want to be quoted on anything."

Just as Alexander finished his meal and asked for a bathroom break, the doors of City Hall swung wide, and in stepped Milton J. Ferguson. The 50-year-old Ferguson was Alexander's uncle. He carried formidable weight as the brand new West Virginia State Tax Commissioner, appointed on March 1, 1953.

Alexander's uncle rushed up the marble stairs of city hall to the mayor's office where he was greeted by Copenhaver's receptionist who said, in answer to Ferguson's demand, that Arch Alexander

---

[68] Ibid.

was being questioned in the police chief's office, on the third floor, near council chambers.

Ferguson turned on his heel, and flew out the door, climbing yet another set of steps, turning left at the third floor, moving rapidly toward the police chief's office, intent on demanding to know why his nephew was being held for questioning.

Ferguson stopped short in the hallway, almost bumping into his nephew and Detective Lieutenant Joe Craft as the two left a third floor men's room. Alexander, tall with dark hair, was dressed in a light summer suit.

"Are you alright?" Ferguson shouted to his nephew.

Alexander assured his uncle that he was submitting to interrogation of his own will.

Alexander turned to Detective Craft and, attempting to assure his uncle, said, "That's right, is it not? I am not being detained by anyone?"

Craft agreed, with emphasis, "No indeed, you are not being detained. We're holding no one."

Left unsaid was the fact that, while Alexander was not being detained, he was undergoing hours of intensive questioning. The door to the police chief's office opened and out stepped Chief Dewey Williams. Williams entered the conversation, telling Ferguson that his nephew was willing and cooperative.

"Why is this taking so long?" Ferguson wanted to know.

Williams, tired from a day that was already long, explained, "Some of his answers had to be checked out, we retraced the same ground several times." Detective Red Fisher joined the conversation and said of Alexander, "Some of his answers are evasive."

Never one to be left out, Mayor John T. Copenhaver emerged from the chief's office, addressing Tax Commissioner Ferguson as a political heavyweight and friend.

"Arch is being treated with every courtesy, Milt," Copenhaver said.

"It's wearisome, only momentary breaks," Copenhaver added.

Copenhaver told the press, "It would be most unfortunate to point the finger of accusation at one who was examined merely because of the examination itself. The police are striving to fix the responsibility for Mrs. Clark's death. For the purpose of putting together facts which are material in solving the mystery, it is necessary to examine at length members of Mrs. Clark's family."

Seven days later, September 3, Alexander was again at City Hall, for the third time, voluntarily submitting to a lie detector test. He was polygraphed in Lyell Clay's city solicitor's office. Newspaper reports said the mayor had made the decision to use Clay's office as headquarters for Fred Inbau to administer his tests because Clay was out of town and his office was empty.

Reporter Ruth Reynolds wrote that George Morgan, a Charleston motorcycle cop, was also polygraphed. Reynolds said in her article that Morgan was, "a married man of good reputation who knew Julie" and "carried a club when on duty." Morgan passed his lie detector test and his alibi checked out. "While the bloody oak splinter could have come from a policeman's club, it didn't come from the one Morgan showed Red Fisher," Reynolds wrote.

Other news articles said *all* Staunton relatives were questioned by Inbau—all except Lyell Clay, who, a *Bluefield Telegraph* Associated Press report of September 5, 1953 said, was "away on vacation since shortly after the crime was committed."

ARCH ALEXANDER, JR.

The Charleston Gazette also reported that Lyell was on vacation shortly after Mrs. Clark's body was found. Intensive searches of newspaper records reveal scarcely any mention of Lyell Clay during the Clark investigation, other than to mention that he was on vacation, and to report his return to Charleston in September of 1953.

Reporter Reynolds provided yet additional information as she dove deeply into the question of Lyell's absence:

At the outset, Fisher (Detective Red Fisher) *found Lyell uncooperative. At first, he refused to account for his whereabouts at the time of his mother's murder. Then he refused to take a lie detector test. After that, Fisher discovered that Lyell had been the center of a family dispute over money matters. This, however, was cleared up long before his mother's death. In the midst of his investigation, the detective received an anonymous telephone call from someone who said, "Lyell's fixin' to leave town."*

Lyell did leave town. He went to South Carolina for a week "to get over the shock." When he returned he was ready to be helpful and has been ever since.

Reynolds ended her story, writing:

None of the usual sources of information—bootleggers, taxi drivers, ginmill operators, madams—have given Charleston detectives a tip on the Clark case. This indicates that someone outside the usual criminal circle is responsible. No average murderer battered in Juliet Clark's head.

The Charleston Daily Mail observed that the city administration documented Inbau's polygraph questioning—"a city hall stenographer was kept at the long and arduous task of making shorthand notes of the question and answer session."

The stenographer's report was to become yet another record to disappear.

The city solicitor's office where Inbau and the stenographer worked was adjacent to that of the mayor. It was a crowded second floor as polygraph tests were administered and reporters swarmed around the mayor's office where notables waited. Joining His Honor were Chief Williams; county prosecutor Herbert Bryan; Bryan's assistant Charles Walker; the prosecuting attorney's investigator, Angus Peyton; and Arch Alexander Jr.'s attorney Robert H.C. Kay, one of Charleston's most respected lawyers.

Kay, tall, white-haired, and patrician, made headlines when he arose from his seat and went to the door of the mayor's office. He opened the door and faced reporters. He said, "We have nothing to hide."

The door to the mayor's office was then closed, but Kay's statement did not remain in the room, it was emblazoned the following day on the front page of both Charleston newspapers and shouted from street corners by newsboys who quickly sold out, as did papers in vending machines around town.

Alexander was not named as a person of interest. But, the grueling session he faced with investigators and Dr. Inbau may have given the public reason to believe that he was, indeed, a person of interest in the death of Mrs. Clark.

Sixty-six years later, Buffy Wallace thought back:

They tried to, of course, pin that murder on Arch Alexander. I think Mayor Copenhaver, I believe it was, was very anxious to find who did it. My parents always felt like that was a very unfair accusation. My father said he never thought Arch Alexander had a thing to do with it. He liked him, first of all, and he thought he was a very nice young man. In addition to that, he said, "No father would leave their baby in a house with a dead grandmother." My father was very convinced that Arch Alexander was not the guilty party.

ARCH ALEXANDER, JR.

Elizabeth (Betsy) Staunton Johnson, the eldest daughter of *Daily Mail* publisher Fred Staunton looked back on the Clark murder. She was 20 at the time and already in college:

Shadows keep coming back to me. My father had a different view of Arch Alexander than that of Buffy's father. He (her father) *was very anti-Alexander, but, as Buffy said, you wouldn't kill your mother–in-law if your child were in a crib in the same house. I don't really remember the angst that Dad thought Arch had with Aunt Julie, whom I saw a lot on Sunday evenings when she would come up for dinner.*

My father did not like Arch as a person and never changed his mind about Arch, but I don't remember that he belabored it. I don't think he (Arch) *treated his wife very nicely.*

John Merrill, Buffy Merrill Wallace's older brother, also remembered Arch Alexander:

Julie had horses and the night of the murder my dad said to me, "Arch has to feed the horses, go with him." I rode with him that night to feed them. The horses were stabled either down on MacCorkle Avenue at what was called the "We Wanna' Ride" club (on the river bank where C&P Telephone's headquarters later located), or out Johnson Road.

Dad also had horses where Julie's were kept. She and Dad often rode together. I recall that Arch was considered to be a suspect, but I did not know that at the time. There was no serious discussion (during the trip to the stables). *He seemed perfectly normal to me.*

Julie was into photography and was taking pictures. Some were used in the Daily Mail. My father, of course, owned Merrill Photography. That, and riding horses together, created a bond. Julie greatly admired my father.

Years later John joined Merrill Photo as a full-time employee.

He eventually was asked by his father to run the business, where he often encountered Arch Alexander. John had definite feelings about Arch Alexander.

Arch was a customer of mine. I liked him and had no feeling one way or the other whether he had or had not done it. He would come in and charge purchases. He ran up several hundred dollars in charges and I, running a small business, needed to call those who owed that amount and request payment.

Merrill called Alexander at his office one evening around 6:15 and they exchanged pleasantries. Arch was effusive—"What can I do for you, John?"

John referenced the reason for his call and said he would appreciate it if Arch would pay his bill.

There was a silence on the line.

Then, John recalled, Arch said, "John, I work from eight in the morning until five in the afternoon. I do not do any business at all after 5 p.m."

John said his temper gauge went through the roof and he replied, "Arch, if you would just pay your goddamn bill, I wouldn't bother you!"

Merrill said it was the last time he ever spoke to Alexander.

—EIGHTEEN—
A FAMILY GATHERING

Mayor John Copenhaver and polygraph expert Fred Inbau agreed that a complete list of those to whom Inbau had given a lie detector test should not be made public. Revealing those names, they said, might "do serious damage" to the reputation of innocent persons.

But names *were* known. Family members were polygraphed, as well as Juliet Clark's household employees. Those names were leaked to the media. While Lyell Clay was out of town, his half-sister Julie, Arch Alexander, Jr.'s wife, was polygraphed in the city solicitor's office, voluntarily submitting to the test.

Inbau applied polygraph sensors to Mrs. Alexander, and Mayor Copenhaver stuck his head out of the office next-door. A panting press corps waited outside the solicitor's office and Copenhaver began to field reporter's questions about polygraph findings. Striding into the scrum of correspondents, he said, "Dr. Inbau and I agree that his findings will be released at a later date after he has a chance to analyze the testimony at hand."

No results were ever released.

Copenhaver added, "The investigation is continuing on the grounds that a hammer might have been used as the murder weapon." The mayor said, "Some items in the case have been submitted to the state police laboratory for analysis—there might be a delay getting reports on them."

The *Charleston Gazette* reported further family involvement with polygraph experts on November 21, 1953. A meeting between Inbau and his associate John Reid and members of Juliet Clark's family took place at 1:00 p.m. in the mayor's conference room just adjacent to Copenhaver's reception area. The room featured a long wooden conference table with a full complement of chairs and additional seating for observers. A bevy of pictures of former mayors of the city adorned the walls of the room. The large framed photos of those who had led the city in the past, among them Edward "Will" Staunton, featured few smiles—the former mayors seemed to realize the session before them that Saturday in November was indeed serious.

The mayor called the meeting to order as the doors to the conference room were closed. It had to have been an important session, underlined by the fact that Inbau had asked fellow polygraph expert Reid to assist him. Inbau introduced Reid, who had flown in from an assignment in Pittsburgh, as Mayor Copenhaver, police chief Williams, Charleston detectives, and assistant prosecutor Herbert Bryan looked on.

The session dragged on for five hours and, after it was over, reporters demanded answers from those attending the gathering. Mayor Copenhaver, strangely quiet, exited the conference room and said only that the polygraph consultants were leaving town. "They will not be called back again unless unforeseen developments arise in the case," Copenhaver said.

Seeking more information on what was obviously an unusual event, reporters insisted on knowing more. WCHS radio news director Ross Edwards poked a microphone in front of the mayor and asked, "What was the purpose of the meeting? Did the family learn what was in the polygraph results?"

Uncharacteristically, Copenhaver simply walked away, closing the door to his office, declining to say what results, if any, the meeting with the polygraphists produced.

Daily Mail publisher Fred Staunton, brother of Mrs. Clark, attended the meeting. Reporters cornered him as he left City Hall, shouting questions, but with more respect than they gave the mayor, given Staunton's newspaper credentials.

"It was a period of discussion," Staunton said, quickly departing, walking rapidly down Virginia Street toward *Daily Mail* offices.

Arch Alexander, Jr., true to form, declined to comment about the conference.[69]

Assistant prosecutor Bryan crossed the street to the courthouse, reporters trailing him. Bryan said "some progress," was made at the session, but declined to elaborate.

Contacted by the *Daily Mail*, Lyell Clay said only, "I did not attend the session." Clay was also quoted as saying he "knew nothing of what had taken place."

Mayor Copenhaver could have filled the reporters in. He had results of *all* the polygraph tests Inbau conducted; those results were in his keeping, where they would remain, guarded, *never* to be disclosed to the public.

Mayor Copenhaver's appetite for crime stopping should have been sated for the day. But it was not—the Clark family gathering ended at 6:00 and Copenhaver was on police prowl six hours later.

At midnight he accompanied detectives on raids of the city's taverns. A *Charleston Daily Mail* report said of the chief executive's Saturday night presence at police headquarters, "Chief (Dewey) Williams, weary and ready for bed two hours earlier, couldn't say no."

---

[69] *Charleston Gazette,* November 23, 1953, page 1.

A FAMILY GATHERING

The mayor watched police clean out one Kanawha Boulevard tavern of drunks, followed the patrol wagon in with its load, observed Desk Sergeants E.D. Smith and J.V. Brown as they booked prisoners, sat in on the radio call of the midnight platoon, and learned the best way to wield a "billy" when needed.

The *Mail's* story of Monday, November 23, 1953, read, in part:

By evening's end, His Honor was so impressed by the wide variety of jobs police do that he probably would have turned in the headaches of his office for a badge, if only Chief Dewey Williams had asked him.

Before he left one policeman (Patrolman Jesse Bowe) had been shot at and returned the fire on Court Street, two young men had been arrested on "molesting" charges, and Lt. Lawrence Morris invited him to come along on a raiding party on the West Side.

So off they went at 12:30 a.m. in a convoy of three cruisers to a house where police suspected whiskey was being sold illegally. The mayor and chief didn't go in, but listened to the crash of falling doors from a safe vantage point outside.

"When folks refuse to open doors," explained the chief, we have to use a sledge hammer."

The wagon rolled up again, loading four men, and hurried back to the station. Officers came out with their arms bulging with wine and whiskey. Lt. Morris captured a long .410 gauge pistol during the search.

"By gollies," the mayor explained, "this is something."

When the midnight madness finally quieted down, the mayor headed homeward in the chief's car, satisfied that 'his boys' had well earned their pay that night. So had he.

Copenhaver told the *Mail* he thought he would return the following Saturday night, "If my wife will let me out."

—NINETEEN—
NOT A PRIVATE MURDER

In the era before such publications as *The National Enquirer* and the airing of salacious television crime shows, the Charleston newspapers of 1953 were eager to report the most sensational crime and murder stories from around the globe. Editors quickly snatched up Associated Press accounts of knifings, shootings and murder most foul. Such mayhem was emblazoned across their front pages.

But *now! Here!* In Charleston! "XTRA!" newsboys shouted as they rushed from the *Mail* and *Gazette* with freshly-printed special editions detailing any new aspect of the Clark murder.

It was a diabolic mystery that fascinated not just the Kanawha Valley, but newspaper readers throughout the country. No wonder the Clark bludgeoning was the talk of the town. Daily newspaper and radio accounts were full of leads and tips that sent police scurrying—but producing no results.

The watering holes and restaurants of Charleston were deliciously rife with rumor, innuendo, facts, and fables about the murder. In the *Hideaway Room* at the Kanawha Hotel, "Tell" Lafollette, Denver Morgan, P.P. Wilson, P.G. Meador, Jack Patton, M.B. Goldman, Garland Wilkerson, and Zeke Hatfield followed the case with great interest.

NOT A PRIVATE MURDER

The same was true in the dining room at the Daniel Boone Hotel where Houston Young, Hayes Picklesimer, John Dickinson, Nathan Poffenbarger, and Harry Stansbury lunched. Across town, the peculiarities of the murder buzzed in the booths at Scott's Drug Store where notables H.B. Lewis, Carl Early, and Dr. Bedford Westfall gathered.

Down at the long table at the Diamond Cafeteria on Capitol Street, Hugh Curry, Fred Summerfield, Wehrle Geary, and A.W. Cox found it almost impossible not to dissect the case many times as lunch was consumed and opinions voiced.

Cocktails were refreshed and consumed at the bar at the esteemed and private Edgewood Country Club at the top of Edgewood Drive as members speculated who might have murdered Juliet Clark. Buckner Clay Sr. stared down at them from his portrait in the Buckner Clay Room.

Multiple opinions also were being offered at the *Charleston Gazette* where Managing Editor Frank A. Knight sat before his Underwood typewriter, heedless of the noisy clatter echoing from the newsroom beyond his office. He pondered over Arch Alexander, Jr.'s marathon grilling and, on Sunday, August 30, 1953, just days after the Clark murder, Knight wrote in his column, *Today*, that he had experienced a tough week.

Knight metaphorically wrung his hands as he wrote—one hand defending the *Gazette* decision to reveal Arch Alexander's name—the other hand assuring readers the *Gazette* felt *compelled* to print the fact Alexander had been grilled for 13½ hours.

He again stressed the fact that police never forcibly held Alexander.

He emphasized that the *Gazette*, in reporting on the Clark murder, was not withholding facts or names, hinting that the *Daily Mail* might be doing just that. Knight quoted his own editorial to make a point:

ON LAST MONDAY IN ITS LEAD EDITORIAL THE GAZETTE TOOK THIS POSITION ON THE JULIET STAUNTON CLARK MURDER:

"No crime in a generation has inspired all of us with so great a desire to assist in any way we can. Because of this united determination on the part of the community a word of caution is in order. In the absence of clear-cut evidence false reports are certain to start. Some of them may be planted by thoughtless people, and as they grow could become harmful, even dangerous. Good citizens would do well to spike them before they start."

As we wrote the words we already had in our possession a hundred rumors, most conflicting with each other, which the police were running down as fast as they popped up. And we knew, as they did, that there would be hundreds more for here was a hideous killing that fired the imagination of thousands upon thousands of citizens.

With the crime now more than a week old, the rumors, again mostly ugly, will continue to come crawling out like the many-legged bugs from under rocks. Even a sudden announcement that the case had been solved would not stop them now.

PROCEED WITH CAUTION

What should be done with them? There isn't a police department in the world that could tab them true or false in time enough to satisfy every one of the taxpayers. Nor is there a newspaper that could print them all without investigation, even if it dared run the risk of libel.

Yet, literally thousands of calls have flooded our switchboards since the Clark case first broke, asking if this or that was correct. Our answer must always be that we publish only that which we find to be factual, and beyond that we can only check on any other information we receive.

As the opposition newspaper to the Daily Mail, of which Mrs. Clark was the principal stockholder, we are aware that unless we take every precaution there are some readers who might surmise we are taking an unfair advantage in printing some of the news on her murder. Yet, we also realize that the management of the Daily Mail is cooperating with public officials in every way possible in an effort to reach an early solution to the killing.

RUMORS NOT WANTED

Summed up, the Clark murder has not only placed both newspapers in an uneasy position, but it also has embarrassed the radio stations, the news services and, to an even greater degree, the city and state administrations. These latter two are involved because the city administration is of the same general political faith as the Daily Mail and the state administration because of persons in influential places who bear a personal concern in their outcome.

It has every one of them on the spot and no matter how careful and diligent all of us are there will be those who will charge we are withholding information because of fear and friendships. With this in mind every member of The Gazette staff has been warned that we are interested in only two points, (a) the arrests and conviction of the guilty persons or persons, and (b) keeping our readers informed of the absolute facts and to hell with the rumors.

With this policy established we were the first

to publish the story that Arch Alexander, Jr. was being questioned by police although others had the same information and were not revealing it. No one asked us to withhold it, and even if they had it is extremely doubtful if we would have obliged them.

NOT A PRIVATE MURDER

Gathering and printing the news is not always the most pleasant job in the world and we had some bad moments last week before making some of the decisions we did. Yet, beneath any personal reactions is the training of newsmen that their first obligation is to the people who subscribe to their papers.

To have withheld the news of Alexander's questioning, as some were momentarily tempted to do, would have served no good purpose. Indeed, it probably would have added fuel to the fire of reports which were then and still are making the rounds. In the end the fact that he was being questioned, and not held on any charge, would have become completely distorted. I have seen this happen many times.

The difficulty with murder is that it is not a private matter and to the credit of the city administration, the county prosecutor's office and the state police, it must be recognized that they are not pulling any punches in their efforts to find the killer, or killers.

TOUGH ON THE COPS

Conceivably, the Clark murder could drag on for weeks, even months, before a solution is reached. If it does, a number of people are going to be hurt by its far flung implications. No one regrets this more than The Gazette, but murder is never pretty and to reach the reason for it often requires bold methods. The police are experiencing some tough times as a result. Because of the prominence of the dead woman every move they make is subject to question by some interested party and the spotlight of public attention is drawn to it. Their job would be much simpler if the victim had not been so well known.

From a national standpoint the murder is one of the most publicized in several months, which is a long time when you consider the number of killings that occur annually in this country, and the very fact that it remains unsolved at this writing has resulted in top play in newspapers from New York to Los Angeles. Four and five column headlines are not uncommon.

WHEW!

Personally, I'm glad last week is over. It's never any fun invading private lives, and it becomes tougher when someone may be hurt. When it is a relative of an acquaintance it becomes even more personal.

Some people will say we newsmen write to sell newspapers first and to serve second. I wish I could have left some decisions to some of those critics in the last eight days.

Things always look different from the other side of the fence.

Frank A. Knight, Managing Editor

September 2nd, three days after Knight's column was published, the temperature in Charleston reached 100.7 degrees.

—TWENTY—
I SKETCH YOUR WORLD EXACTLY AS IT GOES

Juliet Clark's son, Lyell Clay, ran for a seat in the West Virginia House of Delegates the year before his mother was murdered. He was unsuccessful in his quest. One year after his mother's death he again campaigned for the House. His second effort was also unsuccessful, and Lyell abandoned his dream of a political career.

In 1956 he chose to move to *The Charleston Daily Mail* where he, his brother Buckner, and half-sister Julie (Mrs. Arch Alexander, Jr.) were bequeathed ownership in the *Daily Mail*. Lyell then became fixated on building a media empire.

The Charleston Daily Mail story of June 29, 1956, announcing Lyell's move to the *Daily Mail* mentioned that the mother of Lyell, Buckner and Juliet, Mrs. Walter Eli Clark, was deceased, but not that she had been murdered.

At the *Mail*, the story said, Lyell would be in an "administrative capacity" at the newspaper.

That would soon change.

Lyell Clay
-*Charleston Daily Mail*

CLAY QUITS CITY OFFICE; JOINS MAIL

Charleston's city solicitor today announced his resignation from that position, effective Monday, to become directly associated with The Charleston Daily Mail in an administrative capacity.

Named to the city post only five days after Mayor Copenhaver began his first term of office, Clay is one of six city officials who have served without change since his original appointment.

The mayor accepted the resignation regretfully and said, "This young man leaves behind a public record to which he can always point with pride and satisfaction."

Lyell said, "It has been a very enjoyable and rewarding experience to have worked with you during these last five years and one which I shall treasure always. I consider it an honor to have served in your administration, and in my opinion, the people of Charleston can never repay you for the countless benefits and improvements which you have brought to this city."

Mayor Copenhaver must have been delighted to have the man he mentored move to the *Daily Mail*—it would be difficult for Lyell Clay to question the city's mayor on the editorial pages of the newspaper Clay would soon control.

Copenhaver returned the bouquet given him by Clay, replying, "While I regret to see him go, I rejoice in the knowledge that Lyell will take with him into the field of journalism those qualities of honor and moral integrity upon which a free press must stand for survival and public respect. Our loss will be the newspaper's gain. I predict that in not too many years this young man will stand foremost among the publishers of strength and moral uprightness."

January 1, 1958, two years after leaving his law firm and the post of city solicitor, Lyell fulfilled Mayor Copenhaver's prediction that he would be an innovator in the news publishing business. On that New Year's Day, Lyell, as president of the Charleston Mail Association, and Fred Staunton, as publisher of the *Daily Mail,* announced a consolidation of the *Charleston Gazette* and *Charleston Daily Mail* business and printing practices.

The announcement came in the form of a front-page message from the two men, next to a story by writer Chuck McGhee that gave details of the agreement and histories of the two newspapers.

Clay's innovations did not sit well with publisher Staunton, who never had any ownership of the *Daily Mail.* Soon, Staunton was gone. Some said Lyell wanted total control of the newspaper, and that he pushed Staunton out.

Publically it was said that Staunton retired, but many observers believed such was not the case. Those familiar with the matter said Staunton, a relatively young man, was quite distraught.

Fred Staunton was never again employed.

—TWENTY-ONE—
SLICING "BALONEY" WITH AN AXE

The Charleston newspapers of the 1950s were, to say the least, exciting to read. Their Damon Runyon reporting style and the sheer volume of newspaper journalism, when newsprint was cheap and profits were high, led to verbose reporting and colorful language by both reporters and newsmakers.

Charleston Gazette political columnist and chief editorial writer Harry Hoffmann not only tagged Mayor John Copenhaver as Jumpin' John, at times he called the mayor, "Toreador"—underlining Copenhaver's instinct to always be in the ring, waving red flags to any who opposed him.

Copenhaver also was known to have a lighter side, loving baseball and circuses. One day, as he left town, bound for the "Big Top", he was quoted in the *Daily Mail* as saying, "Boy, it's going to be nice to see one again...eating hot dogs...no bother, no fuss, no answering questions...reminds me of the time I was a country boy." The mayor *could* loosen up at times. On one occasion, he danced at a city event in such an accomplished way city workers dubbed him, "Twinkle-Toes".

Hoffmann and editor Frank Knight, however, found nothing amusing about the mayor's demeanor, providing unrelenting criticism of Copenhaver as Jumpin' John sought re-election to a second term. Hoffmann said in his column of Decem-

SLICING "BALONEY" WITH AN AXE

ber 12, 1954, headlined, *Life and Slander On the Lay-Away Plan*, that Copenhaver and his publicists "already have announced, positively and irrevocably, that anyone who runs against John T. Copenhaver will be a tool of gamblers and other racketeers."

Hoffmann charged Copenhaver with political skullduggery and "irresponsible ravings." The columnist said Copenhaver had effectively pre-accused anyone who might have the unmitigated gall to run against him. Hoffmann wrote:

As a lawyer, John T. Copenhaver has represented his share of the underworld element. Among others, one Franklin Calloway—a man who has as much claim to being the king of the numbers racketeers as any man since Big Bill Lias turned legit—has found John T. Copenhaver in his corner.

Big Bill Lias[70] was a notorious racketeer in Wheeling, West Virginia, considered the state's most infamous town, riddled with crime that had Big Bill's name written all over it. Franklin Calloway, Hoffmann reported, headed the numbers racket in McDowell County and later went to prison. Hoffmann said when the Feds came for Calloway, "the man who now wears a halo," jumped to his defense.

Hoffmann went on to call Copenhaver a "McCarthy in knee britches", comparing him as a pint-size Joe McCarthy, the Wisconsin senator who made unsubstantiated charges against hundreds of Americans he claimed were communists.

Hoffmann wrote:

If a person is to be convicted as a racketeer for doing nothing more than running for mayor of Charleston, what then is to be the decision on the mayor who has actually associated with known racketeers?

---

[70] "Lias controlled the illegal rackets in Wheeling, West Virginia with an iron fist and an extensive web of mob ties"–Legendary Locals of Wheeling, West Virginia (page 62), by Sean Duffy and Brent Carney.

Hoffmann then went into overdrive, his typewriter clanging through *The Charleston Gazette* newsroom as he puffed incessantly on his ever-present *Cigarillo*, writing:

Ever since he has been mayor, Copenhaver has ranted about vice in Charleston. To hear him tell it, there wasn't an honest person in Charleston when he took office. The town was infested with gangsters, prostitutes, thieves and other purveyors of corruption.

Hoffmann summed it up by saying, facetiously:

Copenhaver, of course, cleaned it all up, but it still is a subject of constant conversation with him. He never makes a speech without donning his halo.

Needless to say, Copenhaver probably had little use for Hoffmann, excepting that Hoffmann considered him good copy, and the mayor had to be extremely appreciative of that. Hoffmann might not have liked him, but the Copenhaver name was increasingly in print.

Each afternoon, *The Charleston Daily Mail*, Juliet Staunton Clark's Republican newspaper, gave Jumpin' John little critique, massive coverage, and editorial support. It tended to clean up all that mess from those complaining folks at the morning newspaper. Charlie Connor was the *Mail's* City Hall reporter and he had scoop after scoop as Copenhaver fed him stories. Connor was an easygoing reporter with a wide smile and engaging way. One could not help but like him as he easily chatted up office holders, veteran journalists, and even cub reporters, calling them "Kid" in an affable manner.

Connor's ear was always at the mayor's door and reporters who came for a Copenhaver news conference would usually find him by the mayor's side as they came through the door. Connor, however, never kowtowed to Copenhaver. All agreed Connor's reporting was unfettered, balanced, and fair. The fact that Connor could walk the journalistic tightrope with integrity while being wooed by the strongest of personalities—Copenhaver—earned him the highest respect at both the *Mail* and *Gazette*.

During the intense 1950's competition between *The Gazette* and *The Charleston Daily Mail* it would have been unfathomable for reporters at either paper to think they would one day work in the same building on Virginia Street. But the morning newspaper would be invited in the late 1950s to move to the *Daily Mail's* new structure to share the state-of-the-art presses and business functions, saving money for one and all, an innovation by Lyell Clay.

The business offices would be housed on the first floor, the second floor would hold the two newsrooms, separated by a staircase and hall. The mammoth presses, and offices that were leased to the Associated Press, would complete the space within the building.

The *Mail* newsroom, if one stood on Virginia Street, facing the front of the building, was to the right, naturally. *The Gazette's* was to the left, far left, some complained. From those perspectives the writers and editorialists wrote far different stories, but it would continue to be patently obvious they agreed on one thing—John T. Copenhaver was too colorful to be ignored.

Before and after the consolidation, the *Mail* endorsed the Republican who controlled City Hall while the *Gazette* considered him an unmitigated ham, vigorously opposing and regularly attacking him on its editorial page. The paper said his announcement that he would run for a second term was tantamount to "slicing baloney with an axe," a reference to the manner in which he ordered his police to break down doors of supposed iniquity. *The Gazette* said it was shameless that Copenhaver declared that he *must* "present his candidacy in that he had been swamped with endorsements and pleas that he again seek the mayor's office."

Harry Hoffmann did give Copenhaver credit as being counted on to do "tremendous things" and said in the political arena Copenhaver was the bull that always "laid low." Hoffmann likened the mayor's political gambits as "ventures into outer space." When he criticized Copenhaver for those celestial trips, Hoffmann said Copenhaver would grin and shrug his shoulders, "for it put him where he likes best to be—in the spotlight."

Copenhaver often let Hoffmann slide off his back by seeking once again the mayor's special respite, slipping off to New York to find relief from the issues, heading for the Big Apple to take in Ringling Brothers *Greatest Show on Earth*.

—TWENTY-TWO—
BALLPEEN HAMMER

As reporters covered the first week of the sensational murder story of the slaying of Juliet Staunton Clark, the mayor of the city of Charleston was the talk of the town. Jumpin' John Copenhaver assumed the position of chief investigator, interrogator and spokesman to the press.

The daily doings at city hall and the rumors of big names involved fueled the daily gossip at the *Hub Restaurant & Poolroom* in the heart of the city at the corner of Quarrier and Dickinson Streets. Ironically, in a town where the mayor had pledged to wipe out crime, the *Hub* openly ran illegal tip boards and facilitated sports betting.

The diner's vast interior featured a long lunch counter to the right and booths to the left. Where the counter and the booths stopped, the expansive poolroom began, separated from the eating customers by large swinging doors. A youngster with an extraordinary future practically grew up there. In the late 50s baby-faced Danny Jones, one day to be a four-term mayor of Charleston, lugged food through the eatery, earning dining privileges as he grew up a street kid who hailed from Staunton Road in affluent South Hills. As young Danny strode through the *Hub* he often passed former Charleston mayor and candidate for governor, Daniel Boone Dawson, who regularly took lunch at the *Hub*.

BALLPEEN HAMMER

In the *Hub* poolroom, giant blackboards on twenty-foot-high walls enabled one and all to keep track of major league baseball or professional football scores, updated periodically by Faze Moses who rolled a ladder on wheels under the blackboards, climbing up with a large eraser to chalk up the latest as sport scores changed. Moses' work enabled customers at the counter or in the booths to stay current with the bets they had placed with the *Hub*'s bookie.

The bookie himself was a colorful character who held court from a raised podium to one side of the poolroom, enabling him to watch all activity and accept cash from bettors. This was done in the full presence of the regular customers, prosecutors, former mayors, an abundance of attorneys, and several Charleston patrolmen, lunching free, as they did each day.

Many of the *Hub*'s patrons reflected a popular opinion, nudging one another, some grinning, some grimacing, saying that Mayor Copenhaver might be lax on sports betting, but he seemed to be quite the opposite in what some thought appeared to be an intent to protect the city's elite residents who might be suspects in the Clark murder case. Prominent names were passed back and forth as burgers and beer were consumed. It was complicated—what might have occurred up there on Staunton Road—was there a cover up?

Mayor Copenhaver ignored the innuendo and many opined that the public and the newspapers should let Jumpin' John be Jumpin' John, that he simply could not help himself. This murder was the biggest news ever to hit the town and Copenhaver *had* to grab headlines as the self-described crime-fighting mayor—it was in his DNA.

Years later, *Daily Mail* reporter Charlie Connor would write, "He...changed his mind about small clubs and pool halls as 'dens of iniquity,' and issued a statement that poolrooms were the country club of the laboring class."

Copenhaver told Connor, "I still like to sit in a poolroom and eat a bowl of beef stew."

As the *Hub's* regulars watched, ate *their* beef stew, and listened to the rumors, yet another juicy topping was added to the daily buzz—had the murder weapon been discovered?

It was Saturday afternoon, August 29, 1953, one week after Juliet Clark was found horribly bludgeoned on Staunton Road and the day after Arch Alexander had been marathon-grilled by city police. A line of moviegoers waited at the Virginian Theatre on Virginia Street, where Alan Ladd stared in "Shane". At the "air-conditioned" Capitol Theatre on Summers Street, Leslie Caron had the lead role in "Lili".

Mayor Copenhaver had his own show that Saturday—he called a news conference and, for the cameras, held high a ballpeen hammer that he said, "might be the murder weapon." It had been found in a basement, a significant basement—the home of Arch Alexander, Jr., son-in-law of the murdered woman. The *Gazette* story appeared under a picture of Copenhaver addressing radio reporters Gilbert Brooks of WKNA; Ross Edwards of WCHS; Bob Bower of WTIP; Don Seagle (Marsh) of the *Gazette*; and Walt Sutton, United Press. Their reporter's notebooks were in high gear.

Later that same day, Police Chief Dewey Williams described the hammer pretty much as the mayor had. "Possibly the murder weapon." But the chief declined to elaborate, pending a technical explanation by state police experts.

Then, the next morning, confusion seemed to reign. In stories carried in two of the *Daily Mail's* three Sunday editions, the paper reported that Chief Williams had discounted the hammer as a murder weapon. The Sunday editions said: "A small ballpeen hammer, which police said they took from the basement of Arch Alexander, Jr.'s home, was in no manner connected as a murder instrument in the death of his mother-in-law, Mrs. Juliet Staunton Clark, Chief of Police Dewey Williams told the *Daily Mail* last night."

Police Chief Williams read the *Mail's* story and called the newspaper. He flatly denied the *Mail's* report of his comments. The chief said he "had no idea why I was quoted erroneously by the *Mail*. I'm far from discounting the hammer as a weapon and at no time have I said differently. I don't know how the *Mail* could have misquoted me. I can state definitely that the hammer has not been eliminated in this case."

Some took the chief's statement with a grain of salt. Had Williams been called on the carpet by the mayor and, seeing the wrath of Jumpin' John, reversed course?

Williams was quick to change the subject. He let slip that the Criminal Identification Bureau of the State Police had made its report on the hammer.

Gazette reporter Don Seagle (Marsh) was tired of the double talk. He pressed Williams, "Well, what are the findings? Is the hammer the murder weapon, or has it been eliminated?"

"I would say no..." Williams said, and then bowed once more to Copenhaver—"ask the mayor about that."

Seagle did.

The mayor was quick to respond, saying, "The hammer is an important element in this case. The degree of its importance must be determined from additional information, which the police are now seeking and putting together. The hammer is still regarded as an important clue."

Chief Williams then assured the reporters that "the investigation is going full speed and will continue until a solution is reached." He said statements were being taken but did not elaborate.

"Statements from whom?" reporter Jim Hill asked.

"Certain people," Williams replied, edging away.

The surge of scribes followed the chief, and he felt compelled to add more to the story, saying over his shoulder, "Police departments in other cities, both in and out of West Virginia, are cooperating fully in running down leads. Our state police and police in other states are working with us and we're following every possible lead."

That wasn't enough for the hungry reporters and questions rang out. The chief continued to try to appease the surly band and added, "We're trying to offset lack of an apparent motive by hard work in tracking down and checking information as it is obtained."

He then seemed to withdraw his previous timeline for state police criminal tests for the ballpeen hammer, saying, "It'll be at least tomorrow before certain objects will be scientifically tested for any possible connection with the crime."

"Is another weapon being tested besides the hammer?" reporters asked.

Apparently exhausted, Williams closed his office door.

Later that day, Hill, relentless, sought out Arch Alexander, Jr., calling his home.

Julie Alexander, daughter of the brutally murdered Juliet Clark, answered the call.

"This is Jim Hill at the *Gazette*," said the voice on the line.

"Yes?" Juliet quizzed.

"May I speak with Arch Alexander?" Hill asked.

"He's not at home."

"Who is this?"

BALLPEEN HAMMER

"His wife."

Hill jumped at his chance and related the story that a ballpeen hammer found in the basement of her home was being tested as a possible murder weapon in the death of her mother.

Mrs. Alexander, still convalescing from childbirth of twins, the death of one, and a mother murdered, listened to what she must have considered an abrasive call and calmly responded.

"As I said, Mr. Alexander is not at home, but he has asked me to tell anyone who might inquire that he has absolutely nothing to say. I don't want to say anything either."

Hill pressed on, asking yet another question.

"Neither I, nor my husband, have any comment to make," Julie said, hanging up. One can hardly imagine the emotions she must have felt in the wake of Hill's call.

The *Gazette* story cared little for Julie's feelings, noting that Mrs. Alexander, with the death of her mother, was, "apparently the largest single shareholder in the *Daily Mail*."

Then, the ballpeen hammer disappeared as a potential murder weapon. The scientific tests from State Police stated that the wooden handle of the hammer, "did not match the piece of splintered wood found near Mrs. Clark's body."

The ballpeen hammer possibility as the murder weapon tended to drive home the incredible brutality of the death of Juliet Clark. That terrible hot summer night in 1953 surely culminated with a heated argument, mounting tension, gusts of anger, and a horrible, forceful, swinging of a weapon, brutally striking Mrs. Clark in the face, totally obliterating one of her eyes and its socket, creating a ragged hole in the back of her skull. She must have fallen with the first blow, her life ebbing from her as blood gushed from the first strike to her head.

The coroner's report said *seven* blows were struck to her face. An enraged murderer obviously continued to bludgeon Mrs. Clark's body as she lay dying on the floor of her home, her face mutilated, her body bleeding from the barbaric attack.

If a ballpeen hammer were indeed the weapon used to strike the seven sadistic blows, the murderer would have had to carry it to and from the Clark home, indicating a premeditated crime. The assailant left behind a grisly scene—Juliet Clark's crumpled body, lying face down, her blood flowing onto a rumpled green rug.

—TWENTY-THREE—
A DEEP DIVE

We would go out walking with Daddy and comb the woods, looking for some sign—that somebody might have run through the woods over the hill and dropped something. I remember doing that forever. I remember my father undergoing a lie detector test, voluntarily, and I'm not sure if my Uncle Fred did that or not. There is a possibility that Uncle Fred was in Nags Head on their family vacation. Members of the family were very willing to take lie detector tests to be, you know, sure they weren't involved.

Aunt Julie, as I said, was very well educated. She was a smart, responsible woman and strong willed. Daddy always felt somebody that had worked for her came to the door, and came in asking for money. He thought that she perhaps recognized them and—he said she would have done this—she would have said, "John Smith, I know who you are and you'll be in trouble for doing this!" Daddy said it would have scared them and they would have started hitting her in the head.

That was Daddy's theory, because he said she was very feisty and would have stood up to anybody.
                      -Buffy Merrill Wallace

Lie detector tests were the order of the day at Charleston City Hall. One of the subjects being polygraphed in the Clark case mentioned the Kanawha River, in a quavering voice.

A DEEP DIVE

The Kanawha River!

Mayor Copenhaver jumped on the shaky reference, thinking the person who waivered might know that the weapon used to murder Juliet Clark could be found on the river's bottom. On September 4, 1953, 75-year-old Tom McGuffin of Point Pleasant was hired at $65[71] a day to search the Kanawha. McGuffin donned a deep-sea diver's suit and patiently explained what he would do.

"I'll begin the search near the mouth of Porter Hollow on the south side of the river, just below the front of the hill where Mrs. Clark lived," McGuffin told reporter Jim Hill.

McGuffin said he would then move downriver to below the South Side Bridge. His 42-year-old son Harold, 14-year-old grandson Thomas, Jeff Meade "and a crew of assistants" would man an air pump and barge mooring lines that would give him air and assist his movements.

Diver Tom McGuffin
–*Charleston Daily Mail*

Large crowds of passersby gathered along MacCorkle Avenue to watch the show. Police officers Dallas Bias, Tommy Young and George Nunley kept order. Underwater, McGuffin followed a 108-foot cable fastened to a heavy weight on the riverbed.

An assistant along the shore held another cable. McGuffin moved slowly, feeling every inch of the river bottom with his bare hands. Upon reaching the weighted end of his cable, he moved a few inches downstream. The assistants ashore moved their end of the cable a few inches to compensate. McGuffin also utilized a magnet to search for metal objects.

WSAZ-TV's camera, at the ready, waited at riverside, hoping to see the diver emerge from the deep with an object held high in

---

[71] Estimated as equivalent to $611 in 2019.

his hand. McGuffin broke the water surface, and then re-submerged many times. But, no murder weapon was found.

Finally wading from the river at the end of his search, McGuffin, described by reporter Hill as, "a wizened, gray-haired man with bushy eyebrows," said the river bottom was "part mud, part rocks, and part junk." But none of those parts contained anything that seemed as though it might be used to mutilate a prominent Charleston socialite. The event was, however, great excitement for those who lined the riverbank, eagerly awaiting a break in the Clark case.

The night of the first dive in the Kanawha River, September 4, just before 9 p.m., rains came, breaking the back of Charleston's heat wave of 100 plus degrees and reinforcing the city's dwindling water supplies.

In this cooler weather, the diving searches for a murder weapon went on for four days, to no avail.

Tom McGuffin emerges from the Kanawha River search for the Clark murder weapon.
–Charleston Gazette

—TWENTY-FOUR—
THE QUIET OF A THOUSAND LIVING ROOMS

By October of 1953 the *Charleston Gazette* was extremely agitated that the Juliet Clark murder investigation had apparently stalled. *Gazette* Editor Emeritus Jim Haught recalled the *Gazette* frustration at the slow progress.

Haught said, "I was a callow young police reporter during the Clark case. We printed a front-page photo of a ballpeen hammer and asked if a weapon like this killed the wealthy newspaper owner. Frank Knight had me write daily notices saying, 'no progress yet,' in solving the case. Detective Red Fisher got annoyed when he learned that I wrote several in advance, assuming that he'd never make any progress." A veteran detective with red hair and slim build, Fisher was not a man easily agitated, but he bristled that the Clark murder eluded him—he wanted, with every bodily fiber, to solve the case.

Months had gone by and no solution of the sensational murder had been achieved. *The Gazette* editorial board felt it had to act, particularly so since *The Daily Mail*, Mrs. Clark's newspaper, was strangely silent about the case.

October 25, *The Charleston Gazette* editorialized that the city's housewives were "bolting their doors" as the Clark investigation was going nowhere. The editorial set off a chain of events that played out over the next three days with Mayor Copenhaver, the

THE QUIET OF A THOUSAND LIVING ROOMS

Gazette, the *Daily Mail,* and the statewide Republican Ogden newspaper chain all casting their opinions into murky water.

Fiery exchanges began that Sunday morning with a bold headline at the top of the *Gazette* front page that screamed the question:

HAS JUSTICE FAILED?

CLARK MURDER, NOW TWO MONTHS OLD, GOES UNSOLVED WITH REPUTATION AT STAKE

Two months ago Juliet Staunton Clark, prominent Charleston socialite and publisher, was found murdered in her South Hills residence. For several weeks following, police and city officials conducted a relentless investigation in an effort to find her killer.

But now the search seems to have ended or, if it is being continued, there is nothing new to report. There are no new clues; no additional persons are being questioned.

The clamor for the killer, or killers, of Mrs. Clark is dying down. An aroused community is no longer demanding that no stone be left unturned to bring them to justice. Oh, in the quiet of a thousand living rooms it may still be the No. 1 topic of discussion when the rest of the day's news has been scanned, but the dreadful truth is the bludgeon slaying is being forgotten.

Yet, here was a murder so dreadful that only two months ago housewives who had been previously neglectful were suddenly bolting their doors securely before retiring for the night. Newspaper editorial writers were joining with public officials, civic and church leaders in promising that Charleston's most sensational killing in 20 years or more might be solved.

Police were moving fast in those hours and working around the clock. Persons acquainted with Mrs. Clark, or even remotely suspected of being in the area of the scene of the murder the night it occurred, were being subjected to long hours of questioning. Worse still, some submitted to lie detector tests conducted by an expert of national recognition.

A section of the Kanawha River was dragged, several items were examined as possible weapons, and the house and grounds were carefully gone over several times.

In the wake of such a diligent investigation may well rest the reputation of every person who had been consulted, questioned or approached and later released. What the future holds for them cannot be settled until the tongues stop gossiping or the murder itself is solved.

The rumormongers never will be silenced for they thrive on the lackadaisical attitude of the police and their bosses. When the newspaper headlines are burned with last week's trash they look for new, more positive glories. To most of them the Clark murder is as dead as the woman herself.

The Gazette doesn't believe this should be permitted to happen. In fact, we think we are safe in stating that neither does the Daily Mail, of which Mrs. Clark was the principal owner. But we are not handicapped by the proximity of the slaying as is our competitor, and so we do not hesitate to say that justice is not being accomplished here.

If it is as the police say, there are no new clues and the trail is cold, then let us start afresh. To do this may require a new set of investigators, public or private.

> Should this require additional funds then let us hear so. And if there is not a significant amount in the city's treasury then let us have a public subscription.
> This is a rich and growing community. Its citizens, for the most part, are honest and respected. They should not permit this crime to go unsolved.
> The solution of this murder is not the only thing at stake. There is safety and integrity of the living to consider, too.

Mayor Copenhaver, in his stately home that Sunday morning, October 25, had to have stared long and hard at the *Gazette* front page. His thoughts must have run the gamut from anger to exhilaration. *The Gazette*! Pure scum! Criticizing an investigation to which he had lent hundreds of hours from his busy schedule!

Storming into City Hall on a Sunday, the mayor summoned his secretary to his office and wrote a letter that outlined in a rambling manner his disgust with *The Gazette*.

—TWENTY-FIVE—
GAZETTE VENOM

Addressing the *Charleston Gazette* editorial that asked if justice had failed, John Copenhaver castigated the newspaper for trying to embarrass him, his police force and even the family of Juliet Staunton Clark.

The Gazette gleefully printed his response on its front page October 26, 1953, under a headline that said the mayor ripped them, commenting that he seemed bitter. And how:

Gazette front page as Mayor Copenhaver throws salvo at the newspaper.
–Charleston Gazette
October 26, 1953.

GAZETTE VENOM

Copenhaver aimed his missile at editor Frank Knight. The mayor was steamed. One can imagine smoke coming out his ears as he rambled from the Clark case to an investigation in Logan County, saying the *Gazette* would stoop to anything to gain its point, even publishing fake letters to the editor and all-out fraud.

> *Frank A. Knight, Managing Editor*
> *The Charleston Gazette*
> *Charleston, West Virginia*
>
> *Dear Sir:*
>
> *Subject: Clark Murder Case and Gazette Demagoguery*
>
> *It would be wrong to allow the editorial appearing on the front page of your newspaper yesterday entitled, "Has Justice Failed", to go unanswered. Let me say at the outset that the editorial was not written in good faith and that it represents another step in your newspaper's policy to unjustly embarrass the family of Juliet Staunton Clark; the Daily Mail, a competing newspaper and one you often refuse to refer to by name; the police department; and the present city administration.*
>
> *The effort put forth and the money expended to find a solution to the Clark murder case is unequaled in the history of Charleston. The city police, aided by the state police, the sheriff's deputies, and the prosecuting attorney's office, have done everything humanly possible to build a case around the killer of this prominent woman.*
>
> *At great expense to the city a national figure in the person of Fred E. Inbau of Chicago, professor of law at Northwestern University and an authority on crime detection, was brought into the case and kept here for a week. A professional diver was employed to search the floor of the Kanawha River. For the purpose of finding the killer's weapon great areas in the vicinity of the Clark home and elsewhere were*

carefully searched. Every clue was methodically sifted. The investigation is still in progress and it will not end until the killer has been brought to the bar of justice.

Professor Inbau worked on the case with our police for a whole week. Upon completing his assignment Professor Inbau, in answer to a question of mine, said our police are capable, honest and unsurpassed in ability by any with whom he had ever worked. Our police would gladly give up most any object they possess and cherish to solve the case. They refuse to quit until it is solved: They deserve the praise of the people for a courageous effort, which they receive, not the venom the Gazette is spewing upon them.

The police must not only know the identity of the killer but they must put together proper and relevant evidence which can be used in a court of law before the murderer can be indicted and convicted.

For some time now the Gazette has been building up to the editorial of yesterday. When something is so bad for even the Gazette to print as its own, the Gazette writes itself a letter. The Gazette has some phony name affixed to its letter and then publishes it in that "section" of the paper called the Reader's Forum. By this trick the readers are deceived and often feel that there is some merit in the letter. Such practice is nefarious and perpetrates a fraud upon the readers. Such letters appeared in the Gazette last week. They dealt with the Clark case. Of course, it is a cowardly way to strike at an adversary, a competitor, or a political foe, but that does not deter the Gazette.

The time has come to expose some of the fraud this newspaper has foisted upon its readers. The Gazette pretends that its only concern about the Clark case is in bringing the killer to justice. I don't believe it. Why was the Gazette's feeling so different a few months ago concerning the brutal slaying of Sarah Reed at her home at Logan? Sarah Reed's murder was planned by Melvin Loveless, who was king of the numbers racket at the time my administration came in power. He was indicted, tried and promptly convicted. He was sentenced to be executed.

The Gazette set out to snatch this dangerous criminal from the executioner. Did those who run the Gazette—and some of their political friends cringe when they thought upon what this racketeer might tell just before the switch was turned? Evidently so. To lay the groundwork for saving Loveless from the chair the Gazette went to Logan where he was in jail awaiting removal for the death house at Moundsville and obtained from him a "statement". This "statement" was then published on the front page of the Gazette under banner headlines.

In the story the Gazette saw to it that the criticism directed at our police was used for all that it was worth. It must be remembered that it was our police who drove Loveless out of business and to his present plight. The Gazette then sent its reporter to Moundsville to obtain statements from those who had engaged with Loveless in murdering Sarah Reed and who were then serving life sentences for their part in the crime planned by this criminal. These statements were also publicized.

The Gazette's purpose in giving great publicity to the statements was to create in the minds of the people the thought that this thug had been dealt with unjustly. The Gazette wanted to prepare the public for clemency.

Next, the Gazette visited the Capitol building a few days before the execution, pleading for commutation of sentence. This was before the Supreme Court granted the writ of error in the case.

While the Gazette was trying so hard to save Loveless from the electric chair another statement came into its possession which has never been published. Why? Because it would destroy the Gazette's very purpose. Then contents of the other statements were in conflict with what the newspaper was trying to do. It disclosed what the Gazette was trying to conceal. I challenge the Gazette to refute what I have said.

From what I have said it is plain to see why I have no confidence in the integrity of this newspaper. It will stoop to anything to gain its point. There are many facts and reasons that could be given to show that the Gazette does not believe in law enforcement to the extent indicated by its editorial.

October 25, 1953

Respectfully,
John T. Copenhaver

The *Gazette* editors, in all probability, wondered about the use of the word, "Respectfully".

—TWENTY-SIX—
THE POOR MAN'S MICKEY SPILLANE

On October 27, 1953, the *Gazette* reacted to Mayor John Copenhaver's response to its question, "Has Justice Failed?" Editor Frank Knight said Copenhaver had "roamed all over the lot" in his oversight of the Clark murder and should leave the business of finding the killer to his police department. Journalists across the state admired Knight as a crusading journalist and many newspapers reprinted the editorial.

Knight wrote with a passion, lifting a journalistic ballpeen hammer of his own:

TIME FOR ACTION

The Mayor of Charleston, in an obvious moment of wrath, has endeavored to discredit this newspaper while defending his administration's handling of the Juliet Staunton Clark murder case. The procedure is an old one with the Mayor. Next week, when we write something he likes, he will use the same number of words while praising us.

But we are not interested in his opinions of the press at this moment and we are of the opinion that the public, which has been extremely patient, is not either. What everyone hopes for,

THE POOR MAN'S MICKEY SPILLANE

and has a right to expect, is a solution of the most sensational killing in a generation or more. For the city's chief executive to roam all over the lot in trying to protect his political record and not take definite action is becoming more tiresome by the day.

To put it frankly, the Mayor's chickens have come home to roost. When the Clark case broke more than two months ago, Mr. Copenhaver immediately installed himself as the poor man's Mickey Spillane[72] and to the confusion of both the public and the police department, he has been hamming up the act ever since. Now, the murder has gone unsolved and because the Gazette mirrors the thinking of an alarmed citizenry in expressing growing impatience, he has seen fit to question our methods of publishing a newspaper.

We are content to leave this decision with our readers and we think that the Mayor should leave the business of trying to find the killer, or killers, of Mrs. Clark with the men who have been trained in this kind of work—the police department. If they are no nearer a solution, which they have indicated for the past several weeks, then we can see nothing wrong with the proposal that they seek additional help.

We join with the Mayor in sharing his concern over the cost of the Clark case and we repeat that if the city's finances are endangered because of it, then a public subscription is in order. He need only say the word and the Gazette will do everything in its power to further such a campaign.

Meantime we can assure him—and anyone else interested—that we will not be content until everything humanly possible is done to find the

---

[72] Novelist Frank Morrison Spillane was an American writer known as Mickey Spillane.

murderer of Mrs. Clark. If he wants to make political hay out of such a challenge he may proceed under his own power.

The same afternoon Knight's editorial appeared, October 27, 1953, *Daily Mail* publisher Fred Stanton felt compelled to speak. He did so on the *Mail's* front page:

A STATEMENT IN REVIEW

With a little over two months time since the brutal slaying of Juliet Staunton Clark, a sister of the undersigned, it is pertinent that a brief review be given the public of the facts to the subsequent investigation looking toward the apprehension and conviction of the murderer.

Some may think the reward of $2,500 too small a sum. This newspaper and members of Mrs. Clark's family are able and willing to increase the reward many fold if such would in any way expedite apprehension of the criminal. The amount was arrived at after consultation with authorities with proven experience. Advice was given against the adoption of a larger figure.

From the outset the family has proffered financial and any other aid in the employment of outside investigators or anything else of help. But from repeated conferences with able representatives of the municipal and state authorities and the Federal Bureau of Investigation, as well as Dr. Fred Inbau, a nationally known criminologist, we have concluded that the investigation is in able hands.

We have intimate knowledge of the tremendous amount of work which has been done. We know what is being done and we know much of what is planned. This newspaper has published all of the pertinent facts, but it has not seen fit

> to publish rumors and the host of details in the investigation which might well damage reputations of innocent people and also help to render impotent the work of the authorities.
>
> It is a foul business—it is heartbreaking business. But it will be solved. The authorities are determined to solve it. We of the family and this newspaper know it will be solved. It is an extremely baffling and difficult case, but much has been accomplished. A solution will not restore our beloved sister and gracious working partner, but it is now the first and last order of business.
>
> Our Heavenly Father does not plan that this crime go unpunished.
>
> —*Fred M. Staunton, Publisher*

Meantime, 70 miles away in Parkersburg, the *Parkersburg News* was receiving orders from its owner, Ogden Newspapers, based in Wheeling. The dictum was most unusual—the Ogdens of Wheeling, Republicans all, were endorsing the opinion of the Democratic *Charleston Gazette*[73] that the Clark murder investigation was not going well.

The *Parkersburg News* was the Republican member of the Ogden group. The directive from Wheeling was that the *News* would not only endorse the *Gazette* position, it would give the *Gazette* an advanced copy of its editorial. The *Gazette* then ran the preview, scooping the *Parkersburg News*.

The *Gazette* said in its story of October 27, 1953, that the *Parkersburg News* (and the Ogden family) was saying, flat out, that the Clark investigation had been bungled, noting "officious" oversight by John Copenhaver:

---

[73] Decades later, the Ogden chain would pursue purchase of *The Charleston Gazette-Mail*–they were unsuccessful

"UNSKILLED OVER-OFFICIOUSNESS"

CLARK PROBE "BUNGLED," PARKERSBURG NEWSPAPER SAYS

PARKERSBURG, OCT. 27—The Parkersburg News, Republican member of the statewide Ogden newspaper chain, in its lead editorial tomorrow will charge that the Juliet Staunton Clark Murder case was "bungled" from the "very start of the investigation" last August 21.

Stating that Charleston authorities "are seemingly no nearer a solution than they were 24 hours after the dastardly crime had been committed." The News adds that it "fully" supports the highly pertinent suggestion The Charleston Gazette has now made, namely that this horrible crime should not be permitted, in any circumstances, to go unsolved."

At the same time the News, saying it has had "great respect for the candor and integrity" of Charleston Mayor John Copenhaver, declares, "We nevertheless are convinced his obviously unskilled over-officiousness in this case has been unfortunate.

And his recent importunate public criticism of The Gazette, challenging the integrity of that newspaper's motives in demanding a better and swifter degree of law enforcement, in our opinion, is even more unfortunate," the editorial said.

The *Gazette* printed, on the same page, *Daily Mail* publisher Fred Staunton's statement as to how the *Mail* arrived at the sum of its reward for the killer's arrest, and a statement from police chief Dewey Williams that there was, "nothing new" in the investigation. He said, "I wish we did have something new on the case, but we just don't have at this moment.

I'm sorry."

The certainty of a solution to the murder continued to diminish and the *Daily Mail,* attempting to reignite interest, would eventually raise its $2,500 award to $15,000.[74]

The *Charleston Gazette,* on November 23, 1953, also used numbers, noting the lack of progress through its art department:

Charleston Gazette

Who Killed Mrs. Clark?

Ninety-nine days have passed since the brutal murder of Mrs. Juliet Staunton Clark in her South Hills home.

Police Chief Dewey Williams yesterday replied "no comment" to a reporter's question concerning progress of the murder investigation.

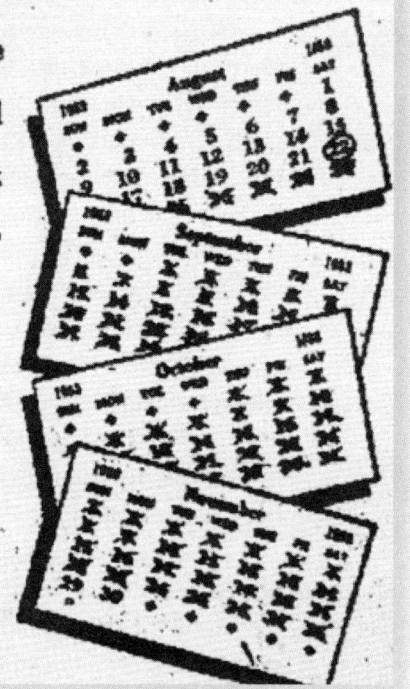

---

[74] Estimated as equivalent to $150,000 in 2019.

—TWENTY-SEVEN—
A SNEAK PUNCH

The year 1953 melded into 1954, and *Charleston Gazette* reporter Jim Hill was back in action on Saturday, March 4, with a headline that read, *"City Police Grill Suspect In Murder of Juliet Clark."* Hill's report said a Kanawha County man who had made a routine burglary complaint to city police had undergone a daylong grilling. The man had been sought for more than a year and a half, they said, after his name "cropped up" during the initial stages of the investigation.

Detective Dallas Bias[75] answered Hill's questions as best he could. The suspect had "reported a burglary about his house and asked for an investigation." Coincidentally, three days later, detectives were sifting through burglary reports in a routine check. Bingo, they found the burglary report dated March 4. The complainant's name was recognized as a person being sought for questioning.

But, Bias said the fellow, upon being picked up and taken to police headquarters, was extremely uncooperative. "He flat out refused to submit to a lie detector test and he kept ordering us to either book him or release him," Bias said.

---

[75] Bias later would become a legendary Charleston police chief who ran for mayor, donning an Indian chief's headdress as he filed for office. Each winter Bias, as chief-of-police, would summon media as he stripped to his Speedo, diving into an ice-cold Kanawha River.

A SNEAK PUNCH

Police found their suspect continued to be uncooperative throughout the day. They referred to their new lead as the, "Mystery Man." The questioning led nowhere and the suspect left police headquarters without being polygraphed. The release caused many to scratch their heads in disbelief. A suspect would not cooperate, so police released him.

So many leads, so many disappointments, so many strange goings-on.

The pace of governing and policing was brutal for Mayor John Copenhaver and he was overly tired the night of April 6, 1954. C. Oral Lowe, pastor of Boyd Memorial Christian Church, had asked him to speak to the church's men's fellowship dinner that evening. Copenhaver accepted the invitation, and it was a fine affair.

The mayor did not feel up to a speech and, after a few jocular remarks, said he was simply going to open the floor for questions. Copenhaver said later he spoke as though he were at a friend's home and what he said was to be taken, "casually." The men's group asked questions that covered a lot of territory about municipal government, zoning in on the city's vice squad and controversies surrounding it. The mayor easily fielded the questions—he knew his job.

All was well, and then, Reverend Lowe, as the evening's discourse was wrapping up, asked *that* question.

"Can you tell us what the current status is in the Clark murder?"

Unknown to Copenhaver, *Gazette* reporter Lewis Abbot was in the room. The *Gazette* had inquired earlier about Copenhaver's date with the church group, and the mayor's office assured the newspaper that the mayor would have nothing newsworthy to say.

The *Gazette* decided to send Abbot to the dinner anyway. The mayor learned of the reporter's presence only as he was leaving the dinner. A short time later Reverend Lowe called the *Gazette* city desk and asked that it not report the mayor's comments to the dinner group.

That guaranteed publication, and Abbot had a scoop that appeared the next morning, April 7, with a bold headline that probably spoiled the mayor's day:

MAYOR SAYS CLARK KILLER IS "KNOWN"

By Lewis Abbot
(Staff Writer for The Gazette)

Mayor Copenhaver said last night that "there is not much doubt" in his mind or that of the city detectives as to who killed Mrs. Juliet Staunton Clark, but that it is "doubtful" if the case will ever be "solved."

The police department today perhaps knows the identity of the person who committed that crime, but "knowing and proving" are two different things, Copenhaver added.

He said that unless some new piece of evidence is turned up there is little chance that the person guilty of the crime will ever be prosecuted.

Copenhaver blew his top. The next day, April 8, he began to shake the hinges on the door to the *Gazette*. The following morning Copenhaver's rebuttal was reported in the paper with a headline that was assuredly softer than the mayor's outrage:

GAZETTE 'UNFAIR' IN CLARK STORY, MAYOR CHARGES

Copenhaver was quoted as saying he thought it was "unfair" to print his remarks that were meant to be "casual" and not to be published. The *Gazette* report said the mayor insisted he did not know a reporter was present or he would have been "more cautious" about what he said.

Reporter Abbot quoted Copenhaver as saying several times during his talk that certain specific comments of his were "not for publication." Abbot said those comments were not used in the *Gazette* story. Abbot added that the Copenhaver comments the *Gazette* published were not ruled off the record by the mayor.

Copenhaver said in the *Gazette* story that it was a "pity" that he could not speak at a church meeting without being "spread all over the front page." He said, "I informed the *Gazette* earlier that my speech would be of no importance but they sent a reporter anyway."

Copenhaver imperiously added that anything concerning municipal government he (Copenhaver) wants published should come from him (Copenhaver) officially. The mayor said the church meeting was "no place for a newspaper reporter."

The mayor's faux pas would not go away. On April 9, three days after the mayor's speech, the *Daily Mail* slapped the mayor's hand. But, at the same time, tried to give Copenhaver some assistance in cleaning up the mess.

OPINION AND REVIEWS

WAY OUT ON A LIMB

If Mayor Copenhaver knows who killed Mrs. Walter E. Clark, it is his solemn duty to go before a grand jury and give it such information as he may have. The grand jury is the only agency competent to decide if it warrants an indictment.

And if the Mayor does not know who killed Mrs. Clark, then it is his equally solemn duty to reserve his comment on this subject for the privacy of his conferences with the detective force.

The Mayor's troubles stem from two commonly accepted meanings of the "need to know". In the form accepted for casual conversation on the street corners, it means little more than a positive conviction on a subject. Thus a man knows that the sun will rise tomorrow.

Why? Because it always has.

"To know" something legally, however, is quite another matter. "To know" something in this sense means you have evidence which is admissible as an attempt at proof, the decision resting with the judge and jury.

As a lawyer, the Mayor knows of this distinction, and it is his custom to practice it. Like a great many other people, he has his theory on who killed Mrs. Clark. As he quickly acknowledged after the initial misstep, this kind of knowledge has no place in a court of law, and the attempt to introduce it there would simply jeopardize the whole investigation which his (sic) Honor has directed so vigorously.

There is no need to be too hard on him on this score. He was tired. He had had no time, as he explained, to prepare a formal address. The best course, then, seemed to be to make himself available, and the conversation turned inevitably to the slaying. His Honor could have turned it aside. Instead, he plunged in, yielding to the familiar temptation to astound the audience, which had paid him the compliment of inviting his appearance.

It might prove to be a valuable lesson in the occasional wisdom of the "No Comment" response, the point being that the Mayor, because he is Mayor, is news and no newspaper can guarantee to keep him out of trouble. The Mayor will have to learn that trick for himself. It is pretty largely a trick of learning when to say nothing which will not make sense in print the morning after.

Mayor Copenhaver was, in all likelihood, driven to near apoplexy when he read the *Daily Mail* Editorial. The *Mail*! It was ordinarily the friend of the chief executive. How could Fred Staunton have done this? Once again, Copenhaver summoned his secretary and blistered a reply:

> Is Fred Staunton honest in his request, made in the lead editorial of his newspaper today (Friday), that we present to the next grand jury such evidence as is now available touching upon the murder of Mrs. Juliet Staunton Clark, his sister, or is it just another sneak punch which he and his newspaper are so adept at throwing from the gutter?
> If the request is an honest one, then Mr. Staunton has changed his position completely since my last conversation with him. As a brother of the murdered woman and as a spokesman for the family, he has been kept fully informed of all developments in the case.
> He knows as much about the facts as I do. I have never told anyone that I knew the identity of the killer. A day or so ago in one of its headlines, the Daily Mail falsely and maliciously represented me as saying that I did know who killed Mrs. Clark.
> I have formed an opinion and so has Mr. Staunton. Our opinions, I would say, are one and the same.

The *Mail*, addressing Copenhaver's letter, said, "So far, there have been no arrests and no motive advanced for the brutal crime."

—TWENTY-EIGHT—
FREDERICK M. (FRED) STAUNTON

Fred Staunton and Elizabeth (Dip) Brightwell were married on January 11, 1928, at St. John's Episcopal Church in Charleston. The Reverend John Gass performed the nuptials. The Reverend Rhuel Merrill, husband of the groom's mother, Ma Merrill, assisted. Ma Merrill wore a black chiffon waistcoat, a black velvet skirt, black hat, and a necklace of pearls.

The wedding reception was held at the home of the bride's parents on Edgewood Drive, Mr. and Mrs. H.P. Brightwell. Newspaper society pages said Dip was, "acknowledged as one of the most charming members of the young social set in Charleston...a member of the family of statewide prominence, being the great granddaughter of the late Dr. I.C. White[76], geologist."

Fred Staunton was cited as being employed by the George Washington Life Insurance Company[77] and having attended the Haverford School in Pennsylvania and Princeton University. The newlyweds honeymooned in the Bahamas.

Fred and Dip resided temporarily with Ma Merrill and the Reverend Merrill at their home on Staunton Road. Shortly after, they

---

[76] White was a celebrated geologist who was honored with a building carrying his name at West Virginia University.

[77] He later would become the publisher of the *Charleston Daily Mail*.

FREDERICK M. (FRED) STAUNTON

began their family "on six acres on a slope" above his mother's house. His three sisters and a cousin were sprinkled in similar manner on the front of South Hills.

Staunton's daughter Fan said her father felt his property was his Eden and he worked the land regularly to perfect it. Father and daughter planted gardens and picked cherries and apples from fruit trees to make pies.

Staunton was accomplished with tools that filled a large workshop—used in wood making and as farming implements. A photographer, he printed his photographs in his own darkroom. He played tennis. Wine was kept in the basement and bourbon was his choice of spirits.

As publisher, Staunton suffered through a major typesetter union strike at the newspaper and spent days and nights with non-union workers to man the presses, doing all he could to publish a newspaper during a walkout. His daughter was alarmed at the stress that punished her father.

Fan, in her memoir, *YOU, Selected Poems and KNOT: A Life*, wrote:

In the daughter's eyes, the father's face, which had been lively and charming, became stern. His eyes narrowed, his mouth tightened, his shoulders bent as the costs of the strike bore on him. When the mother drove to pick up the father in the evening, the daughter saw "pickets", as the strikers were called, walking outside the father's building carrying signs that said, "Scabs go home." The father was jeered.

Fan Staunton says there was a time as a teenager that she rebelled. One day when the family planned to go to their farm, Fan announced she was staying home. Family gone, she invited her friends to her home and they joined her in a joy ride in her father's blue Buick station wagon. She had never operated an automobile until that Saturday afternoon. After dropping off her

Fred Staunton
–Charleston Daily Mail

friends, she ascended the road to her father's house and rammed the Buick into a stone retaining wall. The father said the daughter must be grounded.

Betsy Staunton Johnson, Fan's older sister, idolized her father. She also remembered the struggle her father had as publisher when a typesetter's strike threatened to bring *Daily Mail* presses to a grinding stop:

What I can feel is the emotional load that was on my father. It was very hard on him because he got so much criticism from members in the family that he was spouting all this in the paper—writing all this stuff that was not friendly news. He quoted the wonderful quote the Daily Mail used to have, "Without Offence to Friend or Foe, I Sketch Your World Exactly As It Goes[78]"—he just held on to that. He said, "Just because it's your group, you can't suddenly squash it." That was really tough on him, other than his sister being killed.

Many said that Lyell Clay, once he decided to pursue journalism, forced Staunton out of the *Daily Mail*. Betsy said such was not true, that her father was not happy that Lyell was taking over at the newspaper, but that he did not bluntly ask Staunton to leave:

No, definitely not. Dad had at that time shingles and he had been miserable for years. He could not stand that those Clay boys came in. He loved Buck. Buck was somebody you could not dislike, he was, you know, totally amenable, where Lyell was very egotistic and a very much a climber.

Dad just saw how he came in and he was just suddenly pumped into these higher jobs. He really didn't feel that he (Lyell) knew what he was doing, because he had not been trained. Dad started

---

[78] The quotation carried on the *Charleston Daily Mail* editorial page masthead.

FREDERICK M. (FRED) STAUNTON

out working in advertising. He used to call on all the movie companies. It was wonderful because he kept bringing home treats from these people that were advertising in the paper. Like, bubble gum during the war. That was immensely wonderful. I was the most popular kid in the 8th grade.

I think Dad really just couldn't wait to leave. You could say Lyell bumped him out, psychologically, but not with any means of force or verbiage or anything. Lyell has done so many wonderful things for people with his money. But he was just a very self-centered young man.

He had an opportunity to move ahead and he saw it and he did it. Dad had gotten all these guys in from different places, different papers. He had a team that was so wonderfully special—Charlie Connor, Jack Maurice, Jimmy Martin. Oh, gosh, eight or ten of them. They had a horrible strike. I think it was before Aunt Julie was killed.

Dad had these guys up (to the Staunton home) because they were all filling in for typesetters and whatever. He had them up to the house almost every night. I was a bartender, and it was hysterical. I didn't know Jack Daniels from Southern (Comfort)—whatever. I just loved these people. They kind of spelled out what they had done all day. They kept it going.

And then, you know, Lyell pops in, and he's just—he's not even there at this time, and when he comes in he has no background. He had just family and money. He wasn't a dummy at all, he was a smart guy. So, like he could just—it just worked for Dad—I really do—I think he was very eager to leave. And he wouldn't have, probably for another five years, if Lyell hadn't been there. But, you know, it just seemed to be the right time.

Staunton's nephew, John Buffington Merrill, Jr. said:

I was very close to the entire Staunton family. From the time I could walk I would walk up there every day and spend time with them. Their home was just 100 yards up the hill from us. I saw a lot of Uncle Fred. I did not know the particulars but Lyell came back and said, 'I am taking over,' and he forced Uncle Fred into retirement. They gave him a Mercedes car when he retired. Then Lyell took over. Dad talked about how Uncle Fred was not happy about the way he was forced out. Buck came in later after that.

First row, left to right: Elizabeth Staunton (Dip), with daughter Fan on lap; Juliet Staunton Clay Clark with granddaughter Buffy Clay next to her; Platt Staunton, sitting on the lap of his grandmother, Fan Brightwell; Richard Merrill, sitting on lap of his grandmother, Florence (Ma) Merrill; Mrs. J. R. Thomas (mother-in-law of Katharine Staunton Thomas); Katherine Thomas; Buffy Merrill, and Betsy Staunton.

Second row, left to right: Fred Staunton; Tom Fleeson; Fred Staunton (Betsy's oldest brother); Mary Louise Merrill (just her profile); John Merrill, Jr.; Joe Peck (married to Buffy Merrill's cousin Florence); Toni Clay (married to Buck, brother of Lyell); Sidney Staunton (brother of Betsy); Ruth Thomas (standing in front of Sidney); Buck Clay; John Merrill, and Newton Thomas.
–Merrill Family

—TWENTY-NINE—
THE FATHER CRIED

Both Fan and Betsy Staunton had poignant memories of their father's selfless effort to guide the *Daily Mail* through tumultuous times, causing him physical and emotional pain. For them, Lyell Clay's displacement of Fred Staunton as publisher of the newspaper remained a bitter remembrance.

Fan Staunton Ogilvie wrote in her memoir, *YOU, Selected Poems and KNOT: A Life:*, that she told her father he should fight for his position as publisher at *The Charleston Daily Mail*:

She felt bold enough to tell the father he should fight harder at the newspaper to keep his position as Publisher. His nephew (Lyell Clay) *had financial control of the newspaper and told the father he wished to be Publisher and President. The father felt he had no alternative but to concede. The daughter saw this concession of the father as weak, and told the father. The father cried. He cried. The sick, proud father cried. In pain, confusion and defeat. He looked at her dry challenging eyes, told the young woman she would not make him cry again, that never would he cry in front of her again.*

Staunton suffered two heart attacks before he died. Following his death in November 1976, the *Charleston Daily Mail* published an editorial that lauded the 73-year-old former publisher. The editorial is not signed, but it is assumed editor Jack Maurice penned the thoughts:

FRED STAUNTON, 1903-1976

When he retired in 1968, Fred Staunton had logged in 38 years with this newspaper, beginning in its advertising department and rising thereafter to become its publisher. After his retirement, even as he wished to move into the background, he could not sever the close connection. None of us would let him.

Over so many years, he had entwined himself into the fabric of this enterprise and left upon it the deep imprint of his character and personality. Some of those years were hectic ones. Mr. Staunton met them with confidence and serenity. All of them for those who worked with him were rewarding. Almost without seeming to, Mr. Staunton saw to that.

He could and did demand respect. It was scarcely necessary. His gift was to inspire affection and with it a profound interest in the serious business of putting out a newspaper.

If he ever had a mean motive, he never betrayed nor acted upon it. If he ever lost his patience, he never showed it or his displeasure. In his private and his public demeanor, he was exactly the same—somewhat reserved, unfailingly civil, his good manners, good sense and good wishes his chief reliance.

It could have been mistaken for diffidence. It was not. Once, one of this newspapers advertisers sought to buy what the Daily Mail does not offer for sale. Mr. Staunton refused and bore the outraged disappointment. He did not budge, and as it turned out, he did not lose the friend either.

A great and good man whose loss all of us here feel deeply and share with the family that meant so much to him.

The writer felt Staunton refused to sell what the newspaper did not offer for sale, but that did not stop a political campaign accusation that the *Daily Mail* was a confederate of the Republican Party. In what today would be called a "smoking gun" attack, "Voters for Smith" placed a full-page paid political advertisement in the *Charleston Gazette*. The ad ran on October 30, 1964, just days before the general election.

Hulett Smith was running against former West Virginia Governor Cecil Underwood in what was perceived to be a close campaign. The smoking gun was a years-old memo within the State Road Commission that suggested that the publisher of the *Daily Mail* was a mouthpiece for the Republican Party, and that he accepted favors from the Underwood administration in 1959.

The headline said, in questionable grammar, "*Underwood's State Road Commission Repair Jobs To Private Farms.*" The ad asked, "*Why is the Charleston Daily Mail the chief propaganda organ of the Republican Party?*" Followed by yet another query, "*Why has it been the chief tool of the Republican smear campaign?*" And finally, "*These documents may prove part of the answer.*"

The ad featured a memorandum dated July 11, 1958. The memo was from Robert Hanna, Business Manager of the West Virginia State Road Commission to State Road Commissioner Pat Graney. It read:

Yesterday I had the opportunity of discussing the condition of Rt. 119/12 which leads from Walton to Gandeeville and upon which the farm of Fred M. Staunton is located. County Superintendent Hildreth advised me that the road has been twice graded this year (and) *that drains have been installed at certain locations which will be of immeasurable help to this road. He states that it is now entirely passable but that it would be desirable some time in the future when money is available to add base material to the road. The farmer adjoining Mr. Staunton appears to have been non-cooperative in certain respects with Mr. Hildreth but he feels that he will be able to work the matter out himself. I have advised him that in the event he needs any help in this respect to let you know so that we might ask Mr. Staunton's influence in clearing the matter up for Hildreth.*

There follows in the ad the Staunton letter, on *Daily Mail* letterhead, dated January 23, 1959, addressed to Robert Hannah, Business Manager for the West Virginia State Road Commission:

Dear Bob:

Just about the time that you very kindly drove me to Roane County my secretary was called for jury duty and for a number of weeks my correspondence was a little bit hit and miss, which explains in part this great delay in thanking you for your courtesy and help.

Willy Hildreth did follow through installing four cross drains and really went to town with that bulldozer from the point of the road where my property line commences out to the entrance gate. They took out the fencing, fence posts, trees and anything else which got in the way of a plan to widen the road and permit better drainage. On first sight the change was a bit of a shock and I was afraid that they had totally ruined my farm. Each week-end since my son and I have been cleaning up the trees and debris with a chain saw and when I get the freshly graded area planted it will improve the whole situation immediately. So I am as happy as a lark.

When the road is thawed and soft as mush we stay off of it, in spite of the fact that we have a four wheel drive jeep. And I have been rather pleased that others have seemingly been giving the road like consideration. But last week-end we saw where some dadblamed joker with a jeep had ploughed through making deep ruts. So I am hoping that this spring when it dries a bit, and Willy has his scraper in the vicinity, he will give it a quick going over as to remedy the worst of the damage done by the ornery fox hunters. From then on until next winter we can retain it fairly adequately with the scraper blade on our tractor.

I guess it is too much to hope for that the Democratic Legislature will go along in any degree with a constructive road program. But I am hoping that it won't be as bad as we might contemplate. Thanks again for your kind help and drop in for a chat when you can find time.

    Sincerely,

    mjb/Fred

Robert Hannah's reply was just below Staunton's letter. It was dated January 26, 1959, the same day he received the correspondence.

Dear Fred:

Thank you very much for your kind letter of January 23.

I will most certainly commend Willie Hildreth for having done a good job. I feel sure that he will follow through this spring when the opportune time arrives and put the grader on the road.

We sincerely appreciate the help which you have given us and in any manner that you can influence the Legislature will be extremely helpful to our program.

I expect to drop in and see you in the very near future. With kindest personal regards, I am

    Sincerely yours,

    Robert W. Hanna
    Business Manager
    RWH/mt

THE FATHER CRIED

Hulett Smith was elected governor, defeating former Governor Cecil Underwood by almost 100,000 votes. The impact of the ad was impossible to measure.

—THIRTY—
A STRANGE PARALLEL OF MURDER

Some called them the "Bloody Buffingtons".

On October 17, 1936, 50 miles away from Staunton Road, in Huntington, West Virginia, 63-year-old Mrs. Juliette[79] Buffington Enslow was found murdered in her home. She had been strangled with a towel and beaten with an ice pick.

The *Charleston Gazette* of September 6, 1953, carried a lengthy special report on the murder, titled, *Strange Parallel of Two Cousins*, saying, "Mrs. Enslow was the first cousin, once removed, of Juliet Staunton Clark, and a member of one of West Virginia's most prominent families. Her father, Peter Cline Buffington, was the first mayor of Huntington." He also once owned most of the land between Seventeenth Street and Twenty Fourth Street in Huntington, was a veteran of the Confederate Army and a member of the state legislature.

The Enslow name became prominent in the 1870s when Andrew Jackson Enslow was instrumental in helping to build the Chesapeake & Ohio Railroad. Enslow's son, Frank Enslow, grew up in Huntington and had extensive interests in oil and gas banking and other fields.[80] It was Frank Enslow who built the Enslow mansion.

---

[79] Unlike her cousin Juliet Clark, Mrs. Enslow spelled her name "Juliette".

[80] *The Herald-Dispatch* "herald-dispatch.com" site.

"Certainly his opulent 26-room mansion at 1307 3rd Ave. was a showplace, with silk wallpaper, oak paneling, marble fireplaces, Tiffany chandeliers and stained-glass windows. Even the garage out back, which once housed the Enslow family Stanley steamer automobile, was a fancy affair. It had a turntable on the floor so the auto could be turned around inside. Built in 1893, the Enslow mansion was a center of Huntington social life in that long-ago era.[81]"

Juliette Buffington Enslow was married twice, as was Mrs. Clark. She lived in her Huntington mansion with a maid, one of two regular servants, and her son by her first marriage, Charles Baldwin. Charles had been a captain in the Air Corps during World War I.

"He had lost part of a leg in a railroad accident and walked with a noticeable limp. The pain from his accident was intense during the years and he became accustomed to quelling it with narcotics," the *Gazette* article reported.

Eventually, the article said, "He relied on drugs to such an extent that he registered as an addict. The registration was required by federal authorities and gave him legal permission to purchase and use five grains (of narcotics) a day. His mother was in charge of his supply."

Early on the morning of Oct. 16, Mrs. Enslow's servants saw one of her pocketbooks on the lawn. The servant was alarmed and searched the house. She found Mrs. Enslow's body in her bedroom. Police were summoned and they quickly theorized that a burglary had gone bad.

The murder occurred on a Friday, the same day of the week that Juliet Clark would be murdered 17 years later in Charleston. As in the Clark murder, first assumptions were soon changed, to homicide, as detectives went about investigating the Enslow slaying.

---

[81] Ibid.

Despite the reference to stabbing with an ice pick and strangulation, an autopsy showed that the Huntington socialite died of head injuries, as had Juliet Clark. By October 22, police emphasis shifted to tracing two valuable diamond rings missing from the victim's fingers. The next day the family offered a $1,000[82] reward for information leading to the arrest and conviction of the guilty party.

Then, a bombshell.

On October 25, police arrested Enslow's son, Charles Baldwin. They charged him with murdering his mother. Baldwin denied any knowledge of the killing, "hobbling," the *Gazette* report said, "because of his bad leg."

Police said they had a perfect case against the 41-year-old son. They had discovered a can opener from his room in the house that they said apparently was used in the killing—rather than an ice pick. Baldwin was ordered held for grand jury action and rumors flew through Huntington. The grand jury met in February and indicted Baldwin. His trial was set for March 16, 1937. The Associated Press reported that the witness list read, "like a social register."

The state's case against Charles Baldwin rested on the theory that he killed his mother because he was desperate—she was trying to break him of his drug habit and was limiting his use of drugs. Prosecutors also said blood found on Baldwin's pajamas would be proved to be of the same type as his mother's and that his clothes became bloodied in the struggle in which she was killed.

Two bloodstained handkerchiefs and a bloody key were found in the basement of the ornate home. Prosecutors said Baldwin had hidden the key to a bathroom in Mrs. Enslow's suite. They added that there was no evidence that indicated the murder was anything other than an "inside job."

---

[82] Estimated as equivalent to $18,000 in 2019.

A STRANGE PARALLEL OF MURDER

Baldwin objected, and said on the stand that the blood on his pajamas was from embracing his mother's body after she had been found dead.

As for the drug theory, "Ridiculous," Baldwin said. "I obtained more than 400 grains of narcotics while in Canada. I had far more than the five daily grains supplied by my mother."

Baldwin's lawyers contended the murder was by a robber who was surprised by Mrs. Enslow. They summoned character witnesses that included his mother's daughter by a second marriage. Baldwin, the *Gazette* reported, claimed there was nothing but affection and understanding between him and Mrs. Enslow.

Then, the defense called an expert witness who said the police method used to analyze bloodstains found on Baldwin's clothing had reported, "Nothing conclusive could be proved from the tests." Baldwin said, "I did not kill my mother." The scene was dramatic and Baldwin was moved to tears in his testimony. He said, "I don't know one single thing about it and I have spared myself nothing in trying to make this clear."

The trial ran nine days. It took only two hours before the jury returned its verdict, not guilty. Spectators in the courtroom broke into cheers when the jury's decision was announced. Judge Clay Wrath, said, "Mr. Baldwin has conducted himself admirably but this was a case which had to be tried." Investigators rolled up their sleeves and continued their search, trying to find a killer.

The Enslow mansion was boarded up following the murder of Juliette Enslow. In 1937, R.R. Steele, who operated the Steele Funeral home two blocks from 3rd Avenue, purchased the mansion and moved his business there.[83]

The Enslow Mansion was destroyed by fire in August 1977.

The murder of Juliette Buffington Enslow was never solved.

---

[83] *The Herald Dispatch* "heralddispatch.com" site.

—THIRTY-ONE—
JULIE CLARK ALEXANDER

The years 1950-1954 were cataclysmic for Julie Clark Alexander, daughter of the owner of *The Charleston Daily Mail*, Juliet Staunton Clark. Within four years' time, she lost her father, became pregnant out of wedlock[84], was married to a man her mother apparently detested[85], lost a child at birth, lived through the brutal murder of her mother, suffered through the agonizing death of her three-year-old son, and was divorced.

The marriage of Julie and Arch Alexander, Jr. took place on September 29, 1950. Despite Alexander's accomplishments as a young man, it was rumored by some that Mrs. Clark was not happy with the union, considering Alexander beneath her daughter's standing.

The wedding was quietly held at home with few attendees. It was a major social event—the marriage of the daughter of a former governor and newspaper owner of renown. A socially prominent mother, it would have seemed, would invite hundreds to the marriage of her only daughter.

Yet, there were no crowds, only family. However, the marriage *was* at the top of the *Daily Mail* social page on October 1, 1950.

---

[84] This is according to reporter Ruth Reynolds in her story *Murder on the Rumpled Green Rug*. Reynolds said this was considered scandalous at the time.

[85] Ibid.

MISS JULIET CLARK MARRIED TO MR. ARCH ALEXANDER, JR.

A wedding of much social prominence is that of Miss Juliet Staunton Clark and Mr. Arch Johnson Alexander, Jr., which took place at high noon Friday at the home of her mother, Mrs. Walter E. Clark on Virginia St. Mr. Alexander is the son of Mr. and Arch J. Alexander of Noyes Ave.

Rev. Bernard Vanderbeck, pastor of Kanawha Presbyterian Church, performed the ceremony before an improvised altar of white flowers and greenery in the presence of the immediate families and relatives.

Mr. Buckner Clay gave his sister in marriage. She was attired in her traveling costume, a suit and hat of sapphire blue gabardine, taupe accessories and corsage of yellow rosebuds. Her aunt and only attendant, Mrs. John Buffington Merrill, was wearing a wine-colored crepe frock with a matching hat and corsage of green orchids. Mr. B. Stanley Gill served as best man.

After a wedding breakfast, Mr. and Mrs. Alexander left for Lexington where they will make their home until he completes his studies at the law school, Washington and Lee University.

The former Miss Clark, a member of distinguished families in Kanawha Valley, is a graduate of the Oldfields School, Glencoe, Md., and attended Barmore School in New York City. Her late father served as governor of Alaska for three years and was owner of the Charleston Daily Mail. She is a granddaughter of Mrs. Rhuel Hampton Merrill of Staunton Rd. and the late Mr. Edward Wilber Staunton.

Mr. Alexander, whose father is chief of the

State Department of Mines, is a grandson of the late Mr. and Mrs. J.W. Alexander of this city and the late Mr. and Mrs. Lucian B. Ferguson of Wayne. A veteran of World War II, he was graduated from Virginia Episcopal School and W. and L., belonging to Phi Kappa Psi Fraternity, the Cotillion Club and Calax. He is also a member of the Army-Navy and Toastmasters Clubs.

Three years following the marriage, Julie Clark's life began a nine-month period of tragedy. Pregnant with identical twin daughters, she gave birth August 13, 1953—only to see one of the twins die at birth. Eight days later, her mother was beaten to death on Staunton Road.

Tragedy, for the third time in as many months, struck again November 25 of 1953. Julie's three-year-old son Jay, who had been sleeping in the small bedroom just off his grandmother's living room the night she was murdered, suffered extensive burns in an accident in the basement of his home. Painters had left a paintbrush in a can of kerosene on the floor in the basement.[86] Jay, playing alone in the basement, picked up the brush and began to paint a hot water tank. The brush caught fire and the can exploded.

It was not at first believed Jay was critically burned. Initial findings were that only first and second-degree burns covered his legs and lower abdomen—serious but not lethal. The reports proved correct, but complications arose. Jay suffered for thirteen days and died December 8, 1953 at 8:10 pm. He was buried at Mountain View Memorial Park Cemetery.

It was a terrible timeline of death and despair that took a dreadful toll on young Julie—little doubt dooming her marriage. She filed for divorce six months after Jay died, on June 9, 1954, lashing out at her husband Arch, charging him with "mental cruelty,

---

[86] *The Morning Call*, Allentown, Pennsylvania, March 9, 1958.

neglect and false accusations.[87]" She also indicated that if she were "accidentally killed," someone should investigate.[88]

William A. White wrote in the *Pittsburgh Press*[89] that the bill of complaint filed June 9 was by, "a blue-eyed matron of 24." White asked around town about the atmosphere surrounding the divorce. Those who knew about the details told White that Mr. Alexander would not contest the suit.

Arch Alexander's lawyer, Robert H.C. Kay, a major player in Charleston legal circles. who had said to reporters when Alexander was being questioned by police, "We have nothing to hide," was vacationing in Alaska. Attorney Kay's office told White that Kay would not return for two weeks.

Juliet Alexander's lawyer, D.J. "Jack" Savage, when contacted by White, said, "Mrs. Alexander will not comment on the suit. Divorce hearings are held in secret before commissioners in West Virginia and testimony can be seen only by court order." Savage, considered a legal eagle who had but three fingers on one of his hands, said, "Local newspapers don't publish divorce cases."

Savage then said to reporter White, whose subsequent story centered on the fact that the divorce had reignited interest in the murder of Juliet Clark, "This divorce has absolutely nothing to do with the murder of Mrs. Clark."

Nonetheless, White wasn't going to abandon his angle and his report would scream in blazing headline form in the *Pittsburgh Press*:

---

[87] *Pittsburgh Press*, August 8, 1954.

[88] *The Morning Call*, Allentown, Pennsylvania, March 9, 1958.

[89] *Pittsburgh Press*, August 8, 1954.

MYSTERY DEATH TALK REVIVED BY DIVORCE SUIT

UNSOLVED SLAYING OF MRS. CLARK BACK IN WEST VIRGINIA SPOTLIGHT MAYOR SHRUGS OFF CHARGES
By William A. White

White agreed in the story that attorney Savage was correct that the divorce and murder were not connected, writing, "And there is no reason to believe it does, but it has stirred up comment again on a case that many persons outside of Charleston—and quite a few inside—were under the impression that the case had been 'hushed' because of the powerful interests and prominent persons involved."

White reported that Mayor Copenhaver was the target of sharp barbs hurled from many sides. His story said there were accusations that the mayor "bungled the case" by an "alleged desire" to assume the proportions of a "super sleuth". The report went on to say that Copenhaver was criticized for taking the investigation from recognized police heads to "bask in the sunlight" himself, interfering with "all and sundry" who were legitimately trying to solve the case.

Copenhaver spoke with White, and the mayor admitted he had second thoughts about not incarcerating a suspect in custody because jailing him might have brought about a confession.

The mayor said, "If I did anything wrong at all, it was the turning loose a suspect who had been under long questioning and against whom we had no convincing evidence. I had to make the decision. I turned him loose. He was and still is available. He has not run away. But now some persons say I should have jailed him, that it might have broken him, which I very much doubt."

White was not able to get Copenhaver to name the man he turned loose.

White said that the case had been dormant for "some time" because nothing had developed of consequence. He added that there was "rivalry between the two local newspapers, the afternoon *Daily Mail*—Mrs. Clark's paper—and the morning *Gazette* regarding the Clark story."

White's story concluded, "The most-often heard criticism of the mayor and police is that questioning of some 'local suspects' was delayed too long—until after Mrs. Clark's funeral. But he (Copenhaver) says he does not believe this stymied the investigation in any way."

—THIRTY-TWO—
THE PERFECT CRIME

The *Pittsburgh Press* divorce story of August 8, 1954, noted that, for a long time after the murder of Juliet Clark, *The Charleston Gazette* persisted in mentioning it in some way *every* day. It cited the October 25, 1953, editorial written by Frank Knight, "Has Justice Failed?" and the responding blistering blast from Charleston Mayor John T. Copenhaver.

The Pittsburgh newspaper repeated the well-known fact that within a few hours after the murder of its owner was discovered, Fred M. Staunton, publisher of the *Daily Mail*, and brother of Mrs. Clark, offered the reward of $2,500 for apprehension of the killer. Nothing came of it and a little over two months later, there was hardly a nibble in the case. Police received many tips, heard telephone callers accuse almost every person in any way connected with the case, and received sketches saying, "This is the man."

Charleston Police Chief Dewey Williams said the Clark case was "still very much open," and that he had done some very recent work on it. The rumor was he might soon take a trip out of town to check out a possibility. Further, it was said, Detective Lt. W.W. "Red" Fisher had been almost exclusively on the case for some time, but authorities would not discuss what if anything he might have uncovered.

THE PERFECT CRIME

The Mayor, the Police Chief and many other persons said openly they felt sure they knew the identity of the killer. But they admitted they hadn't a "nickel's worth" of convicting evidence.

The killer was still at large, and the mayor's confidence in a solution of the crime waned. "If it isn't solved soon," he said, "I'm afraid it may never be. It could be the perfect crime."

Betsy Staunton remembers a startled family when it learned "Aunt Julie" had been brutally slain:

We were at the beach when we learned she was killed. It was like outer space. It's like, almost like, "Tell me about murder!"

Somebody's killed, with a blunt instrument, it was horrible. And then to know it was my dad's sister. I imagine they were close because they were in the business together. Aunt Julie got Dad into the Daily Mail.

At Nags Head, we got the call at the Parkinson Hotel, and he (her father) *just came in to all of us and said, "Julie's gone, Julie's dead, Julie's been murdered!" And we all went "What!" It was a very strange thing to happen to a family. You think you are so secure in life, and you are so beyond what you read in the newspapers and suddenly, you know, it happens. What would you think?*

What would anybody think who had lived this protective little South Hills life? It wasn't country clubs and it wasn't to the manor born. We all, we had a knowledge of work. We all grew up with such a work ethic. Such an appreciation for the land.

It was idyllic and Dad had this wonderful job that he adored and people working with him that he adored and all of a sudden this black stain comes in your family and it's like, what? That's somebody else. That doesn't happen to us.

One year after the Clark murder, *The Charleston Daily Mail* headline of Sunday morning, August 22, 1954, reviewed the year-old case with eye-popping headlines at the top of the front page:

MYSTERY CLOAKS CLARK MURDER AFTER YEAR

The recap featured this subhead:

ANNIVERSARY OF BLUDGEONING BRUTAL CRIME NEAR PERFECT
By CHUCK MCGHEE
Of The Daily Mail Staff

A year ago this morning the savagely beaten body of Mrs. Juliet Staunton Clark was found in the living room of her Louden Heights home and today the Charleston police department knows as little about who killed her as was known the instant the murder was discovered.

Then, McGhee provided some additional observations:

MYSTERY CAR SOUGHT

"On the night Mrs. Clark was last seen alive, nearby residents recalled seeing an automobile parked in an isolated spot near a path that could be used to reach the Clark home through a woods. It created no speculation on that night, but one passerby recalled that the number of the license plate was "3" and that it was a West Virginia tag.

"It appeared not unreasonable to assume that the automobile was the car in which the killer departed the somewhat isolated residential area. To this end the Daily Mail, in its own offices, checked the more than 5,000 state license tags beginning

THE PERFECT CRIME

with the figure.[90] The gigantic task provided no positive lead."

McGhee's story went on to provide these added details:

- There were three massive skull fractures, any of which would have caused death.
- Thirty members of the city police department were originally assigned to the case.
- No fictional character fashioned by a master plotter of imagined crime could have left a fainter trail.
- Mrs. Clark had been sitting on a divan in her living room, reading, when her killer entered through the front door that was seldom, if ever, locked.
- There has been much "unestablished assumption" that she knew her killer.
- The police refusal to move the body for hours was an, "amazing reluctance."
- The partially burned cigarette found in an ashtray was Mrs. Clark's, McGhee's report said.[91]
- A small red billfold was missing from her purse—it was thought to be an apparent ruse to indicate robbery as a motive. Mrs. Clark never carried large sums of money.
- The minute piece of wood found in blood on the rug of the living room was not, as had been earlier described, a highly polished fragment of wood. Rather, as analyzed by state police, it was a piece of wood half as long as a little fingernail. The piece was white oak. It had either been kiln dried or had long seasoned in a protected place. The sheen on it that initially prompted the varnish reports was dried blood plasma.
- Much of the area surrounding Mrs. Clark's property was in high and tangled brush land. This was searched as thoroughly as possible and teams of trustees from the city jail chopped and cut through the area in a search for the weapon wielded

---

[90] McGhee did not elaborate as to whether the number 3 was the sole numeral on the plate or one of several numbers.

[91] However, Mrs. Clark's son, Buck Clay, was quoted in *The New York Sunday News* as saying it was not possible to say if it was her cigarette because she had no preferred brand.

by the murderer.
- There was about a mile of road leading from the Clark residence to the South Side Bridge admitting into the downtown section of Charleston. Both sides of the road were minutely combed.
- Mayor Copenhaver, "who had taken an intense personal interest in the case and assumed virtual command of the police investigation, said it was time for the city to employ outside help.[92]"
- Police commended Fred Staunton, Lyell Clay and Buckner Clay for increasing the reward leading to an arrest and conviction in the case.
- Then, a bit of reportorial whimsy in McGhee's last paragraph—"Police feel that one person has accurate knowledge of who killed Mrs. Clark, why she was killed and with what she was killed. It follows that that individual is not interested in the reward."

In the same issue of the *Mail*, Charlie Connor had a sidebar that said,

RECORD COSTS CITY $12,000

The lead had the Charlie Connor touch:

> Acting Police Chief Dewey Williams spun the dial on the big, black safe that sits in a corner of his third floor office in City Hall. He worked the combination carefully, swung open the door and extracted a bulky file fully four inches thick.
> "This represents a year's investigation on the Clark murder case," he said, flipping the pages. "It contains four or five times as much information as that collected on any other murder case handled by city police. It sill isn't complete."

---

[92] Copenhaver enlisted Dr. Fred Inbau's assistance as a polygraph expert on September 3, 1953.

THE PERFECT CRIME

> The Clark case—the state's most widely publicized unsolved murder—is something the chief discusses only with the utmost care.
>
> He does say, however, that it has cost the city and state police, "roughly...$12,000[93]," during the investigation which began last Aug. 22 when the body (was found).

Connor continued his probe, quoting the chief:

> "And I will say that I think we have accomplished much since that time," he said. "It has been a process of elimination one of the most involved murder cases I've ever worked. I will say, also, that there is still more than one suspect."

"How many?" Connor asked.

"More than one...less than five," the chief said.

"Do you agree with Mayor Copenhaver's statement that police know the killer but, 'knowing and proving it' are two separate matters?" Connor asked.

"No comment," the chief said.

"Do you think the case will ultimately be solved?" Connor continued.

"Yes, I do, definitely," he (the chief) said. "It is my hope to lead the investigation to a successful conclusion before I retire from the Charleston police force."

Connor's report continued:

---

[93] Estimated as equivalent to $108,000 in 2019.

The chief has less than two years to serve before he is eligible to retire after 20 years service.

In estimating the cost of investigation Mrs. Clark's murder, Chief Williams listed the following:

Overtime hours paid to city police officers—737½ total man hours at a cost of a total amount of $895.91[94]; Prof. Fred Inbau, polygraph expert, $989.34[95]; John Reid and Associates crime specialists, $368.68[96]; Charleston Boat Club, $27.15[97]; Jeff Meade, $25[98]; and Tom McGuffin and son, $215.[99]

Meade and the McGuffins were diving specialists hired by the city to explore the bottom of the Kanawha River along the south bank and beneath the South Side Bridge in search for the murder weapon. The Charleston Boat Club lent aid in this respect.

"This does not include the extra man hours spent by Mayor Copenhaver, City Solicitor Lyell Clay, members of the street department and trustees from the city jail, nor does it include hours or expense devoted by the prosecuting attorney's office, the state police and other police organizations," the chief said. "It does not include car expense or added food expense for investigating officers."

The chief, in making a rough estimate of $12,000[100] said that would include state police expense in his opinion, however.

---

[94] Estimated as equivalent to $8,000 in 2019.

[95] Estimated as equivalent to $9,000 in 2019.

[96] Estimated as equivalent to $3,300 in 2019.

[97] Estimated as equivalent to $244.00 in 2019.

[98] Estimated as equivalent to $225.00 in 2019.

[99] Estimated as equivalent to $1,936 in 2019.

[100] Estimated as equivalent to $108,000 in 2019.

THE PERFECT CRIME

Capt. N.C. Reger, head of the criminal identification bureau of state police, said he could not estimate expense in that organization for its help in the Clark case.

Seventeen city police officers worked overtime during the first frantic days of the murder investigation. Since then, Sgt. W.W. Fisher of the detective bureau has been assigned permanently to the case, reporting his findings to the chief personally.

Mayor Copenhaver, who took great interest in the case from the beginning and actively directed its investigation for several months, turned it over exclusively to the police four or five months ago.

"The investigation is continuing," Chief Williams says.

—THIRTY-THREE—
"SOMETHING STINKS"

The notice of cancellation of the Charleston Mail Association reward for information leading to the conviction of the person or persons who killed Juliet Clark took place March 2, 1955, quietly, in a classified ad that appeared that day in the *Daily Mail*. The Association's $15,000 was taken off the table in what was considered to be a most unusual moment.

NOTICE OF WITHDRAWAL OF OFFER TO PAY REWARD

On August 23, 1953, the undersigned, The Charleston Mail Association, offered to pay a reward of $2,500 for information leading to the apprehension and conviction of the person or persons guilty of the murder of Mrs. Walter E. Clark (Mrs. Juliet Staunton Clark) during the night of August 21, 1953. On February 9, 1954, the Charleston Mail Association and the family of the late Mrs. Juliet Staunton Clark increased the reward to $15,000 and notice thereof has been published from time to time in the Charleston Daily Mail. No such information has been furnished to either the Chief of Police of the city of Charleston or the prosecuting attorney of Kanawha County, as specified in such last mentioned notice.

The undersigned, the Charleston Mail Association, and the family of the late Mrs. Juliet

"SOMETHING STINKS"

Staunton Clark hereby give further notice that the offer to pay such reward will be withdrawn and become null and void and of no binding or effect on and after 12 o'clock noon on Monday, May 2, 1955, and will remain in force and effect until then, subject to the provisions contained in the published offer to pay said sum of $15,000.

THE CHARLESTON MAIL ASSOCIATION
By F.M. Staunton, President
March 2, 1955

Eleven days after the ad was published, Sunday morning, March 13, 1955, the *Charleston Gazette* had its chance to further the chances of Jumpin' John Copenhaver's mayoral opponent, Judge Joe Thomas, as the challenger went on the attack, reviving major interest in the murder of Juliet Staunton Clark.

The *Gazette* slyly cited the *Daily Mail* legal notice that the Mail Association was cancelling the Clark reward, *effective election day*, quoting Thomas in headlines as saying he would pursue the Clark case that Copenhaver had left "lying on a shelf, gathering dust."

THOMAS TO REOPEN CLARK INVESTIGATION

JUDGE DECLARES PROBE "STINKS," RIPS COPENHAVER

Municipal Judge Joseph Thomas said, "something stinks" about the investigation of the Clark murder case and promised yesterday he would redouble efforts to solve the mystery if he is elected mayor.

"It is strangely significant," said the judge, "that a $15,000 reward offered by the Charleston Daily Mail Assn. is being withdrawn on May 2 — the very day a new mayor takes office."

The association is publisher of the Charleston Daily Mail, a newspaper which has strongly endorsed the candidacy of incumbent Mayor John T. Copenhaver.

Juliet Staunton Clark was principal owner of the paper. She was found murdered at her South Hills Home on Aug. 22, 1953. Despite the wide interest in the case, police have made no arrests and have never said if they've found a motive for the death.

Within days after Mrs. Clark was killed, the Mail Association offered a $2,500 reward for information leading to conviction of her murderer. A few weeks later, the amount was increased to $15,000.

Then, on March 2, 1955, the newspaper carried a notice the reward offer was being cancelled, effective May 2.

A spokesman said the reward had been in effect for a year and a half without results. For that reason, he added, it was being withdrawn.

Judge Thomas, who puts his mayoralty ambitions on the line in tomorrow's Republican primary, said he would strive to raise a new reward if his election hopes are successful.

"In the event I become mayor," he added, "the investigation will be reopened. So far as I can learn the record of the case has been laying on the shelf, gathering dust."

Criticizing Copenhaver's interference in the case, Thomas said, "I think the whole thing stinks."

Thomas pointed out that Copenhaver once said police thought they knew the identity of the murderer but couldn't prove it. If such information is available, Thomas continued, he would turn it over to the prosecuting attorney's office for further action.

"SOMETHING STINKS"

> Judge Thomas also recalled the same suggestion was made editorially by the Daily Mail shortly after Copenhaver made his "knowing and proving are two different matters" statement.
>
> After the editorial appeared, Copenhaver fired back that both he and Fred Staunton[101] were of similar opinions and Staunton had as much access to the prosecuting attorney as he.
>
> Thomas said, "the public is entitled to know what information, if any, the police department has uncovered."
>
> He said he had received no specific news of progress made on the case but candidly added, "I don't think anything's been done for several months."
>
> Thomas also rapped the mayor for the manner in which elected officials were selected. He said Copenhaver "broke all precedent" by taking the naming of officials from the city committee and entrusting it to city council.
>
> "It's pretty obvious what he's trying to do," said Thomas. It goes along with the old theory that the man who controls polls is the man who wins elections."

On the same front page, Frank Knight could not miss the chance to once again gig Copenhaver. Knight wrote of the Thomas-Copenhaver election fight:

> "Then there's the matter of the police department in politics and its bungling of the Juliet Staunton Clark murder. Copenhaver, playing Dick Tracy on this occasion, presumably kept his cops from catching the killer. Left alone, it's an even bet the Clark murder would have been solved today.

---

[101] Mrs. Clark's brother, and at that time, publisher of the *Daily Mail*.

MURDER ON STAUNTON ROAD

Here again, the mayor has controlled the police as if they were subservient to him alone. The ones who have wilted beneath his demands are

Cartoon by Kendall Vintroux
–*Charleston Gazette*

the ones who have received the gravy jobs and frequent promotions. Law enforcement? Bosh!"

The *Charleston Daily Mail* was concerned. The *Gazette* was fiercely out to defeat their man—Copenhaver. The *Mail* was equally determined to keep Copenhaver in City Hall.

Conferences were held in the *Mail* editorial offices and a new tack was ordered—the *Mail* unleashed its heralded political columnist Bob Mellace, introducing yet another aspect into the Republican primary, the underworld:

AS TO POLITICS

HOW TO TWIST A SOLEMN TRUTH

By Bob Mellace
Daily Mail Political Editor

One of the ugliest aspects of the GOP city primary campaign that ends tomorrow has been

"SOMETHING STINKS"

the horrible twisting of the truth by the anti-Copenhaver forces. In so doing, they have blinded the people of Charleston to a truth that should not be overlooked.

It is, simply, that the underworld element of Charleston is out to get Copenhaver's scalp and will go to any ends to do it.

Instead of spotlighting that truth, Copenhaver's enemies, particularly the Democrats trying to drive a wedge in Republican ranks, have come up with this version: Copenhaver has accused his Republican opponent, Joe Thomas, of being in league with the underworld.

That attack has the double-barreled result of smearing Copenhaver and Thomas at the same time. A more devious bit of political propaganda by the Democrats you will never witness.

Copenhaver has never attacked Thomas' integrity, his honesty, or his standing in the community as an upright, law-abiding citizen. And no Republican of any responsibility would do such a thing and especially not to a man who might be the party's nominee.

What Copenhaver has said is that the underworld is out to get him, Copenhaver, and that is the gospel truth. It is not that the same underworld is "for" Thomas, but that it is "against" Copenhaver. It would be for any man, Democrat or Republican, named Thomas, Smith, Jones or Brown, if its support of that man meant the end of Copenhaver's campaign against them.

But you cannot infer from that statement that Joe Thomas is hooked up with the underworld element and Copenhaver is not. You can't, at least, unless you want to destroy both men.

It is a fact, as Copenhaver has pointed out, that gamblers are against him, and for good reason. One of them, a man with a long criminal record, is campaigning hard from the Summers St. place of business that Copenhaver's vice squad hit and harassed for four years. Ask yourself: Is he for Joe Thomas or is he against John Copenhaver, and what is his purpose?

Another anti-Copenhaver campaigner owns a long string of properties that formerly were rented to operators of bawdy houses. When Copenhaver cracked down on them, this man's tenant moved out and he has trouble renting them for lawful purposes. Ask yourself: Is he for Joe Thomas or is he against John Copenhaver, and what is his purpose?

Similar examples could be cited from all other elements of the underworld, and John Copenhaver is telling the people of Charleston the truth when he says they are out to get him at all costs.

If he wins the nomination tomorrow, they will shift their allegiance to his Democratic opponent in the general election. They will raise more funds and they will spend them. Again, it won't be because they love the Democratic candidate more, but because they hate John Copenhaver and his administration most, and with a viciousness that surpasses the understanding of decent citizens.

Frankly, we thought Copenhaver would have been better off campaigning on his record of civic improvements. This was based on the further belief that his record would carry him through, no matter what the racketeers might devise.

But the "hate Copenhaver" forces on the Democratic and Republican side would have none of that. They deliberately halted and goaded the mayor into taking cognizance of this shadowy force arrayed against him.

Being human, and subject to human feel-

"SOMETHING STINKS"

> ings, the Mayor struck back, and he struck back hard. And when he did strike, he did it with the truth. He told the people of Charleston the underworld is against him with all the resources it can command.
>
> If he is defeated tomorrow, it will be a victory for Joe Thomas. It will be a bigger victory for the underworld. Joe Thomas didn't elect to have it that way, but that doesn't change the fact: That is the way it is.

The *Daily Mail* was flirting with reprisal from rough elements with the Mellace column that did everything but name names of serious criminals. However, the *Mail* obviously thought Joe Thomas might have a chance to be elected and, further, that he might be serious about reopening the investigation of the murder of Juliet Staunton Clark.

True to its legal notice, the *Daily Mail* cancelled its $15,000 Clark reward effective Election Day. The *Mail* worried for no reason—the Joe Thomas threat was eliminated with John Copenhaver's primary win.

—THIRTY-FOUR—
THE KILLER WILL BE FOUND

On July 13, 1955, Charleston Mayor John Copenhaver called reporters together once more, confirming he had not forgotten the Clark investigation.

"My police officers have interviewed two prisoners at Moundsville and I'm bringing two life termers from the state penitentiary to Charleston for questioning in the Clark case," he told reporters.

"Do you think there is a confession?" reporters asked.

"The two men we are bringing here are 27-year-old Thurman Rice of Charleston and 28-year-old Robert Miller of Nitro," the mayor said.

"My officers obtained a statement from Miller that produced considerable evidence," Copenhaver added, assuring the excited members of the press that there was new material to be had.

"What was in the statement? What did Miller say?" Charlie Connor asked over shouts from the other reporters in the room.

"It's the best lead we've had yet," Copenhaver replied, "the interrogation that will take place here in Charleston might result in a solution to the two-year-old Clark case." The mayor must have sensed a lull in the excitement, and he added, "I understand that Miller told my officers the location of the murder weapon."

Charlie Connor and Jim Hill furiously scribbled notes and WSAZ-TV's camera ground away—this was big news. Finally, this could be the break that would solve Charleston's most notorious murder. Hill raced back to the *Gazette,* Connor to the *Daily Mail,* and Bob Horan to Channel 3. Calls were made and reporters soon had additional verification that the story was indeed big.

Moundsville State Penitentiary Warden Oral Skeen chimed in when Hill reached him by phone. "Yes," Skeen said, "Rice has hardly eaten a thing and has been highly agitated since two Charleston policemen were here."

The prisoners were brought to Charleston. They were interrogated for many hours. The *Gazette's* sensational front-page story of the grilling featured a large picture of Thurman Rice's face with a caption that said, "Haunting fear shows clearly in the eyes of 27-year-old Thurman Rice."

The July 16, 1955, report was vintage Jim Hill:

RICE SUBMITS TO LIE DETECTOR;
MAYOR DOUBTS FELON IS GUILTY

By James A. Hill
Staff Writer for The Gazette

Frightened and near collapse, 27 year old Thurman Rice was grilled on the police department's lie detector yesterday as tension mounted at City Hall over the outcome of the Clark Murder Investigation.

Rice, the principal figure in the renewed investigation, submitted voluntarily to the examination by Detective Sgt. Delbert Stover, the department's polygraph expert.

The wide-eyed, soft-spoken life termer was brought here Thursday night from the state penitentiary along with Robert F. Miller of Nitro.

It was Miller who centered statewide attention on the case with his statement that Rice had boasted of killing Mrs. Juliet Staunton Clark with a mechanic's wrench.

The results of an earlier polygraph test given Miller were not disclosed, but Detective Sgt. W.W. Fisher indicted he would undergo a second one.

The tests were arranged at the insistence of Mayor Copenhaver, who indicated clearly that he isn't satisfied with results so far.

His prepared statement issued to the press showed a noticeable difference of opinion with Police Chief Dewey Williams.

"After an extended conference with Sgt. Fisher," the mayor said, "I think there is yet a grave doubt about Thurman Rice being the slayer."

Chief Williams, who headed the five-man police detail that brought the two prisoners here under guard from Moundsville, was quoted earlier that the case was nearing a solution.

"Our evidence is a lot stronger," he said early yesterday at the end of a six-hour-long grilling of Rice.

Miller, a tough, well-built youth, who fears he may be in for trouble when he returns to the penitentiary, maintained throughout the day that he was telling the truth in his statement made last week at Moundsville.

"My life won't be worth a plugged nickel when I go back," he told reporters during a respite in questioning. "Those boys up there figure maybe I did wrong in talking on Rice."

During the same respite, that came about 2 in the afternoon, Mayor Copenhaver appeared at the detective bureau and requested a private interview with Miller.

While police remained on uneasy guard in the corridor, Copenhaver talked for about 10 minutes with Miller before he emerged from the room.

He remained on the scene until Rice was brought over from the county jail for his lie detector test.

As the handcuffs were being removed from the obviously nervous prisoner Copenhaver was introduced by a detective.

"How old are you, son?" the mayor asked of the prisoner who has stoutly declared his innocence.

"I'm 27," Rice mumbled so low the mayor was forced to ask the same question twice.

Meanwhile, a wrench produced by police at St. Albans was shrugged off by Charleston detectives "as obviously not the murder weapon."

At the same time police disclosed that a number of wrenches of various types have turned up since the Miller statement was released.

Sgt. Fisher indicated police still plan a systematic search of a section of U.S. Rt. 60 near St. Albans for the real weapon.

Miller said the same wrench was used in both the Aug. 21, 1953 murder and the later robbery-beating of an elderly West Side confectioner.

He added that the weapon was hurled from a speeding car near St. Albans as the two sped west for California.

The two were later arrested for a series of burglaries in Rawlings, Wyo., and returned here for prosecution on the robbery charge.

Rice blamed Miller's statement implicating

him in the murder as the result of a grudge that blossomed in Intermediate Court here.

"He's just trying to get back at me," said Rice. "He told me about three months ago that he was going to cop out on me."

Police disclosed further that a Charleston man indicted with the duo for the robbery-beating was being questioned in connection with the Clark murder.

He was identified as a Joe Arthur, who was not tried after an examination determined he was mentally incapable of defending himself.

A sidebar by Jim Haught accompanied the Hill story. *Gazette* reporter Haught had snagged an interview with Rice's aunt and foster mother, Mr. Marie Rice. Mrs. Rice, a cleaning woman, said she adopted Thurman after his mother's death at Thurman's birth. Haught's report said Rice, who lived with her brother Lintford on Thomas Avenue off Pacific Street in Edgewood Acres, said Thurman was at home all night the night Mrs. Clark was murdered.

She said he, "didn't leave the house" on the night of August 21, 1953. "We lived on Ferry Branch Hollow that summer," she told Haught. "And Thurman was working at a service station in Forest (sic) Hills. I picked him up when he got off from work at 9 p.m. and he stayed home with me all night."

"Thurman always was a sickly boy," she told Haught. "He had polio and couldn't walk until he was nine. Then he got typhoid fever and later he was hit by a bus and hurt bad. That's why he's so nervous now. It's not because he's guilty of the Clark killing."

Mrs. Rice accused Miller of "trying to frame my boy." She said, "Thurman and Miller have run around together ever since Thurman was 14 years old. And Miller always mistreated my boy. Thurman was afraid of him and gave him money all the time. He would tell me he 'lost' his paycheck and then I'd find

THE KILLER WILL BE FOUND

out that he had given the money to Miller. I don't know why he gave Miller the money."

When *Charleston Gazette* Managing Editor Frank Knight was on a roll regarding anyone with whom he disagreed, his Remington banged out blistering comment. He also did not hesitate to praise his reporters, especially swashbuckling crime reporter Jim Hill. Knight's typewriter had first struck on August 30, 1953, only days after Juliet Clark was murdered. The editor refused to quit his critique and, two years after Mrs. Clark was found dead in her home, he was again raising the eyebrows of his readers.

This time he heaped praise on reporter Hill, criticized police, and questioned decisions by Jumpin' John Copenhaver in his *"Today"* column of Sunday, July 17, 1955, saying mistakes had been made in the Clark investigation.

TODAY

It was a busy week for Police Reporter Jim Hill, whose life ambition is to be on the scene when the killer of Juliet Staunton Clark is revealed. I honestly believe that it was the compelling force behind his return to Charleston from San Francisco where he had planned to continue his newspapering.

Now back on The Gazette, where he started as a cub, Hill talks about the Clark case at the drop of a hat. It was this persistence that enabled him to break the story on 27-year old Thurman Rice, the latest in a string of suspects. Hill dug that story from behind a wall of police secrecy last Tuesday morning, got Mayor Copenhaver to confirm it, and then held it through the competition's publishing hours to write it for the Blue Streak edition Tuesday evening.

It was a stroke of fine newspapering, and while it now appears that Rice may not be the murderer it remains to Hill's credit that he was first with the most. His story brought Rice's questioning to a head and then, instead of appearing triumphant over the part he played, Reporter Hill said, "I never felt so sorry for anyone in my life."

MAN IN A CORNER

Interviewing a suspected murder always is a challenge to a newspaperman. Rice, with a long record dating back to days as a juvenile delinquent, hardly is deserving of pity.

Yet, Hill could feel the rat-like fear which gripped Rice's soul as he talked to reporters. "He acted like the whole world was stacked against him and that he was going to take the rap for the Clark murder regardless," he said. "From what I've seen, I don't think he did it."

Why didn't Hill say so in his Saturday morning story in The Gazette?

Well, for one thing, reporters don't write what THEY think, or feel, or believe. They write from the facts before them. They quote people in authority...like police and the mayor.

What Are the Facts?

Getting the facts has been tough in the Clark case since it first occurred two years ago next month. For some reason, which no one seems to be able to explain, persons in authority have felt it best to clam up when Mrs. Clark's murder is being discussed. For another, there appears to have been too many conclusions formed without proof to back them up.

One of these is that the murderer's identity generally is known and all that remains is to prove him or her guilty. The Mayor as much as said so in a talk before a men's church group eight months after the crime had been committed. What he didn't realize when he made the statement was that a Gazette reporter was in the room.

It now appears that neither the Mayor nor the police can be so sure. If they were they wouldn't have dragged Rice and his accuser and fellow convict, 28-year-old Robert Miller, here from the penitentiary at Moundsville.

Let's Start Over

The business of coming up with a new suspect may serve a wholesome purpose in the end. The police and the Mayor have now admitted—whether they like it or not—that there is more than one person who might have pounded Mrs. Clark to a grisly death. They now will have to get off their collective seats and go to work in earnest.

They can start by running down every new—and old—clue that is available. And they can continue the search by taking ALL the press, which represent the people as much as they do, into their confidence.

New Reward Needed

Until the Clark case is settled for good there will be a number of people whose lives will be affected. In justice to them, as well as the public which needs protection from potential killers, this most baffling of murders must be solved.

It was disappointing that the reward money was withdrawn early in May. Since this was privately subscribed it appears that the city council should take action to establish a new reward and also appropriate sufficient funds to start a relentless and continuous search for the killer.

Then progress reports should be made from time to time. And, if there is no progress to report, then the police and Mayor should be frank enough to say there is none.

Killer Will Be Found

Such a procedure is going to mean the invasion of private lives, but it occurs to me that enough persons have already been sufficiently hurt by this matter that there can be no stopping. If anyone even remotely suspected of being a party to Mrs. Clark's death turns out to be innocent then it is all the more important that the search be continued.

I suspect that when her killer finally is found—and indeed he or she will be—there are going to be some terribly red faces. First of all, the Mayor never should have said the identity of the killer was known unless he was ready to order an arrest and, secondly, it's probably going to wind up that some obvious boners were committed in the early hours after Mrs. Clark's body was discovered by her colored maid.

In any event, I'm betting that Reporter Hill, who now has decided that Charleston is best for him, will be on the scene when a confession is obtained. Better than that—and this is putting him on the spot—he may get another exclusive.

Frank A. Knight
Managing Editor

Then, another year on the calendar, May 31, 1956, and the *Charleston Gazette* reported that an ex-mental patient from Nitro, West Virginia, had told Chicago police he murdered Mrs. Clark. Mayor Copenhaver did not jump on this report. Two convicts in Mounds-

THE KILLER WILL BE FOUND

ville had burned him, and he wasn't eager to get burned again.

The *Pittsburgh Post Gazette* did, however, pounce on the story, headlining an Associated Press report in a definitive statement: "Socialite's '53 Murder in W.Va. Solved." The sub-head read, "Tramp in Custody Of Chicago Police Admits Slaying."

The story said that an itinerant laborer from West Virginia walked into a police station and "related he killed Mrs. Juliet Staunton Clark." The newspaper reported the man said he had bludgeoned her to death with a hammer and, "wanted to get this thing off my chest."

This time Copenhaver let the police make the statements—and his police chief patiently explained that the Chicago confessor, a 32-year-old Navy veteran, Erwin Shipley, apparently had delusions. His father said he had been treated in several hospitals and suffered from a mental disturbance.

A Chicago police captain, Thomas Alcock, said Shipley flatly denied the confession he had repeated many times. Alcock quoted Shipley as saying, "I might be capable enough to do it, but I lied when I said I committed the murder."

—THIRTY-FIVE—
BY SUFFRAGE OF COPENHAVER

The Clark investigation began to fade as an election neared in 1959 and Mayor Copenhaver had bigger fish to fry. Four years after his successful bid for a second term as mayor of the state's largest city, he again prepared for a tough fight against the 1959 Democratic ticket that sought to take him out of power. The Democratic Party had fielded a strong ticket of well-known Charleston names, and Copenhaver took them seriously.

In a masterful stroke, he sought the support of former foe, Joe Thomas, the man who almost beat him in the bitter 1955 Republican primary. The same Joe Thomas who had scathingly decried Copenhaver's handling of the Clark murder case. "Impossible," some said when Copenhaver floated the idea of Thomas joining his ticket.

Somehow, the politically astute and charming (as needed) Copenhaver persuaded Thomas to join his election team and run as the Republican candidate for police judge. Political junkies at the time scratched their heads and marveled at the audacity of Copenhaver, while greatly admiring his political ability.

Gazette political guru Harry Hoffmann said it was a quintessential Machiavellian move, but admitted it would add muscle to Jumpin' John's bid for re-election as mayor.

BY SUFFRAGE OF COPENHAVER

On March 27, 1959, in the city's primary election, Hoffmann threw every brick he had at Copenhaver, painting him as the worst kind of dictator. He warned the citizenry before the election that Copenhaver wanted re-election for the wrong reason: to run for governor as mayor of the state's capital city.

POLITICS
BY HARRY HOFFMANN

STABILITY IS DEMOCRATIC KEY IN OPPOSING MAYOR

John T. Copenhaver figures he has things set up right cozy with his Joe Thomas coup but there are a few things he must reckon with before laying aside city affairs to run for governor.

One of these is the April 26 city election, which the Democrats are dead serious about winning. More than that, the Democrats have the kind of candidates needed to make up a winning ticket.

Headed by 40-year-old James Kemp McLaughlin, the Democratic ticket is loaded with stability.

McLaughlin, energetic and forceful, will bring new ideas and a fresh outlook to the mayor's office. Backing him up on the Democratic ticket are such men as George W. Reeves, Sr. for city treasurer; John Lynn Goshorn for city police judge; Alvin McCorkle III, Clarence J. Benson, A. Garnett Thompson, John T. Moore and Cullen Hall for councilmen at large, plus a balanced ticket for ward council posts.

That is the strength of the Democratic ticket—balance and stability. There's not a dictator among them...[102]but each is a man of proven ability and sane judgment.

This also marks the big difference in comparison with the Republican ticket...for the GOP ticket, as proved over the last seven years, is composed of one man—John Copenhaver. There are other names on the ballot of course—but only as a formality.

By suffrage of Copenhaver, there is also one other candidate on the Republican ticket this election, but he never has been able to fool the followers of Joe Thomas.

Think back to 1955 and you'll recall that Copenhaver virtually labeled Joe Thomas a crook and a gangster—a tool of racketeers—just because Joe had the effrontery to oppose Copenhaver for the mayoralty nomination.

Copenhaver beat Thomas by a narrow margin...and it took some squeaking to get him by a Democratic unknown in the general election. It was so close that his cause might well be hopeless if he did not have the Joe Thomas following with him this time.

In the Republican primary, trying to balance water on both shoulders, Copenhaver posed as being aloof. After all, that Republican newspaper, which was supporting Copenhaver, also was supporting the incumbent Republican judge, Julius McWhorter. So Copenhaver either had to adopt a hands-off attitude or run the risk of alienating one side or the other.

Thomas, with Copenhaver's help, won the nomination by a narrow margin, chiefly on the strength of support in the so-called back end of town. This is the element that Copenhaver had not been able to fool...simply because those peo-

---

[102] Hoffmann used three periods in his columns as a writing technique. They are not intended to be "ellipsis" periods, designating something has been omitted in his writing.

ple knew that certain individuals were able to get away with things that landed others in jail.

This brings up two more things for Copenhaver to reckon with: (1) will his clandestine embrace of Thomas, after berating him as an evil man four years ago, enable him to win the support of the Thomas followers? And (2) can he get away with what he did without the support of the McWhorter followers?

(Joe) Thomas got there, as a candidate for police judge, because Copenhaver wanted him there. Copenhaver wanted him there because he figured he needed the Joe Thomas voices to win election for himself. And winning this election is most important to John Copenhaver...for, as in the past, he wants to use the mayor's office as a springboard to run for governor.

The importance multiplies for Copenhaver this time, for age is creeping up on him. He'll be 62 when the gubernatorial campaign rolls around next year, which means that this probably will be his last chance to bid for his life's ambition to be governor. And that chance will fade if he fails to win re-election as mayor on April 20.

That's why it became so urgent to get Joe Thomas to run for police judge, and to get him nominated. In the seven years John Copenhaver has been mayor of Charleston, he has fooled a lot of people...but he never has been able to fool the followers of Joe Thomas.

Copenhaver won his third term with ease, but Hoffmann's column was prescient. The *Gazette* political columnist said Copenhaver would soon be 62 years old, and had age against him in any gubernatorial race.

Five months after the above Hoffmann column was printed, Copenhaver was dead, at 61 years of age.

Hoffmann again took to his typewriter:

There can be no denying that Copenhaver died at the height of his political career. He was just four months into his third term as Mayor, which he won by an overwhelming majority; more importantly, he appeared in favorable position to win the Republican gubernatorial nomination which had eluded him two previous times, in 1952 and 1956.

Although still considered an open case, for all intents and purposes, the Clark murder investigation died with Copenhaver, fading into obscurity in reports buried or lost in records of the Charleston city police and those of Charleston's extraordinary mayor, a case never to be solved.

Had Copenhaver lived to see the indeterminate ending of the Clark homicide investigation, he would have had reason to be relieved. It was a convenience that avoided any awkward arrest and prosecution—possibly of a prominent person— thereby resulting in what the mayor said might be the "perfect crime."

—THIRTY-SIX—
THE OLD TOWN WON'T BE THE SAME

At the time of John T. Copenhaver's death, the Charleston newspapers had ceased to consider the Clark murder as newsworthy. Copenhaver himself, however, continued to be, even in death, fascinating news for Charleston's newspapers and their readers who bemoaned the fact that their city had lost the most colorful mayor it had ever had.

The Friday morning, August 14, 1959, *Charleston Gazette* headline read:

CITY MOURNS MAYOR'S DEATH, FUNERAL WILL BE SATURDAY

OVERWORKED HEART FAILS

By Don Marsh
Staff Writer

Funeral services will be held at 2 p.m. Saturday for Mayor John T. Copenhaver whose colorful career was ended Thursday by a heart attack.

The vibrant political figure died as he had lived—unexpectedly.

Dr. Goff P. Lily said that death was caused by a coronary insufficiency. The mayor's over-

THE OLD TOWN WON'T BE THE SAME

worked heart simply stopped beating.

The news stunned and saddened a city and brought a massive outpouring of sympathy for his family.

It seemed impossible that he could die. The limitless vitality and contagious enthusiasm of the man who had directed the affairs of Charleston for eight years appeared inexhaustible.

But they were not. The end came at Copenhaver's fine new home on Elk River. He had gone to take a shower and when he overstayed, his wife became alarmed. She found him dead in the bathroom.

She summoned city electrician Joe Bonham, an early visitor who had come to discuss some landscaping at the home.

They tried unsuccessfully to revive him. Dr. Lilly said death occurred at 8:45 a.m.

Marsh's story said that Copenhaver's death "beclouded" the 1960 political picture and removed the most likely contender in the Republican gubernatorial primary. The West Virginia statehouse had been a lifelong dream for the "poor boy" from "up Elk". He had captured a city's imagination and was respected throughout the state, demonstrated by a poll in northern West Virginia that showed there was no Republican in the state who could challenge his political popularity.

Marsh quoted the mayor's mother, Adaline, who died at 87, a year before her son's death, as saying, "He just sort of grew up. He was a country boy who never caused his parents or anyone else any trouble."

John Shanklin, president of Charleston City Council and a fierce supporter of Copenhaver in his second campaign for mayor, tearfully proclaimed himself temporary mayor. Shanklin's voice was laden with emotion as he said the law required him to assume the post until council would elect a new mayor.[103]

Shanklin, who had not been fond of Copenhaver during his first term, lapsed into tears as he attempted to enumerate the projects undertaken by Copenhaver.

"No one can say," Shanklin said haltingly, "that all of his projects were not for the betterment of the city." Shanklin, who would be voted the new mayor by council, then ordered all offices at city hall closed for the entire week to honor Copenhaver.

The *Gazette* editorial page that same day saw the *Gazette* wrangling with itself. In a strange piece of writing, a eulogy with praise for Copenhaver was ruled out. However, appreciation for Copenhaver's toughness was acceptable. The journalistic approach proved the *Gazette* had a true love-hate relationship with Jumpin' John.

Was he the best Charleston could have had? That, the editorial seemed to say, was debatable. The wandering *Gazette* opinion of August 15 said the newspaper would not lower itself to be "gooey." The *Gazette* editorial headline was:

JOHN T. COPENHAVER

HE WAS THE MAYOR

Unquestionably, the word that spread throughout Charleston Thursday was shocking: Mayor Copenhaver is dead.
A typical remark was one that came from Don Marsh, a Gazette staffer who wrote a series on the indomitable Copenhaver several months ago.
"It just doesn't seem possible," said Marsh,

---

[103] Shanklin would succeed Copenhaver as mayor of Charleston.

THE OLD TOWN WON'T BE THE SAME

"He seemed to be indestructible."

John Thomas Copenhaver, indomitable as he was, had to yield to one inevitable fact of life: death.

As any reader of The Gazette knows, this newspaper did not always agree with Mayor Copenhaver... on the...occasions that he ran for mayor of Charleston, we opposed him.

We have no apologies to make. As an independent Democratic newspaper, which supported the Republican candidate for governor in the last state campaign, we backed the Democratic nominee for mayor each time that Copenhaver ran.

Each time Copenhaver won. There is no way of determining whether Charleston would have been better off if the candidates of our choice had won.

We mention this only because we do not want to appear to be eulogizing Mayor Copenhaver just because he is dead.

In fact, we are not inclined to eulogies. We feel it is better to have our say about a man while he is still alive...when he can either appreciate what we have to say, or fight back—as Mayor Copenhaver often did.

Somehow, we feel there was a certain fondness between this newspaper and Mayor Copenhaver. We felt it: he expressed it on many occasions. He was a guy—he liked that word—who appreciated having an adversary and making up.

When Copenhaver lived and stirred up political storms, we called him on more than one occasion a political demagogue which, by the dictionary, means a popular leader; a political agitator appealing to the masses. We see no reason for changing our opinion now that he is dead.

Mayor Copenhaver was, in his own words, a "controversial character."

He thrived on that characteristic. Just because he reached the milestone in life that is death, we are not inclined to gush over his accomplishments or to become nauseating in eulogy.

We think some of the things John Copenhaver did for Charleston were good—as we said on more than one occasion while he lived. We also think some of the things he did were not as good as we think time will prove.

In the enthusiasm of a political campaign—as is befitting one running for political office—we think he took exaggerated credit on occasions. We say now, as we said in the last political campaign, that there were times when he retarded progress as well as advancing it.

There was, in short, both good and bad about John Copenhaver as mayor of Charleston—as with every mayor that went before him, just as surely there will be with every one to follow him.

As we said, we disagreed with Copenhaver on many occasions, as he did with us—but we also supported many of the projects that he undertook.

We think time will tell what kind of a mayor he was.

John T. Copenhaver was a rough, tough political fighter. We won't spoil his record with a gooey eulogy. We don't think he'd think much of us as an old adversary; we don't think he'd like it. Let us just say The Mayor; he'd like that.

News reports by the *Gazette* also said of Copenhaver:

The Copenhaver years were never dull. The mayor moved jauntily from argument to argument. He was never at a loss for either words or opinions.

At various times, he attacked the President and Vice President of the

THE OLD TOWN WON'T BE THE SAME

United States, a pair of West Virginia governors, newspapers, radio stations, the judicial system, authors, the Charleston Ministerial Assn. and even—on one surprising occasion—the Detroit Tigers.

Much of his first campaign was devoted to cleaning up what he said were intolerable vice conditions in the city. In the process, he ruptured many old friendships and very nearly lost his second campaign for election.

Through it all, the mayor kept his equanimity. He had a genius, it seemed at times, for making enemies.

But he also had the rare quality of making enduring friendships and of inspiring a loyalty that verged on adoration.

Mrs. Mary Case, a secretary in the city building inspector's office, expressed how many felt toward him when she said, "He was almost like a father to us. Everybody in this building loved the mayor."

Copenhaver himself said he held no grudges. "I am sincere when I say I hold no animosity for anyone. So far as I am concerned, I am no man's enemy and no man is mine."

John T. Copenhaver's favorite reporter, the *Daily Mail's* Charlie Connor, had a different take on John Copenhaver and was not afraid of any "gooey" retrospect. Connor did not deal in goo, he was devastated when Charleston's larger than life mayor, a man he considered a friend, died. He did the mayor proud with his usual first-rate reporting. His August 13, 1959, story was headlined:

THE OLD TOWN WON'T BE THE SAME WITHOUT COPENHAVER

By CHARLIE CONNOR
Of The Daily Mail Staff

The old town won't be the same.
"The man who gets things done" is dead.

> Few mayors in West Virginia's history made more headlines than John Thomas Copenhaver, an "Up Elk" farm boy who kept the state's capital city in a tizzy most of the eight years he held office.
>
> He was never dull. Reporters loved him. He would express an opinion at the drop of a hat. Controversial, colorful, outspoken, he stormed into dozens of arguments to have his "say". He made "good copy" and he recognized that fact.
>
> Often, he had several fusses going at the same time. He loved conflict until it began to weary him physically. Then, he'd slip off to go to the circus or a ball game to relax.

Connor related that Copenhaver's father was a county commissioner and assessor, that Copenhaver was a family man, devoted to his son and daughter and the seven grandchildren they had given him.

His last large effort was to create a city park that would encompass 80 acres in North Charleston. It would be named for him, posthumously. He may have been bombastic in nature, but he *was* the man that got things done. Connor quoted a financial adviser who said Jumpin' John had his fingers on everything. "He knew more about the budget than I did. He knew exactly how much he could spend before I figured it up for him," the friend said.

The news of the death of the man of action stunned City Hall. Shocked residents called the *Daily Mail*, refusing to believe Copenhaver had died. "You're kidding, of course," one woman said.

Charlie Connor's final words answered the disbelieving caller. He summarized the end of John Copenhaver's amazing life with these words:

But it was true. The old town would never be the same.

—THIRTY-SEVEN—
2019—A COLD CASE INDEED

An initial West Virginia Freedom Of Information Act[104] (FOIA) request for police files of the investigation was filed during the last days of Charleston Mayor Danny Jones' fourth term. It was filed November 3, 2018, sixty-six years after Juliet Clark's murder. There was no response. It is believed the FOIA was lost in the transition from Jones' administration to that of the new mayor, Amy Shuler Goodwin.

When Goodwin became mayor in January 2019, a second FOIA request was filed with the city.

Tiffany D. Redman, senior staff associate in the Charleston City Attorney's Office, responded to the second FOIA request on January 22, 2019. Redman said in her response that she had spoken with Randy Sampson at the Charleston Police Department Records Division "who advised me that he has searched his available databases and closed filing. He found no documents responsive to your request. Mr. Sampson further informed me that there was a flood sometime in the early 1980s that destroyed most if not all the documents prior to the date of the flood."

---

[104] The West Virginia Freedom of Information Act is a series of laws designed to guarantee that the public has access to public records of government bodies at all levels. West Virginia law defines records as "any writing containing information relating to the conduct of the public's business, prepared, owned and retained by a public body." It allows for five business days for records request response.

2019—A COLD CASE INDEED

Redman's letter did not cite any documentation or attribution from Sampson regarding the flood referenced.

Not until April 30, 2019, did Mayor Goodwin become aware of the first or second FOIA. Goodwin had her hands full, being in office only five months, inundated with activities as she took the reins at City Hall.

Research by the authors complicated the issue—in the 1980s the only flooding of consequence in West Virginia was the flood of November 1985. But its impact was in north central and eastern West Virginia in areas such as Clarksburg, Parsons, Marlinton, Moorefield and others.

There was no evidence in our research of flooding of consequence in Charleston during the 80s. Moreover, research provided no evidence of significant flooding in the streets of Charleston since the completion of the Summersville Dam in 1967. The Charleston police chief who served under former Mayor Danny Jones would neither confirm nor deny that a file on the Clark case existed.

Former Charleston Detective Rick Westfall, who spent 17 years in the city's detective bureau, said he believed the Clark file was there as recently as 2001. "The case files were on the fourth floor of city hall." He added, "I know, I looked through the entire file several times. When the elevator doors opened on the fourth floor, the door to the records room was directly in front of anyone exiting the elevator." Westfall, 69 and retired, said all detectives that worked the Clark case are now deceased.

Detective Dave Dickens, an eight-year Charleston detective, was, in the mid 90s, the Charleston Police Department Information Services Division Commander in charge of information services records and criminal warrants. He had supervision of the police department computer system.

Dickens said, "When we moved records and put them on the new system I took over records as well." Dickens said the department would never have checked the Clark file out. "If anyone would have wanted to take it out, we would have made them a copy," Dickens said. He said he did not remember anyone requesting that.

The former Commander said, "At that time we were still microfilming all of our reports. So, if nothing else, all that would be on microfilm." Dickens said he had a request from the evidence technicians to have one of his people go through their huge stack of envelopes and get rid of the ones they did not need anymore. However, he said, "We would never get rid of a murder case."

Dickens confirmed flooding at City Hall during his tenure. "There was a flood that had damage in the evidence room. That was independent from records unless they moved them after I retired. The evidence room was in the basement."

Dickens said he never put a cold case murder file in the basement. "If it happened, it happened after I retired (which was in 2001). And, I would not have done it for no other reason than it was really damp down there—and there were rats."

Asked if he believed the Clark file would have been on the fourth floor of City Hall in the 80s, Dickens said, "Yeah—this is a long time ago so I guess my recollection could be faulty, but, at that time the only place we would have moved it would have been from the first floor down to the ground floor in the records division and I just don't think that would have happened. We had some really old case files and we never got rid of murders."

Westfall said that yet another detective, George Jarrett, is convinced the Clark files were there as recently as 2001. Westfall said Jarrett had an assistant who personally put the Clark file in a locked closet on the fourth floor. Westfall said, "I may have been the last person that looked at it. I did not check it out, I just perused it."

2019—A COLD CASE INDEED

Westfall is of the opinion the files are still there, but he believes the current police department does not know *where* they are in the depository and will not devote the time to find them. Westfall concurs with Detective Dickens that, in the 1950s, many files were placed on microfilm and the Clark file could have been memorialized in that manner. Westfall says the woman who oversaw microfilming is deceased.

It is plausible, some say, that there may well have been, during the decades following the Clark case, an ongoing cover-up by authorities and prominent citizens of Charleston that was meant to protect people and reputations—something the *Gazette* seemed to have believed. Certainly there seemed to be, at various times, manipulation of the investigation. If the Clark file could be found, Detective Westfall says, police documentation of the case would undoubtedly add additional information to the unsolved murder, perhaps pointing to the individual who killed Juliet Clark.

Westfall, a veteran investigator, said the Charleston police of 1953 and 1954 who wrote reports on the Clark investigation might not have been the best at recording details, but a reading of their remarks would certainly provide significant insight as to what they surmised as they documented their activities—and those of the personalities that hovered over the investigation.

Westfall said his reading of the file indicated, "the detectives (who were assigned to the Clark case in 1953) tended to lean toward the son-in-law, that was the feeling I got."

And then—there is this:

Tom Toliver, who gardened for Mrs. Clark, believed at the time of the murder that the Clark case was filled with inconsistencies. He recounted a chance meeting several years after the Clark bludgeoning with a detective who was integral to the investigation.

Toliver said:

Years later I was in the Sterling Restaurant having a snack. It was late at night and two detectives came in there. I never will forget the name, one of them was W. W. "Red" Fisher. I went over to his booth and I said, "Mr. Fisher, you don't remember me, do you?" He said, "No."

I said, "I'm the guy y'all arrested for Mrs. Clark's murder." He said, "Oh, let me tell you the story." And he sat down—he didn't go through the whole spiel, but he said, "Let me tell you, we had the person in hand, but the mayor wouldn't sign a warrant for an arrest. They were interviewing you to see what you knew."

I don't want to implicate anybody, but I did know for years that the Daily Mail and Gazette—there were relatives on both sides—always wanted to merge, and Mrs. Clark was the blocking factor. I'm just speculating, but after she got killed they merged. Seems kind of strange to me.

The Gazette was over on Hale Street. It was run by, let me see, there was a Smith[105], the Merrills[106]—I knew them all—they were all relatives there. Of course, you are aware that Mrs. Clark's husband was the first governor of Alaska.

Back then they didn't say "person of interest"—they were just trying to get information out of me. I never knew until later in life that my mother called the police station and read the riot act to them. I didn't realize she had part Irish in her. Back then they called us "Negroes" and we didn't talk to people like that. But my mother called that police chief and Mayor Copenhaver and she called them everything but the Son of God.

At that time there was a policeman who worked part time and there was a Shell station on the corner of Walnut and Bridge Road. They claimed they found a wrench there. But, that case was really shut down. So, to me, it was just strange.

---

[105] Robert L. Smith, Sr., publisher of The *Gazette* from 1950-1961.

[106] *The Gazette* was located near Merrill Photo on Hale Street

2019—A COLD CASE INDEED

They tried to put the murder on Mrs. Clark's son-in-law, Arch Alexander, because they never did like him being in the family. I heard about that, because I used to work for Lyell Clay when he was over the Daily Mail. It was rumored by Lyell that Alexander never was welcome in the family. They third degreed Arch and ran all kinds of tests and no one ever knew the results, just like they ran on me.

I'll just tell 'ya, the case just looked funny. Like, right now, the police, they have no record of it. You might see if they'll let you view Detective Fisher's 1953 files, when she was killed. They might—he's been dead for years.

I would look at the time Mrs. Clark got killed and the time the Gazette moved to Virginia Street to see if there is anything to that. If you were investigating, would you put that in your investigation? I'd go back to look at it to see who was the blocking factor.

It was a cold case, but at one time, I was going to ask the chief to open it back up. But, there are no records. Doesn't that sound suspicious? As I got older, the case remained very strange to me.

I'm not implicating anybody, but as I said, the Gazette was over on Hale Street, and they always wanted to merge. Mrs. Clark was the blocking factor. After she got killed, what happened? They merged.

Detective Fisher said that night at the Sterling Restaurant, "We had the man and if you think I'm lyin', my partner will be here in about an hour and I'll let him prove to you that they wouldn't sign the warrant to get him." Again, if you could get into Fisher's files, you might be able to find some information on that.

Mayor Copenhaver said it might have been the perfect crime.

What was not said was, *it may have been the perfect crime because there was a determined effort to protect the assailant.*

If the authorities did indeed know who killed Juliet Clark and failed to move to make an arrest, they not only protected a brutal killer, but also put a shadow of suspicion upon a number of innocent people.

—THIRTY-EIGHT—
SIGNIFICANT QUESTIONS

Six decades after the horrendous event, our plunge into the murder of Juliet Staunton Clark does not provide complete answers to questions that remain about Charleston's most celebrated unsolved murder. They hang heavy in the air surrounding well-known names and legacies.

They are:

- Mayor Copenhaver said it was known who the killer was but there was not enough evidence to convict. He said if he made any mistake it was in not jailing a man in custody—he said incarcerating the suspect might have produced a confession. However, he also said he very much doubted that the individual would have "cracked." Who was the unidentified suspect?
- Did Mayor Copenhaver refuse to sign an arrest warrant for a person Detective W. W. "Red" Fisher is reported to have said was known to be the killer?[107]
- Was there manipulation of the investigation to protect a prominent person and let that individual go free?
- No fingerprints, no footprints, no tire tracks. Why? Published reports of the investigation contained no mention of fingerprints at the murder scene.
- If there were a case file in the Clark case, any remnants of

---
[107] Referenced by Tom Toliver in his April 4, 2019, interview with the authors.

SIGNIFICANT QUESTIONS

- clothing or blood in the file could be subjected to DNA testing today.
- Did the *Charleston Gazette* know who the murderer was but found its reportorial hands tied by a refusal of authorities to make an arrest?
- Did the *Daily Mail*, with a vested interest in the case, soft pedal its coverage?
- Why was the Clark-Alexander wedding, normally one that would have been a huge event, such a subdued affair?
- Did Arch Alexander resent his mother-in-law?
- Did his mother-in-law harbor ill feelings toward Arch Alexander?
- Did she believe he was not worthy of her daughter in marriage?
- Did Alexander make two visits to the Clark home the night of the murder, as reported by Ruth Reynolds?
- Did other family members dislike Juliet Clark?
- Was she the sweet lady some remembered or was she a mean, vitriolic person as others have commented?
- Who would have been so rage-filled that they literally beat her skull to a pulp, as the medical examiner commented?
- Why did the *Daily Mail* cancel its reward for information leading to the arrest and conviction of the murderer on the day of a city election wherein Copenhaver's challenger said, if he were elected, he would vigorously pursue the Clark murder, an investigation he said stank?
- Who lost their composure during a polygraph test when the Kanawha River was introduced into the questioning?
- Why did polygraph expert Dr. Fred Inbau call a family meeting late in the investigation?
- Did Fred Inbau ever polygraph Lyell Clay?
- Was Lyell Clay ever interviewed?
- Was it logical that Lyell Clay went on vacation for several days just after the murder of his mother?
- Why did Lyell Clay not attend the Inbau gathering?
- Why would Fred Staunton not comment on the meeting?
- What was said or revealed in that meeting?

- Where are the polygraph tests that were given in the case?[108]
- Why were the results never released?
- Are the polygraph records in a city file, or have they been destroyed?
- Are there records and evidence from the case that still exist?
- If Clark case records were destroyed, who gave the order?
- Were the records stolen? If so, who would want them to disappear?
- Is there any possibility that the murder will ever be solved?

On April 30, 2019, current Charleston Mayor Amy Shuler Goodwin was asked by the authors to assist them in obtaining any files of the Clark murder that may be still in City Hall, either hidden or lost. She said she had been in office only a few months and was not aware that a FOIA requesting the Clark file had been filed.

Goodwin, a former reporter, public relations specialist, and city employee under the administration of Mayor Kemp Melton, said she found it unlikely that the Clark file had been lost, but easy to believe it could have been misplaced. "I was here (at City Hall) as communications director in 1998 and 1999 for Mayor Kemp Melton, and I remember at that time there was discussion about moving offices and moving files to try to streamline different departments and different floors."

Goodwin said she put a policy in place the first week she was in office to say, "there should be document retention for every office and it should be taken seriously since we are conducting city business with city money and city resources."

Goodwin added, "Let me push and shove a little bit because, obviously, I have, for years, fought for freedom of information—you kind of hit a nerve there. I just find it so hard to believe there is nothing in this building, somewhere. It might be in another file, it might be in another office and people just don't know where it

---
[108] Northwestern University said it has no record of Dr. Fred Inbau's polygraph results in the murder of Juliet Clark.

SIGNIFICANT QUESTIONS

is. I can see that happening very easily. I will revisit everything, have them pull everything and say, 'go look again.' I promise you this—if it is in this building (the Clark file), I'll find it for you."

Goodwin's quick affirmation that she would find the file if it existed, and her exhaustive search, produced no file at the time of publication of this book. Mitch Evans and City employees continued to have extensive email conversation during Mayor Goodwin's search.

On May 29, 2019, Mitch emailed the Mayor's assistant, Tina Stinson:

> Hello Tina, et al,
>
> I just left a message on your voice mail in follow up to the discussion that Mayor Goodwin and Charles Ryan had on April 30th. This relates to the FOIA request I submitted actually on two occasions, once before the transition in City Hall after the election, and once afterward, regarding the murder of Juliet Staunton Clark on August 21, 1953.
>
> May I suggest that I be available to assist in the location of these files after being properly sworn? (As a Registered Securities dealer and Certified Financial Planner in Charleston for 36 years, I have been finger-printed and bonded in a number of areas, and am sworn to confidentiality as part of my trade). The quest to locate these files has been an exceedingly long road, and as Charlie and Mayor Goodwin discussed, there is certainly reason to believe that the files do, in fact, exist in one form or another on the City Hall premises. I would greatly appreciate your assistance in bringing this journey to an end.
>
> Thanks so much.
> Charles M. "Mitch" Evans

On July 8, 2019, Mitch emailed City Hall a third time, with this message:

> May I please receive a response to my email of May 29th?

Ms. Stinson replied on July 8, 2019:

> Hi, Mr. Evans! I have this on Mayor Goodwin's running call list. I'll circle back with her on this issue. Have a wonderful evening!
> Tina

On July 31, no reply had been received from Ms. Stinson. Seeking a response, Mitch thanked her for her July 8 email:

> Hi Tina. Thanks for getting back with me.
>
> As a researcher for a book, I'm eager to get this file, particularly since we have very good reason to believe it does, in fact, exist, and our FOIA requests have been long-gestating. But, as a business owner in the city limits, and as a taxpayer, I completely understand priorities. Especially when tornadoes come our way. (That was crazy[109]).
>
> If you and I could speak for just a few minutes we may be able to knock this out quickly, and we can all move on.
>
> Could we arrange a ten-minute call please? You name the time, or feel free to call anytime.
>
> Thanks so much Tina!
> Mitch

Then, Mitch tried another approach. He visited Lieutenant

---
[109] Referencing a tornado that touched down in the Charleston area on June 26, 2019.

SIGNIFICANT QUESTIONS

Randy Sampson who oversees the records department of the Charleston Police Department. Lieutenant Sampson told Mitch he had never heard of the Clark case, but if it should be found he would simply turn the material over to Mitch. Mitch followed up with an email that read:

> Hello Lt. Sampson.
>
> Thanks for taking a few minutes to discuss the Juliet Staunton Clark murder file with me this morning there at your office.
>
> I left you my business card there that refers to me as "Charles M. Evans", but I go by "Mitch", which is my middle name.
>
> As we discussed, we have every reason to believe that the file existed as late as 2001, based on the statements I shared with you, in which case the flood did not claim the materials. This file enjoyed a place of special record-keeping.
>
> As Detective Westfall indicated, at least for some time in his experience there the file was located in the records room directly in front of the elevators on the 4th floor. Thanks for sharing with me that this has all changed through the years, and there are no records remaining on the fourth floor.
>
> To just provide what I would refer to as somewhat "informed speculation" on my part, is it possible that this file might be located in a special and distinct place, such as a locked drawer or cabinet on the premises of City Hall, and not in the off-site location (I think that's an old elementary school or something)?
>
> Mrs. Clark held such a position of prominence as do her heirs (see link to her case below), that while it may be forgotten or unknown now, my theory is that this file didn't make it to a location where it would be lodged

among several other thousands of other files. Are there any locations in the police department or City Hall otherwise where the file may have been locked away, and those who have access to it periodically don't even really know what they have?

I just think this file calls for a somewhat out-of-the box type search. Would it be possible to send out an internal e-mail to request if anyone at City Hall has information about it? The presumption is that this is not a typical record, and my speculation is that it remains at City Hall in a secure location.

I'm attaching a link that will provide information on the crime. This may be helpful to make you aware of the case, as I know you mentioned that you were not familiar with it.

Thanks so much.

Mitch Evans

—THIRTY-NINE—
THE FINAL WORD FROM CITY HALL

The original Freedom Of Information Act (FOIA) filing with the City of Charleston was served November 3, 2018. Nine months later, on Monday, August 5, 2019, Mitch Evans, determined, tried once again to illicit a response from the City of Charleston in this email to Chief Opie Smith and Samantha Walls:

>Dear Chief Smith and Ms. Walls:
>
>I'm writing to you to respectfully request that you provide me with all materials (files and evidence) for the murder investigation of Mrs. Juliet Staunton Clark on August 21, 1953 on Staunton Road in the South Hills section of town. I am attaching two files, one which is a brief compilation of newspaper reports of the day, so there is no question regarding the case to which I refer. This is the most noteworthy murder case and crime against the people of the City of Charleston of the 20th century. This is due to the prominence of the victim, for whose murder no one has been held accountable. It remains an open case to this date, and my colleague, Charles Ryan, and I are writing a book on this subject which is also very much a history of the city. It simply is not complete without the police materials on the case.
>
>The official word is that the records are either lost,

THE FINAL WORD FROM CITY HALL

misplaced, or destroyed in a flood in the 1980s. See the response from Tiffany Redman on January 22, 2019 (attached) to one of my requests under the Freedom of Information Act (FOIA). While I appreciate the efforts of Lt. Sampson, who has checked his available data bases and closed case files as Ms. Redman's letter indicates, and while I understand that it may be challenging to locate any case records dating back to 1953, this is not just "any" case, and we have significant reason to believe that the records do, in fact, exist. We also suspect that rather than being transferred to the off-site facility for storage, the records have a special holding area within the files maintained on the City Hall premises, perhaps in a locked file, desk drawer, locker, etc. Regardless, two FOIA requests have been served over the last 18 months, and the records have still not been provided.

Confirming our belief that the records were most certainly not destroyed in a flood in the 1980s (and therefore are most likely readily available), we have statements from those who have worked in the Charleston Police Department and City Hall indicating that they have seen the files as late as 2001, and that these records were maintained at City Hall. One such example is that provided by Det. Rick Westfall, who spent 17 years in the detective bureau:

"The case files were on the fourth floor of City Hall. I know, I looked through the entire file several times. When the elevator doors opened on the fourth floor, the door to the records room was directly in front of anyone exiting the elevator."

Westfall told us that a fellow officer viewed the Clark records in 1997, and he is convinced that they were there as recently as recently as 2001. That officer told Westfall he had an assistant who personally put the Clark file in a locked room on the fourth floor.

Det. Westfall believes the records remain on the premises of City Hall but the department may not know precisely where they have been placed and will not devote the time to find them. He also told us that many of the records were placed on microfilm, and the lady who oversaw the microfilming is deceased.

As a taxpayer and business owner in Charleston, I can certainly understand and embrace the challenge the department has in spending the time and human resources to find these records. I'll re-state an offer I've made to Lt. Sampson and others at City Hall. I am finger-printed, bonded, and licensed as a registered securities dealer and Certified Financial Planner in Charleston and have been for 36 years. Would it be possible for me to be sworn and deputized for the narrow purpose of assisting in the location of these records? I am prepared to take the steps necessary to be qualified to assist you, including a binding confidentiality agreement, if you let me know what I would need to do to proceed.

Chief Smith and Ms. Walls, our book will indeed go to publication in the near future with or without these records. In the case of the latter, we will be addressing the efforts and inquiries we've made to obtain them which have been numerous, as well as the failure to obtain them including the timeframe over which we sought them. And we turn now to you as our last resort to kindly assist us please in obtaining all of the records in this case. Actually, I began my inquiries with the Chief of Police prior to the election, so your office was truly our first (and now) our last resort. Should we not be provided with the records, we wondered if you would care to comment. We would greatly appreciate that.

We thank you all so very much for what you do for our town and the commitment you demonstrate to perform what must be one of the most difficult jobs there is!

Thanks so much.
Mitch Evans

THE FINAL WORD FROM CITY HALL

There was no response from City Hall.

In a last exhaustive effort, Mitch again asked for access to the Clark file on August 12, 2019:

> **URGENT RESPONSE REQUESTED**
>
> Greetings Mayor Goodwin, Chief Smith, Tina Stinson, and others,
>
> The exhaustive e-mail below reflects my most recent attempt to obtain all of the records from the City of Charleston regarding the August 21, 1953 murder of Juliet Staunton Clark, on Staunton Road (South Hills) Charleston. My inquiries date back several months before the transition at City Hall, when I visited the former Chief of Police's office. Over this period of time we have filed two FOIA requests, the response to one of which was provided to me by Tiffany Redman, Esquire (many thanks Tiffany), indicating the records were lost or destroyed in a flood in the 1980s. However, after research and taking statements from those who were affiliated with the police department until much more recently, we understand that the files do exist, but are most likely stored in a separate and distinct location other than the off-site storage location to which many have referred in the course of this inquiry. Press reports of the day clearly indicate that these files were protected within City Hall, due to the prominence of the family involved. Moreover, this would suggest a line of custody and succession through the years for these particular records that other case files simply would not have, due to the notoriety of the case and the protection of the reputations of those close to the case, and out of an abundance of caution.
>
> Our thanks to Mayor Goodwin who personally discussed this matter with my co-author, Charles Ryan, on April 30th, 2019. She demonstrated a very strong voice regarding Freedom of Information and a commitment

to unearthing the records. Since we've heard nothing since that conversation other than Tina's steadfast commitment to keeping a priority on this matter's resolution, and we are bringing our book to publication eminently, with or without the records, we ask the following questions:

1. Will you kindly provide us with all of these records by September 15, and will you consider my offer to be sworn and assist with the search, if necessary, due to the credentials I maintain regarding confidentiality among other bonding and licensing?

2. If all of the records are not forthcoming, will you please comment on why they are not being disclosed given the statements we have taken from those who worked in the police department who have seen the records as late as 2001? And will you please confirm for us that the files are not being protected in any way due to the prominence of the victim, her family, descendants, or their legacies which survive to this date? We would greatly appreciate your comments that may be helpful in reconciling the lack of disclosure of the records with the statements we have taken from Det. Rick Westfall and others who attest that they have, in fact seen the files, as late as 2001. We seek to understand.

Please see the two files attached to this e-mail so there is no question about the case to which we refer. Very importantly, see my e-mail below from Friday, August 5, 2019, in which I appropriately describe this case as the most significant and noteworthy crime against the people of Charleston of the 20th century. This suggests that the records may reside in a separate and distinct location, perhaps on the City Hall premises possibly overlooked or unaccounted for over the last several years.

And thanks to all for your commitment to the people of the city!

Mitch Evans

THE FINAL WORD FROM CITY HALL

The comprehensive summation by Mitch proved to be the charm—there was a lengthy reply from Kevin Baker, the city's attorney. In an email dated September 13, 2019, Baker responded to Mitch's requests in a manner that assured him the city was complying with the FOIA he had filed.

Baker said the Clark file could not be found, but the search would continue. The city attorney said, however, that he doubted anything would be found. He also added an interesting new note, saying it was entirely possible a city detective had taken the file home without properly checking it out from the city. There was no elaboration.

All bases were covered in attorney Baker's email, complete with boldface emphasis that the city was not withholding information:

> Mr. Evans,
>
> Thank you for your request and for all of the information you provided. I am writing to let you know that I spent portions of the last three weeks working with our Chief of Police, Deputy Chief of Police, CPD Detectives, and CPD Records and Evidence employees to both personally locate the files and have them search yet again for the files you have requested. I regret to inform you that we have been unable to locate any files relating to Ms. Juliet (or Juliette) Staunton Clark.
>
> I understand that you contest the prior answer given that the files were destroyed in a flood in the 1980s. As you know, there was a recent change in the administration of the City and many of us are new in our positions. I think it is fair to say that we do not know when or how the files were lost or destroyed, but that we believe we have searched all of the locations where the files could possibly be located and are unable to locate any responsive files.
>
> While I cannot confirm the date of the flood that de-

stroyed some records in pre-1980s cases, I can confirm that it occurred and I have seen the remnants of some old documents with pages stuck together and completely unreadable. In addition, I believe it is entirely possible that a former detective took the file home without properly checking it out from the City.

In all candor, I believe there are numerous possible reasons the file is no longer here. What I can assure you is that we looked diligently for it and we are unable to locate it. While we would be more than happy to produce a copy of the file pursuant to the West Virginia Freedom of Information Act, unfortunately we are unable to locate any file relating to your request.

We cannot allow you to personally search through our files due to the confidential nature of the files, but I hope you will accept my assurance that we have scoured the records and diligently sought out files responsive to your request. I apologize again that we are unable to locate any responsive files.

As you can see from my comments above, I can only speculate as to why the files apparently disappeared sometime between 2001 and 2018. I am sure there were many personnel changes during that time and I can confirm that City police records were moved to a different location between 2001 and 2018.

During any of that time or during the move, the files could have been misplaced or intentionally removed by a former City employee. **I can assure you that this administration is not withholding the files or protecting the files in any way due to the prominence of the victim, her family, descendants, or their legacies which survive to this date—or for any other reason. We are simply unable to locate the files and we believe that they do not exist within the City's custody or control.** *(boldface by the sender of the email).*

Finally, as this administration continues to get the offices

THE FINAL WORD FROM CITY HALL

>of the City more organized and as we seek better solutions for storing and cataloging the numerous files maintained by the City, if we somehow come across the files you are seeking we will provide them in accordance with the West Virginia Freedom of Information Act.
>
>I realize that any such potential future discovery, which I believe is exceedingly unlikely, will be well after the deadline for usefulness in your book and I apologize again that the City does not have custody or control of the files.
>
>If you have any other questions or if I can be of any further assistance, please do not hesitate to contact me or my office.
>
>Thank you,
>Kevin
>
>*Kevin Baker*
>*City Attorney*
>*City of Charleston*
>*501 Virginia Street, East*
>*Charleston, WV 25301*

Mitch replied:

>Thank you very sincerely for all your efforts and your response to our inquiries.
>
>Should the file materialize in microfilm or physically, in whole or in part, we certainly will appreciate your letting us know.
>
>Best,
>Mitch Evans

Then, shortly after Baker's email, on Thursday, October 17, 2009, Mayor Amy Shuler Goodwin followed up with this voicemail left for Charles Ryan:

Hey, Charlie, it is Amy Shuler Goodwin calling. It is the 17th of October at 11:28. I hope this voicemail finds you well. Just cir-

cling back with you, I know it's been a while. I know we've had a lot of folks working and searching for documents, to no avail. I just wanted to circle back with you on this and hope everything's going great for you! Talk soon. Bye, bye.

So far as we know, and to her administration's credit, Mayor Goodwin's search is the only comprehensive effort to find the Clark file. Eight city administrations had come and gone since the Clark murder, a fact City Attorney Kevin Baker emphasized when he said, "I am sure there were many personnel changes during that time and I can confirm that City police records were moved to a different location between 2001 and 2018."

Baker's, "In addition, I believe it is entirely possible that a former detective took the file home without properly checking it out from the City," raises some additional questions.

Improperly signed out? Or, intentionally stolen?

By whom?

Mitch Evans wrote one more email to Charleston City Hall in January 2020, as *Murder On Staunton Road* was being sent to the book publisher.

Mitch's email to Kevin Baker said:

> Our book regarding the Juliet Clark murder of August 21, 1953 has been delayed but it is now just about to go to the publisher.
>
> One question that I wanted to ask and confirm before we seal the publication, keeping in mind that there were several documents and files at the Charleston PD that were apparently being saved to microfilm according to the statements we took from former city detectives in our research - DID YOU ALL CHECK ALL OF THE AVAILABLE MICROFILM DATABASES THAT ARE AVAILABLE TO YOU?

THE FINAL WORD FROM CITY HALL

Thanks so much.

Mitch Evans

Kevin Baker's reply was:

Thank you for the inquiry. I checked with our CPD leadership that are most familiar with the storage of old documents related to unsolved cases and this is the response that I received:

To my knowledge, CPD has never had a microfilm database.

Case photos prior to 2017 were stored via hard copy in a photo ledger and filed in the Crime Scene office in CID for a period of 3 years. After 3 years, the files are then transferred to storage at Roosevelt.

Regarding Mrs. Clark's case, I have thoroughly searched the historical files at Roosevelt as well as the files that still remain in CID. In doing so, I exhausted all possible locations that I am aware of in which this file may be located. Unfortunately, my search has not produced any information related to this case. I would feel confident in assuming that the file for this particular case is not in our police department facilities.

I hope this is helpful. If you have any additional questions, please let me know.

Thank you,
Kevin

Sixty-six years later the question remains—was there a protective shield placed around the suspect, or suspects, in the 1953 brutal murder of Juliet Staunton Clark? Failure to find the homicide file continues to block closure for Juliet Staunton Clark's relatives, friends and descendants, and the people of Charleston.

Fan Staunton Ogilvie, the daughter of *Charleston Daily Mail* publisher Frederick M. (Fred) Staunton, in her 2008 memoir *YOU, Selected Poems And KNOT: A Life*, articulated the legacy of the investigation of the death of her aunt Juliet Clark with this astute observation:

They covered up all the fingerprints and footprints and did not leave anything that would help us solve it.

Fan's words ring true to this day.

Juliet Clark's rage-filled murderer was never brought to justice.

—I.—
AFTERWORD

The men and women of the Juliet Clark story led extraordinary lives. Here are additional details of their remarkable accomplishments.

BUCKNER CLAY, SR.

The history of the Spilman, Thomas & Battle Law Firm recorded[110] that Buckner Clay's great grandfather, General Green Clay, was a soldier in the American Revolutionary War and served in the legislature of Virginia and Kentucky. He later commanded the Kentucky militia in the War of 1812. Buckner Clay's grandfather, Brutus J. Clay, was a colonel in the Confederate Army. Following the war, he settled on his estate, known as "Runnymede", in Bourbon County, Kentucky, and raised thoroughbred horses.

Buckner Clay chose a different path. He was graduated from Kentucky University in 1897 and then attended law school at the University of Virginia. He was admitted to the Bar at Paris, Kentucky.

Buckner became a full member of Price, Smith & Spilman in 1907[111], expanding the firm's name to Price, Smith, Spilman &

---

[110] *Spilman, Thomas & Battle's History Of Service, The First 150 Years*, 2014, page 35, by Elizabeth Jill Wilson.

[111] Ibid.

AFTERWORD

Clay. George Atkinson described Buckner Clay as "a young man of sound morals, high-grade integrity, well-educated and thoroughly grounded in legal principles. He is a zealous worker, a close student of sound judgment, and a careful pleader." He was a registered Democrat, but was not interested in political office. Interested in current literature and science, he was described as "an interesting and delightful companion.[112]"

Clay and Spilman worked in tandem on legal cases, going to great pains to prepare each other. Spilman would write a brief in opposition and vice-versa. They prepared thoroughly and challenged each other to ensure that all aspects were covered.

LYELL BUFFINGTON CLAY & BUCKNER WOODFORD CLAY, JR.

Lyell and Buck were raised in the home of Juliet and Walter Clark on Virginia Street, East, in downtown Charleston. After Walter's death, Juliet built a home on Staunton Road near the home of Florence Merrill (Ma Merrill). Lyell Clay adored Ma Merrill's family, and the Merrill granddaughter, Buffy Wallace, said Lyell spent many hours in their home.

Buffy said:

It wasn't until 1950 that Aunt Julie Clark moved to Staunton. She had been married to Buckner Clay. They had two sons. The first child was Buckner Clay (Jr.) and the second was Lyell. While she was pregnant with Lyell, his father, Mr. Clay, died. Lyell never knew his father; he was raised by Aunt Julie and her second husband, Walter Clark. We kids called Mr. Clark "Uncle Doc", because he also had a doctorate.

I remember Lyell adored my grandfather Merrill—he was a father figure to him for many years, before she[113] (Lyell's mother Juliet) *married Doc Clark. Lyell would say, "Daddy Merrill called*

---

[112] Ibid.

[113] Aunt Julie.

me, 'Lyelley.' And Daddy Merrill would say, "Lyelley, come sit on my lap."

Lyell had lovely memories of his, really, step-grandfather, who tutored Charles and Herbert Jones in Latin when they were little boys growing up. Charlie Jones would tell me about coming to Daddy Merrill for Latin tutoring.

Lyell's years at the Lawrenceville School in New Jersey provided a heady experience for a young man. The institution was among the first of its kind to offer advanced placement courses. The school regularly brought internationally known guest speakers to campus to address its students. The young men at Lawrenceville were lucky enough to be enrolled in a system that was a leader in academic innovation. The school featured the "Harkness" method that brought the house system to the classroom, providing an "intimate environment for intellectual discourse around a single, large conference table."

Lyell, eager to learn, took to the curriculum at Lawrenceville with ease. The school offered him both education and exercise while embracing its house system and indefatigable school spirit. Landscape architect Frederick Law Olmsted[114] and architects Peabody and Sterns of Boston, created Lawrenceville's "Circle" at the center of campus. The newly expanded grounds of the school became a National Historic Landmark. The children of wealth at Lawrenceville were cocooned in scholastic splendor.

Lyell and his classmates quickly learned that Owen Johnson wrote Lawrenceville into popular literature in his 1910 novel, *The Varmint*. The story featured the fictional character Dink Stover, recounting his days at Lawrenceville from *New Boy* to the day he graduated. Lyell and his classmates no doubt eagerly read of Stover's exploits in subsequent magazine stories, comparing them to their own.

---

[114] Olmsted designed Central Park in New York City.

AFTERWORD

Lyell was multi-faceted and amassed a fortune. He applied his wealth to many humanitarian causes. His generosity to his Lawrenceville roots was large. He gave $5.5 million to the institution to build the 17,000 square foot *Juliet Lyell Staunton Clark Music Center*, completed in 1998.

He had been active in barbershop music and a member of the Cavaliers Quartet at the University of Virginia while in law school there, and he retained his musical interest until he died. Music, it could be said, was the great love of his life. He composed 30 copyrighted songs and recorded eight CDs.

Lyell became an expert with the Yamaha Disklavier Piano and made a gift of the instrument to the Lawrenceville School where he had played banjo and bass with the Lawrenceville Dance Band. He then purchased and gave Disklaviers to Williams College, the University of Virginia, the University of Charleston, and Marshall University. Eight other colleges in West Virginia also received the prized piano.

Lyell Clay sought to serve through public office. His interest in politics was noted early on. He ran twice as a Republican for a seat in the West Virginia House of Delegates.

The first run was a success, and then it wasn't.

Lyell ran for the West Virginia House of Delegates in 1952, the year before his mother was murdered. The general election vote total that November showed Lyell a winner, but a recount began and candidate Paul Heydrick was winning. The recount, as it proceeded, became a bitter one between Lyell and Heydrick.

On Christmas Eve, 1952, leading by 79 votes, Heydrick felt he had defeated Lyell and withdrew from the recount—but with the right to re-enter should Lyell take the lead in the race. Lyell told the Kanawha County Court that was patently unfair, that Heydrick had a right to withdraw, but not conditionally.

The court rejected Lyell's plea, but Lyell insisted the recount continue. The court agreed to do so, but only if Lyell agreed to pay all recount costs unless he succeeded winning the election in the ongoing recount.

Lyell wanted the House seat; he agreed to the deal.

When the dust settled in early 1953 Heydrick was declared the winner. In August of the same year, Lyell's mother was murdered. It seemed his political career would have to wait.

But, in the next election, he again hit the road for a seat in the House of Delegates. His newspaper advertising featured a head and shoulders shot of the handsome young man staring straight ahead. The copy said:

LYELL B. CLAY
for House of Delegates

LYELL B. CLAY IS EXPERIENCED...
CITY SOLICITOR OF CHARLESTON SINCE 1951

Lyell B. Clay is public spirited...ex-vice president of Charleston Open Forum; Vice President of West Virginia League of Municipalities; director of Charleston Humane Association; Charleston YMCA; Kanawha Clay Chapter-American Red Cross.

Lyell B. clay will work to reduce cost of government through elimination of waste and inefficiency; improve schools through expansion of facilities and higher salaries for teachers; build more and better roads through reorganization of state road commission.

Lyell B. Clay is uncontrolled

Paid for by the candidate

AFTERWORD

The next day, the *Charleston Daily Mail* had no hesitation in giving major coverage to the Clay campaign. The *Mail* ran a lengthy story that any candidate for office would give eyeteeth for. It repeated Clay's campaign promises and featured a large picture of Clay and his wife standing before his campaign station wagon—a sign mounted on its roof said, *"On the Road with Lyell B. Clay, Republican, House of Delegates"*.

The *Mail* loved Lyell Clay. The campaign story referenced Lyell's connections to former prominent politicians, including the country's 9th Secretary of State, Henry Clay of Kentucky—but failed to mention that Lyell was the stepson of the former governor of Alaska, Walter Eli Clark, publisher of the *Daily Mail* or the son of his slain widow, Juliet Staunton Clark.

Lyell said, "I found out that you just can't conduct a political campaign and practice law at the same time, so I decided to spend my vacation touring Kanawha County." His station wagon was equipped with a prominent campaign sign atop the roof. The sign was four feet long. He traveled several thousand miles up and down hollows and into every corner of the county.

A campaign comment of his to the *Daily Mail* pre-dated a John F. Kennedy quote. Kennedy said, "First, you have to get elected." Lyell said it had always been his ambition to have a career in politics, adding, "But, you have to get yourself elected, you know."

Lyell was indeed serious about his ambition—for two years he attended Marshall College at night, working toward a Master's degree in political science, saying, "After I finished law school I came to the realization that in addition to a law degree, an educational background in political science is highly desirable for anyone interested in active participation in public affairs. There is so much to learn."

Lyell considered himself a poor public speaker. He was adamant that he would become a fluent orator on the campaign trail and often filled in for Mayor John Copenhaver at public events—honing his delivery. He said, "The one thing that gives me encouragement is that someone who knew Senator (Everett) Dirksen, whom some consider one of the greatest living orators, told me that he was pretty rough when he started."

He also told reporters that he believed the greatest asset of a man who is interested in a career in public affairs is an understanding wife—"And I've got one!" he said.

His wife was certainly an unabashed cheerleader for her husband. In the Sunday edition of the August 22, 1954, *Charleston Gazette*, 364 days after Mrs. Clark had died, the social pages of the newspaper ran a feature on the wife of the city's solicitor. Its tenor was that of the '50s—she was a homemaker and adoring wife.

The story said, "While Lyell Clay, Charleston's young city solicitor, prosecutes and defends in the city's behalf—his brunette wife plays nursemaid to five huge German Shepherds and two cocker spaniels named Boots and Peter...Mrs. Clay, whose natural pride in her husband makes her a good wife for a rising politician, speaks with a well-modulated voice and frequent hand gestures."

"And just what sort of husband is "Mr. City Solicitor?" the story asked.

The answer was, "His wife says he's kind, considerate to the point of inconveniencing himself, enjoys people and likes to make a self-concocted sauce for spare ribs. He doesn't smoke so she doesn't have the common housewife's worry of ashes on the rugs. He likes almost everything to eat so she doesn't have to worry about preparing meals. She insists she isn't a very good cook."

Mrs. Clay added, "He works so long and so hard at his various duties, that I might feel deserted if I didn't have some interests of my own."

AFTERWORD

The article failed to mention that "Mrs. Lyell B. Clay" had a first name. She was referred to in this, and most every article about her in the city's newspapers, as simply the wife of Lyell Clay, the exception being when Clay himself referenced his wife.

Her full name *was* used in Charleston newspapers when she was admitted into the city's Junior League. In that article she was identified as Patricia Kennedy of New Rochelle, New York. The article also revealed that she studied at Rye Country Day School before receiving a degree from Wellesley and later produced and starred in the ABC television show, *Our Dogs*.

An adoring wife, favorable *Daily Mail* stories, and newspaper and radio advertising certainly aided Lyell's second campaign for office. But disappointment reigned again as Lyell lost his second bid to become a member of the West Virginia House of Delegates.

Lyell rapidly forged forward once he became a newspaperman. Clay Communications was formed, and his enterprise expanded to four television stations in three states and four newspapers in West Virginia and North Carolina. The Clays also purchased two radio stations as a personal investment.

The Clay Empire birth began with a partnership with the *Daily Mail's* fervent competitor. A 1961 *Daily Mail* story announced the formation of a Joint Operating Agreement (JOA) with the *Gazette*. The story said the mechanical and business functions of the two newspapers would remain unchanged and the news and editorial departments would continue to operate with exactly the same degree of independence of one another as in the past. It was, said the story, a national pattern:

This step is but a continuation of the national pattern, Charleston being one of a very few remaining cities of comparable size in which some similar or identical arrangement has not been effected. Economic pressure is the motivating factor. Such consolidations elsewhere have proven of substantial benefit to properties through improved financial stability and, of most importance, benefit to the public through more complete and better-edited newspapers.

The two newspapers incorporated the Newspaper Agency Corporation in 1958, a prelude to the JOA. Incorporators were Robert L. Smith and W.E. "Ned" Chilton III of the *Gazette,* and Fred M. Staunton and Lyell Clay of the *Daily Mail.* Employees of both newspapers were assured that there would be no termination of employment because of the consolidation.

It was a creative and brilliant effort by the *Daily Mail* and *Gazette* to attack the increasing costs of publishing a newspaper. The consolidation worked and the two newspapers remained profitable, so much so that they were considered plum properties by media companies intent on growing their empires.

The *Daily Mail* and other Clay-owned newspapers were sold in 1987 for, according to Editor and Publisher, $135 million. The Associated Press, in 1987, said four Clay-owned television stations sold for $60 million. Lyell and Buck then established the Clay Foundation with a mission to improve the quality of life in the Kanawha Valley. Their efforts were seminal in creating a stunning center for the arts and sciences for West Virginia.

Buck Clay, sitting, Lyell Clay standing; their father Buckner Clay, Sr., is in the portrait behind them. *–Merrill Family, circa 2000.*

A grateful community and state wanted the Clay name to be honored by generations for their largesse and the Board of Directors of the 1999 nascent arts center was determined to assure the name "Clay" would have a lasting legacy.

Lyell and Buck were not at all comfortable to be celebrated in the naming of the new facility, but it was something they simply could not stop. "Clay" was to be forever embedded

AFTERWORD

in the impressive entrance of the world-class $80 million, 240,000 square foot, *Clay Center for The Arts and Sciences of West Virginia* that opened on July 12, 2003.

The bulk of the millions raised for the structure was largely by way of an initial Clay Foundation underwriting and subsequent substantial Clay gifts as the cost of the building, encompassing an entire city block, grew. The infusion of cash was, at the time, one of the largest amounts ever devoted to a performing arts center in the United States. Without the Clay Foundation the center would never have been built.

Lyell made many donations. A favorite enterprise of his was the Charleston YWCA—where his mother Juliet had given much. Lyell became the YWCA's largest contributor, predating the formation of the Clay Foundation. He formed a trust fund in memory of his mother—proceeds from that trust were used to make a $1.5 million donation to the YWCA in 1987.[115]

Lyell owned the parking lot next door to the YWCA and he donated that property to the YWCA several years after his original contribution from his mother's trust. Within a few years he again gave to the Y—this time an historic home on Kanawha Boulevard that had been home to the Clay Foundation offices.

There was great poignancy in the YWCA gifts in that the Y's "Resolve Family Abuse" program centered on interventions for victims of domestic violence. The emotional benefactions by Lyell would help protect women from violence in the home. Charleston historian Brooks McCabe, whose family lived on Staunton Road near Juliet Clark, commented, "This shows that good things can happen, even in spite of bad things."

In 2004, MediaNews Group purchased the *Daily Mail* from Thomson Newspapers. Then, MediaNews Group turned around and sold the *Mail* to the Daily Gazette Company, owners

---

[115] See "YWCA Sets $1.5 million Goal", *Sunday Gazette Mail*, February 18, 2007.

of the *Gazette*. The U.S. Department of Justice moved to reverse the sale, saying that the Daily Gazette Company purchased the *Mail* with the intent of shutting it down, violating antitrust laws.

A settlement without trial was agreed upon that prohibited a *Daily Mail* closure until 2015. The *Gazette* lost little time in melding the two publications when 2015 arrived. Employees of both newspapers received termination notices with the caveat that they could make reapplication for their jobs.

In 2015, a suit was filed by MediaNews Group that alleged the Daily Gazette Company illegally sold the domain name "dailymail.com". The Denver based company said it had retained the rights to the domain. After arbitration, the Daily Gazette Company was found liable on all counts. In 2018, HD Media, owner of the *Huntington Herald Dispatch*, purchased the *Gazette* for $11,487,243.

Lyell and Buckner Clay were among the most notable of Charleston entrepreneurs and philanthropists. Lyell was a public figure and was celebrated by the Charleston community with great enthusiasm. He was out and about even as his health began to suffer. Buckner Clay, however, chose to remain largely in the background throughout his life.

The authors reviewed newspapers from the 1950s through 2003, the year of Buck's death at age 84, and found scant mention of him other than legal notices and his work in establishing the Clay Foundation and Clay Center, and even those mentions were few and sparse. He was, however, remembered by those interviewed for this volume as generous and kind, with a smile for all.

When Buck's mother Juliet was murdered, there were two quotes from him in a *New York Sunday News* article detailing the slaying, but research revealed no post-Clark murder comments from him in Charleston papers.

Buck Clay died at home August 25, 2003, of amyotrophic lateral sclerosis, Lou Gehrig's disease. He and wife Toni were parents

AFTERWORD

of Florence Buffington (Buffy); Buckner (Buck) Woodford, III; and Toni Clay.

Lyell and Patricia Clay had four children: Whitney Kennedy, Ashton deLashmet, Leslie Staunton, and Courtney Clay Peraza. Lyell died of Parkinson's disease November 15, 2007, at age 83.

Lyell's daughter, Whitney Clay Diller, in the *Charleston Daily Mail* April 4, 2014, beautifully described the kindness of her father:

From my earliest memories, the Charleston Daily Mail was a huge part of my family. My dad, Lyell B. Clay, joined the paper in 1956, the year I was born.

The Daily Mail had special meaning to Dad because he had taken the reins from his stepfather, Walter E. Clark. As an attorney, Dad was instrumental in negotiating the Joint Operating Agreement between the Daily Mail and The Charleston Gazette. Many credit the JOA, which merged departments such as classified and composing, yet keeping editorial separate, for helping to assure that both papers had long lives ahead of them. Shortly after, he became publisher.

As a child, all I knew was that the Daily Mail was a magical, Rockwellian place. In the newsroom there always seemed to be a clatter of typewriters as reporters and editors rushed to meet deadlines. I remember the editors—Sam Hindman, Charlie Connor and Rex Woodford. They often wore green-tinted visors and Sam was rarely without a cigar. And I remember my Dad in the midst of it all. In the earlier days, the executive offices were in the newsroom and I think my Dad rather liked it that way.

I have seen my Dad referred to as a businessman, which of course he was, but to me, first and foremost, he was a newspaperman. I remember him telling me about a businessman he knew who decided he'd buy a newspaper. He thought he'd make a little money. Dad shook his head, baffled, saying he just as well could have been selling shoes or anything else for that matter. He felt it was important to be emotionally invested in what you were doing.

To him, the Daily Mail was not just any business; it was part of the Fourth Estate. As a publisher, he had an enormous responsibility, one he considered a great privilege. Folks looked forward to coming home from a hard day's work, sitting down with their evening paper and finding out what was happening in their communities.

I think the reason he felt so at home in a newsroom was he had a tremendous love of the English language. He also had an incredible vocabulary. I remember when I was interning in the newsroom as a teenager during the summers and Dad would sometimes write a piece for the editorial page. I'd hear Rex Woodford holler from his desk, only half-joking, "Now, how do you spell that, Lyell?"

I was fortunate enough to intern in the newsroom while in journalism school, later returning to work at the paper as a reporter. It was truly a family. Many of the staffers had been there for decades. Someone once asked Dad the secret to his success in business and he said, "I hire people who are really good at what they do and then I let them do their jobs." Dad saw the success of the paper as a team effort.

I never heard my Dad say he didn't want to go to work. He embraced it. I remember he frequently worked on weekends and growing up, I would often tag along. I loved getting a paper right off the presses and the ink would be all over my hands. As the years went on, improvements in ink and newsprint quality helped to alleviate that problem, but back then, I never cared. I loved it. Getting a paper as it came off the presses made me feel a part of something immediate, timely and important.

Since my father retired in the late '80s, the newspaper business has changed significantly. With the addition of the Internet, there are countless news sources and timely news has a whole new meaning.

AFTERWORD

But I think Dad would say that the same basic concepts still apply. He believed that integrity and impartiality should be governing principles. He loved the saying under the Daily Mail masthead that his stepfather used as the newspaper's guiding light: "Without, Or With, Offence to Friends or Foes, I Sketch Your World Exactly as It Goes". To Dad, those weren't just words, but rather a promise to the readers, one he never took lightly.

PAULA BUTTERFIELD

Toward the end of Lyell Clay's life and after his wife Pat's death in 1976, Lyell's companion was Paula Butterfield, a pharmacist and owner of Trivillian's Pharmacy in Kanawha City. Her remembrances of Lyell are poignant—and Lyell must have thought most certainly that she was a blessing to him.

Paula readily agreed to talk about Lyell, but said she wanted his family to know she holds them in the highest regard and in her remembrance did not want to in any way be offensive or cause them discomfort.

Paula said Lyell seldom mentioned his mother, and cited her murder only once—but with great emotion:

He told me "That that was the end of my innocence." That after his mother was murdered his whole life changed. That things were good, everything was going perfectly, and then she was murdered—that's the way he put it, "That it was the end of my innocence", but he didn't mean that he had killed her, you understand what I'm saying.

He and I were on a cruise to Norway, and at the summer solstice, we were at the northernmost tip of Europe, and we were in a bus going back, and that's when he talked about it. It was—so beautiful—there was this beautiful ship—he had, we had—a bedroom, a living room, two balconies, a jacuzzi, a bathtub, a this, a that, everything was perfect. Coming back we went to the Shetland

Islands and Edinborough. This was late in his life, and he just wanted to live life to the fullest.

His mother's death is the first murder that I ever remember. I didn't know her, but it was such big news, and everybody read the newspaper then—it was the first murder I ever heard of. I'm sure I asked Mom, "What's murder?"

Someone came in and beat Mrs. Clark in the head with fireplace tools. There were two suspects. One was Lyell's half-sister's husband, Arch Alexander.

Lyell said that he wasn't denigrating his half-sister Julie Clark at all, but he said that she just loved men in uniform. Apparently, she had started having a fling with a policeman or whatever, and she and Arch were in the process, or beginning to get a divorce, or having problems, or whatever. And I think that is one of the reasons—he (Arch) had gone up there that night—and I think that is why he was suspected.

There also was a retarded man that wandered around South Hills. Lyell's aunt, Mary Merrill—I knew her well—told me that's who she thought did it. But, who knows? You just don't know why something like that happens.

He did not talk about his mother's personality—he seldom talked about his mother at all—only how much he cared about her and what a big part of his life she had been—what a hole that was left when she was gone.

I was very late on the scene with Lyell, but I can imagine his pain. My mother died in 1970 when I was 28, and I thought I had experienced the worst hurt that could ever be imagined—and then, from then on, nothing would bother me.

I thought, I have gone through this, and nothing is ever again going to bother me like this. But it does. I got really close to my dad, and when he passed it almost killed me. And the same thing

AFTERWORD

occurred when Lyell died. But, you do mend, and I think Lyell had mended, as far as his mother's death was concerned.

He was a man of many interests. He loved the Olympia Brass Band, opera, and the symphony. He was pretty young when he was diagnosed with Parkinson's, and he had the disease when I came to know him.

He worked hard to maintain his stamina and his strength, doing his best to control his symptoms. He fought the disease—I was told by a friend of his that Lyell would go to the (then downtown) YMCA and do 100 one-arm pull-ups.

Lyell Clay and Paula Butterfield in the den of Lyell's home on Staunton Road. The portrait far left is Lyell's monther, Juliet Clark.
–Photo courtesy of Paula Butterfield

He wanted to keep going as long as he could. He would spend 45 minutes trying to button (his cuff). I'd say, "Lyell, why don't you get somebody in here to help you?" But no, he wanted to do it by himself.

Parkinson's is a terrible disease. Those who have it develop a gait of sorts in their walk. They drool. And if Lyell didn't take his med-

icine, he couldn't move. Conversely, the medicine he took would cause tremors. He was up there in that huge house by himself, and people would tell him, "You shouldn't be up here!" One of his friends brought him a football helmet to wear because he could just stop dead in his tracks and fall at anytime.

He bought his house from his aunt, Florence Fleeson. It was up there on the family property on Staunton Road—a stone house with 22 rooms. The grounds featured a greenhouse, swimming pool, and tennis court. It was a gorgeous property.

Lyell would go to bed, by himself, and he couldn't move until he took his medicines. He had a regimen—certain times he could take his medicine. He would essentially be in bed, unable to move. He couldn't get up to go to the bathroom. And he would call me, and he would say, "I hear something." It wasn't a new house, so it made noises.

I'd ask, "Lyell, what is it?"

He'd say, "I don't know. But I heard something."

I'd ask, "Do you want me to come up there?"

And he would say, "Yes."

I think he wanted me to come up there and he needed a reason. Hearing noises, essentially trapped in his bed, those were as good reasons as anything for me to go to the house.

When I was there, I could hear the noises he was hearing. I thought if I were up here in this huge house up on the top of this hill, nobody around except in one end of it, and I thought of my mother being murdered—well, no wonder he's getting anxious about it.

His mother's death affected Lyell greatly, as it did his older brother Buckner. Buckner was wonderful, but he wasn't a business person. I guess Lyell realized that if the newspaper was going to

AFTERWORD

continue he was going to have to take the reigns.

Buck went to Florida in the winter, I think, but he was here in the summer. He and Toni (Buck's wife) lived up on the hill somewhere close to his mother. Lyell said that his brother was a prince of a man—words from a different generation.

I'm not so sure that Toni wanted to be around us much. I think she wanted to be around their little part of the family rather than being around Lyell—but I'm not certain of that.

The first time I ever saw Lyell—I didn't even know who he was—we were at the University of Charleston at a dinner for contributors. The audience was being addressed and I was sitting at a round table where Lyell was seated. I did not know who he was. He was with Renee Conlin (wife of Charleston Symphony Director Thomas Conlin).

Lyell was sitting not quite straight up. As I watched, his head moved slowly down toward the table. I didn't watch him the whole time, but he ended up with his head resting almost on the table. I thought, how terrible!

Lyell Clay and Paula Butterfield in evening dress
–Photo courtesy of Paula Butterfield

Then, we were at another gathering at the University of Charleston's President's house. I was there because I had gone on a lot of University Board of Governor's trips, and I knew many of the faculty. I'm not certain, but the occasion may have been in honor of Lyell and Buck who were large patrons of the school. I told Bill McDavid (a well-known Charleston lawyer) that I had never met Lyell.

Bill introduced us and I thanked Lyell for what he was doing for the University. He said, "Are you having dinner with anybody— would you join me for the dinner?" And so, that's how I met him.

He then would come into the store (Trivillian's). He would ask if I wanted to do this, or if I wanted to do that.

And of course, I did.

Have you heard any of Lyell's music? He contributed a lot of underwriting to the School of Music at the University of Charleston, and one afternoon some of his music was to be performed at a recital. He invited me to attend. During the recital, one of Lyell's compositions was played. It was announced that Lyell was dedicating it to me. Isn't that sweet? It was something about "My Valentine".

I had stars in my eyes.

There was a big difference in our ages—and he was so wealthy. I remember, he came in the store one day and walked back to the pharmacy department. He was with (University of Charleston President) *Ed Welch. Lyell came to the counter back where I was, stretched his arms wide and loudly said, "WILL YOU MARRY ME?"*

It was so impromptu, and I said, "Yes!"

He went out to his car and told everyone in the car that I'd said I'd marry him. I followed him out and said I couldn't do it. I just could not do it.

I felt that if I married him people would say, "Well, no wonder – he's been footing the bills all along. You know what I'm saying. I had worked really hard all of my life, had no kids, didn't do anything but work! The store had become my whole life, and I was very independent.

But I think about it now—what difference does it make what people think? You know, you're so crazy at different points in your life. Why would I care what anybody thought? Why should I have?

AFTERWORD

Lyell was never the least bit parsimonious, so far as I knew, but I remember Lyell's secretary telling me that spending money on greeting cards irritated him. She said he'd send her out to get a card, and he'd get angry because she'd spent so much for it.

His bias against printed greetings had nothing to do with money—he just thought a heartfelt greeting would have been better written. Perhaps it would have been, but I am sure his disease prevented his writing personal notes.

Lyell was 70-plus, and very ill when I met him. We went so many places, even as the Parkinson's worsened. He would sit at dinner in public places and his head would slowly begin to bend toward the table. When I saw that I'd just gently pull him back up. I thought it had been inhumane the first time I saw that—before I really knew him—people would just let him drop to the tabletop. It was awful to have somebody sitting there with his head bent toward the table. This was recurring at any sitting. He would start to bend down, and I'd pull him back up. I never let him go all the way down. Before me, his head would droop to the table and his dinner partners would just forget about him. Awful.

A customer who had Parkinson's came into the store one evening and was really in a bad way—jumping around. I walked him to his car. He steadied himself by holding onto the car, but the jerking continued. He said his medication caused hallucinations and told me, "When I'm driving home, the whole time I'm saying to myself, there's not a monster out there trying to get me! It's just a hallucination. It's just a hallucination."

I mention this because one of Lyell's caretakers said, "Well, he's going crazy." I said, "What do you mean, he's going crazy"?

She said, "He's telling me that he's seeing snakes coming out of the ventilation system." It was a hallucination. This person who was trying to take care of Lyell knew nothing about Parkinson's effect and assumed the man for whom she was caring was crazy. Lyell called me one night at the end of my 11-hour day and said,

"Can you come up tonight?"
I said, "I'm so tired tonight, but I'll come tomorrow."

He said, "Okay."

That night I closed the store around 8:00. Around 10:00 I got an urgent call from Jenny (his secretary), shouting, "You need to come right away! The house caught fire and Lyell has lost all of his medicines! You need to bring all of his medicines to him!"

When Lyell became aware that his house was on fire he was able to, somehow, thank goodness, get out of the house and make his way up the hill to where the Merrills lived—they called the fire department.

There were several fireplaces in his home. Each had a system that would empty residue from a firewood or coal chute to the lower level of the house where hot embers would cool. It is believed the lower level ash container had been left open and hot embers spilled onto the carpeting, causing the fire.

I worried that if I'd gone there after I got off work, perhaps he wouldn't have lost everything. But someone said, "What if you'd opened the door, it could have created a backdraft!"

The area where the fire started contained fine things—mementoes of opera stars he knew, his albums and books. Helen Hoffman was a favorite artist of his and Lyell displayed many of her works. On the walls of his home's circular staircase was a portrait of Lyell and renderings of each of his children—all painted by Hoffman.

I went to the Marriott where Lyell had checked in as his house lay in ruins. Here was this man sitting there who'd lost everything except the clothes on his back and a necklace with a gold pendant. The gold was from the Alaska Gold Rush. Lyell's stepfather, Walter Eli Clark, the former owner of the Charleston Daily Mail and former gold prospector in Alaska, had given a large gold nugget to Lyell who then divided it into pieces for his family members.

AFTERWORD

Lyell sat there in that hotel room and said to me, "I just did the hardest thing I've ever had to do in my life." I said, "What was it, Lyell?" and he said, "I had to call Helen Hoffman and tell her that her life's work is gone."

The "Llardo" artistic rendering titled, "Figurine In The Gondola", that was given to Paula Butterfield by Lyell Clay
–Photo by Mitch Evans

I just thought that spoke so much of who Lyell was—he'd lost everything he had, and he sat there worrying about someone else.

He said, "They didn't save anything at all, except that old Jeep. It's ten years old. But the firemen knew a car had value and they said, 'Well, let's get the car out!' instead of saving things of real value."

The car wasn't worth what that figurine is worth down the hall. But they just didn't know (Paula pointed down the hall of her residence to an artist's rendering of a gondola that Lyell had given her).

Everyone just beamed when Lyell came in. He was just so nice to everybody. When we'd go to Edgewood Country Club he insisted that we go through the kitchen and say hello to everyone. Everyone knew him and liked him.

Frank, who worked for Lyell for years—Lyell wrote a song for him. Oh, it's the funniest thing. Frank was a black man and he had drinking problems. One night Frank called Lyell, and he told him he was in jail.

"Would you come down and get me?" he asked.

"Okay," Lyell said. This was when Lyell was still able to drive, and I don't know if he had Parkinson's at that point, or not, but he went to the police station.

The police checked their records and even went back to the cells to ask if there was a Frank present. They came back and said, "We don't have any 'Frank' in jail—but there's a Lyell Clay back there." Lyell thought that was hilarious, so he wrote a song about it. Frank then went on the wagon, found a lady friend, and got married to Louise. Lyell bought them a house in Kanawha City.

One evening Lyell and I were at General Seafood. It was casual, noisy and crowded. A physician friend of Lyell's came to our table and said, "Lyell, do you remember me?" Lyell said, "Well sure, how are you doing?" They talked a little bit, and after they left Lyell said to me, "I have Parkinson's Disease, not Alzheimer's. I went to grade school with him."

Prior to the University of Charleston dedicating the Clay Tower, he asked me to go see it. We stood there looking at it and I said, "What do you think, Lyell?" And he said, "I think it looks like a chess piece." And it does look a little bit like that, doesn't it?

Lyell made me feel like a princess. He could put you on a pedestal. Lyell was a lot older than I. I remember we went to the Civic Center, and somebody said something about "my dad." That offended me to no end. I may have been younger and looked younger, but he was not fatherly at all to me, and he enriched my life so much. He could have, had I let him, taught me more about how to better use my money to help others.

The Charleston YWCA came to him many years ago and wanted to know if they could buy the parking lot that he owned across the street from the Y. He said they really needed it for their member parking.

Lyell told them, "Well, I don't know. Let me think about it." He told me, "I thought about it for a good while, and I called them back and told them they couldn't buy it—but I'd give it to them." He said, "It made me feel so good that I've been giving money away like a drunken sailor ever since."

AFTERWORD

So that was the beginning of his extraordinary philanthropy. He built a building at the University of Virginia Law School for students who were having emotional problems. The reason he built it for them is that his best friend committed suicide while in school there.

He came to me one time, and he had this clipping out of the newspaper. It was from some young man who had written the newspaper to say how much he admired Lyell. That just really affected him. He was really proud of that. He carried that around with him. I mean, that meant more to him than a lot of the other accolades that were given him—the fact that somebody who didn't know him, not a monied person, was thanking him for what he'd done for this area.

ARCH ALEXANDER, SR.

Arch Alexander, Sr., the former chief of the West Virginia Department of Mines, and Arch Alexander Jr.'s father, did consulting work for numerous mining entities following his stint in state government. Alexander was associated with Island Creek Coal Company, Eagle Coal and Dock Company, Carbon Fuel, and Appalachian Coal and Lumber Company. His obituary said he attended Washington and Lee University and the University of Illinois.

Widely-known and respected in the industry, he served as president of the Mine Inspector's Institute, secretary of the Independent Coal Association, and as a member of the American Institute of Mining and Metallurgical Engineers.

He must have known Walter and Juliet Staunton Clark well, for he was at one time president of the Charleston Rose Society. A joiner, he belonged to the Elks, Masons and Scottish Rights bodies, and the Grandparents Club. He and his wife were members of First Presbyterian Church of Charleston. Alexander's survivors were his wife Lucille, son Arch, and daughter Mrs. Richard E. Ford of Lewisburg. Arch Alexander, Sr. was 78 at the time of his death.

ARCH ALEXANDER, JR.

Arch Alexander, Jr. died February 22, 1977, at the age of 52. His obituary was brief, relaying that he lived at 2913 Noyes Avenue and died on a Thursday as a patient in the Memorial Division of Charleston Area Medical Center. It related that he practiced law for more than 23 years in the town of Marmet in Kanawha County and that he was a World War II veteran and captain in the Air Force.

The obituary recorded that he was a native of Logan and was survived by his wife Helena (his second wife) and daughter Shelley Cuisset of Paris, France, and a son, Guy J. of Charleston.

His death notice cited his mother as Mrs. Lucille F. Alexander of Charleston. It listed as survivors his sister, Mrs. Richard E. Ford of Lewisburg; his stepdaughter, Mrs. Pamela Jane Bailey; and his stepson, Steven Bailey. Both stepchildren lived in Marmet.

There was no mention of a marathon grilling of Alexander following the murder of his mother-in-law in 1953.

JULIET CLARK ALEXANDER

Juliet (Julie) Clark Alexander, daughter of Mrs. Walter Clark, died October 18, 1985, at her home in Charleston, after a long illness. She was 55 years old. After her mother's death she was employed for a brief time as a member of the newspaper's women's department and was listed as the assistant secretary of Clay Communications at the time of her death. She was a major stockholder of the business.

Julie lived the major portion of her life in France, residing for years in Paris, before settling in Chantilly, where she raised Arabian horses. She became fluent in French and traveled extensively in Europe. During her 24 years abroad, according to a *Daily Mail* article of October 19, 1985, she had a daughter, Roge Antoinette Monnier-Thuret, by Pierre Monnier.

AFTERWORD

Richard Merrill recalled that Buck and Toni Clay visited Julie in France. When Toni returned to Charleston, she told Richard that she could not believe the conditions in which Julie lived. She resided, Toni said, above a stable in "appalling conditions."

Julie returned to Charleston in 1983 and resided at Chilton Manor in South Hills. Daughters Shelley of Charleston and Antoinette of Shepherdstown, West Virginia, survive her.

JULIET LYELL SHELDON ALEXANDER CUISSET

"Shelley" Alexander Cuisset returned from France to build a luxurious home in Charleston's Quarry Creek development and open the Café de Paris, a French restaurant at the corner of Capitol and Quarrier Streets in downtown Charleston. The restaurant has since closed. Shelley continues to live in Charleston. The authors attempted to contact her by email and telephone during the writing of this book, but she did not respond to those efforts.

GERARD CUISSET

Shelley Cuisset's husband, Gerard, was born in 1951 in Saint-Aubin, France. He was a member of the French Air Force and held a Masters Degree in Mathematics. He attended flight school in Toulouse, France and earned his commercial pilot's license in 1975. His commercial pilot career lasted 30 years. He flew for Air Provence Charter, flying Airbus' 300-A and Boeing's 737 and 747. Gerard died in 2018 and was survived by his 94-year-old mother, Ginette Wery Cuisset; his wife Shelley Alexander; his two sons, Phillipe and Nicholas; his daughter Virginia; and two grandchildren, Zion Cuisset and Michael Scott Cuisset, Jr. He is interred beside his father, Michael Cuisset, in France. His obituary said Gerard would always be remembered for his, "wise and, at times, funny comments."

BUFFY MERRILL WALLACE

Buffy Wallace and her husband Harry, now deceased, purchased the home that Elizabeth and Frederick M. (Fred) Staunton built. She is an extraordinary woman of great cheer. Her husband Harry had quick wit and humor. Buffy credits "Wally" with coining the phrase, "The Bloody Buffingtons."

Buffy's brother John walks his hunting dogs on Staunton Road at 6 each morning and, walk completed, knocks on Buffy and Wally's door and enters the beautiful home built by Fred Staunton.

Buffy recalled:

Strangely enough, I have the wedding gown my grandmother (Ma Merrill) *wore and Aunt Julie* (Juliet Staunton Clark) *wore, in my attic. And then my mother wore it. I wonder what can I do with this wedding gown from the 1890s? It should not rot in my attic. When I die my kids will throw it in the trash!* (She laughs goodheartedly.) *I wonder what you do with collector's items like that?*

JOHN BUFFINGTON MERRILL, JR.

John Buffington Merrill, Jr. ran Merrill Photo for many years after his dad turned the business over to him and finally closed it down with the advent of digital photography. He is retired and each morning walks his hunting dogs from Lindy Road, across Louden Heights Road, to Staunton Road. Annually, he visits South Carolina for two weeks and South Dakota for three weeks to hunt quail. He spends each Sunday afternoon at a local shooting range to keep his shotgun prowess in fine tune.

Buffy and John are full of humor and gently kid one another when they get together, which is often. John is fondly remembered by the tens of thousands of customers who patronized Merrill Photo for decades. He was known as a merchant of the highest ethics and one of the kindest businessmen that custom-

AFTERWORD

ers ever encountered. His employees were long-term and held their boss in the highest esteem. The word "gentleman" best describes John Merrill, Jr.

RICHARD MERRILL

Richard Merrill is the CEO of Tyler Mountain Water Company, a business his father bought and ran at an advanced age. Richard is a world-class squash player at Edgewood Country Club in Charleston and has the family trait of extreme kindness. He regularly assists young players who have taken up squash.

Richard and future Charleston mayor Danny Jones were buddies, even though Danny was a few years younger. Together they often visited, late in the evening, the Sterling Restaurant downtown. Richard remembers that Danny became frustrated one such evening waiting for service as the late night crowd drifted in. Richard has a vivid recollection of the future mayor of Charleston sitting in their booth, slowly beginning a low "Moooo" sound, increasing the volume of the "Moooo" until a waitress rushed over to take the boy's order, thereby silencing young Danny.

Merrill memories include that of a powerful storm that felled a number of trees on their property. Appalachian Power came with chain saws and denuded the slope in front of the Merrill home, revealing a stunning view of the Kanawha Valley.

Once the Merrills had the view, others wanted it, and joined in the chain saw party, broadening the panorama.

Today, Richard and his family own and live on Staunton Road in "Briarwood", the home built by his grandparents.

FREDERICK M. (FRED) STAUNTON

Fred Staunton was born March 10, 1903, and died November 2, 1976. His father and mother were Edward Wilber[116] Staunton and Florence Garland Buffington.[117]

Publisher Staunton's wife was the former Elisabeth (Dip) Brightwell. The couple was married January 11, 1928. They had five children: Frederick Marshall, Jr., (Freddy); Sidney Augustus, II (Sid); Elisabeth Brightwell (Betsy); Henry Platt Brightwell; and Fanny White Brightwell (Fan) Staunton.

Sidney Staunton became board chairman of the New York Investment Banking firm *Laird, Inc.*

Freddy died young. A *Daily Mail* headline of Wednesday March 28, 1972 read:

Ex-Publisher's Son Claimed in Greenbrier---Fred M. Staunton Jr., 43, found dead in driveway of his Greenbrier County home at Caldwell. His death was attributed to a heart attack. He was commercial manager for C&P Telephone at Lewisburg.

ELISABETH (BETSY) STAUNTON JOHNSON

Betsy Staunton Johnson is in her 80s and abundantly gifted with memory and health—she sees things through a poet's eye. She and all the kids on Staunton walked to school at Fernbank Elementary on Bridge Road. "We were pretty fit children because we walked to and from school," she said.

The school-bound youngsters trailed down Staunton past a large sycamore tree to Lower Ridgeway and on to Louden Heights Road, crossing Louden Heights onto Abney Circle, accessing Forest Road and then on to Walnut Road, finally ending at Bridge Road and their school.

---

[116] Some printings say "Wilbur".

[117] Ma Merrill

AFTERWORD

It was not an easy trek. Occasionally they would shorten their trip by climbing Bird Road off Louden Heights and exiting on Forest Road at the home of Bob and Jenny Hawkins.

Betsy has a portrait of her father, *Daily Mail* Publisher Fred Staunton, commissioned by Lyell.

She did not like the painting. She still has it, but does not display the rendering:

March 3, 1968 photo of Robert Baranet[118] painting the portrait of Frederick M. (Fred) Staunton.
—Charleston Gazette

> I remember taking a group of Boy Scouts down to the newspaper and Lyell had had a painting done by a very fancy person in New York. I remember walking into the pressroom and the painting was hanging up there and I remember looking at this painting. I've got it in the basement and it's all covered with mildew. I said (during the visit to the newspaper), "That is not my father!" All these people, some I still knew, said, "Oh, we didn't dare say that! We would not have dared say that!"

FANNY STAUNTON OGILVIE

Fanny Ogilvie, Betsy's sister, resides in Martha's Vineyard. Her 2008 book *YOU, Selected Poems and Knot: A Life*, says the following:

Fan Ogilvie is a poet, teacher of poetry, and organizer of poetry workshops and events in Washington, D.C., New Jersey, CT, New York City and Martha's Vineyard. In 1984 she received a Chester Jones Foundation commendation award. She is included in two chapbooks[119], "The Other Side of The Hill" and "In a Certain Place".

---

[118] Baranet was a native of Pittsburgh who studied art in Spain and Italy. He became a noted artist after forsaking a career in oil and natural gas "wildcatting".

[119] Paperback booklets of poems.

Her poems are published in The Poet and the Poem Anthology, Poet Lore, Three Sisters, Z'Arts, Fulcrum, An Annual of Poetry and Aesthetics, The Martha's Vineyard Journal of Writing, online on Fieralingue, the Poet's Corner, and others.

Her public readings include the Folger Shakespeare Library, the Corcoran Museum of Art, Georgetown University, the Stirling Library, Massachusetts Institute of Technology, among others.

She established the Folger Shakespeare Library's Poetry Board and served as its chairman from 1986-1995. In addition, she helped to organize the Martha's Vineyard Writers Program. She taught poetry at the Featherstone Center for the Arts on Martha's Vineyard from 1996-2007. She is co-founder of Martha's Vineyard Point Way Writers' Residency Program 2008.

She graduated from Smith College in 1966 and earned an MA from George Washington University in 1971. She now lives on Martha's Vineyard with her husband Donald. They have two children, Jennifer and Adam.

FLORENCE AND TOM FLEESON

Buffy Wallace remembers: "Aunt Florence had married this man named Gordon King[120], who was very wealthy, from Pittsburgh. I think they were involved in Jones and Laughlin Steel. They were a pretty renowned family in Pittsburgh. Gordon King was killed in a car wreck. Aunt Florence then married Tom Fleeson, whom my grandmother always called, "Mr. Veeson"—she had a hard time saying Fleeson.

He had been married before, too. He had a daughter and he had a brother, Neville Fleeson, who wrote the song, "I'll Be With You In Apple Blossom Time". And after he died, Uncle Tom still received the royalties from ASCAP.[121] We were always quite fas-

---

[120] Gordon Coltart King, Jr.

[121] American Society of Composers, Authors and Publishers.

AFTERWORD

cinated with Uncle Tom's brother who wrote that song, because it was pretty famous.

Aunt Florence and Tom Fleeson moved down here from Pittsburgh and built that—to me that was the prettiest house in Charleston—they built that house when I was in about the fifth grade, so it was around 1948. They lived there—she lived there a long time and when she finally went to live on Long Island in a retirement community where her youngest son lived, that's when Lyell bought the house."

BESSIE SMITH AND JOHN WOODSON

The authors could find few references to the lives of Bessie Smith and John Woodson after the Clark murder, other than a lifetime trust given to Woodson by Mrs. Clark that would provide him with a monthly income for the remainder of his life.

Buffy Merrill said she had no memory of Bessie Smith, but knew Woodson well. "John was getting up there—he had worked with Aunt Julie and the newspaper for years. Maybe he was in his sixties. I know he worked a lot with Julie (the Clark daughter) and her horse. The name of her horse was Gray Dawn."

"John Woodson worked with her (Julie) a lot and helped take care of the horse. He was not a real young man, but he was in good physical shape. I would see him down at the newspaper cleaning up the *Daily Mail*, working at the newspaper as well as with Aunt Julie. He was someone who had been with the family for years," Buffy recalled.

FRANCIS ANTHONY KNIGHT

Frank Knight was considered to be one of the most readable journalists in West Virginia. He wrote until he died at an early age—respected as a man of strong opinion with a desire to aid the underdog.

Knight, Mayor John T. Copenhaver's nemesis, was born in Chicago in 1907. His family moved to Canton, Ohio when he was a small child. He was educated in parochial schools, graduated from Canton's McKinley High School and attended Wittenberg College in Springfield, Ohio.

Precocious, he became at eight years of age an office boy at the *Canton Daily News*. He watched and listened, adopting an approach to journalism held by Donald "Ring" Mellett, the crusading editor of the Canton newspaper who was killed by a hired assassin as Mellett conducted a crusade against vice conditions in his city. Mellett's intensive and aggressive approach to matters in Canton instilled in the young Knight a journalistic mind set to right the wrongs of the world.

In 1929 Knight earned a job as sports editor for the *Charleston Gazette*. He stayed at the newspaper for seven years and then moved to New York, joining the public relations firm of Carl Byoir Associates in 1936—he then worked on the 1938 Roosevelt presidential campaign.

Prior to returning to Charleston, he moved to Miami Beach where he became director of public relations for several hotels. He returned to the *Gazette* and served as promotion manager and assistant to the publisher. Several years later, he became managing editor at the *Gazette*, whereupon he began writing his Sunday column, *Today*, which also appeared on occasion during weekdays.

Knight's interest in politics saw him run and win a seat in the West Virginia House of Delegates where he served six two-year terms. Many years later, his son, Tom Knight, would also run for and be elected to the House.

In 1951 Frank Knight moved on up the *Gazette* chain of command when he became managing editor of the *Charleston Gazette*, following the death of its president and managing editor, William E. Chilton, Jr.

AFTERWORD

Frank Knight was 48 when he died on July 6, 1956. His death was bemoaned by thousands of readers. The *Gazette* article recounting Knight's early death said his column, "ranged in content from personal whimsy to politics and world affairs."

Associated Press Bureau Chief Harry Ball, a longtime Knight friend and colleague, eulogized Knight, saying, in part:

One of the time-honored clichés of every newsroom is a death "shocking the community." The AP dusted off that oldie and used it again, because it was literally true in the case of Frank Knight.

Knight did, indeed, carry a big needle, for both his friends and his enemies. Most of all, he enjoyed jabbing it into stuffed shirts. He abhorred sham and its accoutrements, whether for waging editorial war or battling politicians, including neither tact nor diplomacy. He was the brash upstart, always jumping into the middle of the melee and expecting to slug his way out on top.

Once when Knight had stirred up a political tempest with a Fairmont angle, Ned Smith, the esteemed editor of the Fairmont Times, called up to complain.

"That damned Charleston Gazette. It just can't stand tranquility."

Charleston Gazette Editor Frank Knight.
–Charleston Daily Mail

Knight considered that a great compliment.

Ball then credited *Charleston Daily Mail* editor Jack Maurice with insightful comments:

The Gazette's principal competitor, The Charleston Daily Mail, summed up the life and times of Frank A. Knight in a scholarly editorial by Editor Jack Maurice. Here are some cogent excerpts:

"Most of the time and on most things we disagreed."

"It would have annoyed him, we think, that his untimely death fell on our time."

"He was an able newspaperman—alert, imaginative, aggressive and enterprising, who deserved his honors and honored his profession."

HARRY HOFFMANN

Harry Hoffmann, a native of Wheeling, began his newspaper career in 1929 on the *Wheeling Register*. He joined the *Gazette* in 1939 as its statehouse reporter and became editor in 1947. In 1953 he was named chief editorial writer, and editor in 1956.

He served twenty years as editor of the *Gazette*, retiring on November 1, 1976. He continued to write his *Gazette* political column. His insight and lack of fear of reprisal caused politicians throughout the state to turn first to Hoffmann when taking their newspaper off the front porch. He had clout with office holders and wannabe candidates throughout his journalism career. The *New York Times* called him in its January 6, 1977, story of his death as one of the state's best-known and most influential political writers.

Gazette political editor and later editor, Harry Hoffmann
–Charleston Gazette

The *Times* noted that Hoffmann died at his typewriter as he worked at his home on one of his political columns. The newspaper called him courtly and amiable in personal and professional conversation. But, the *Times* said, in his columns he wrote scathingly of those regarded as incompetent or demagogic and those he thought were not liberal. Upon retirement Hoffmann said of his continuing as a political columnist, "I guess you might say I'm taking retirement like a federal judge, going on senior status."

AFTERWORD

DON MARSH

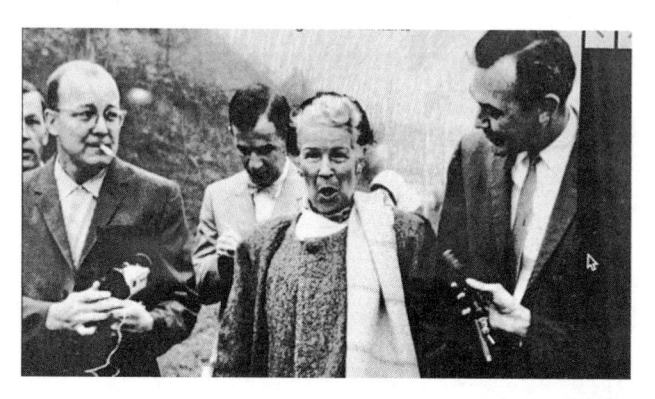

Don Marsh, extreme left. Behind Marsh, Jack Davis, Associated Press. Left of Marsh, Dick Toren, United Press International. To Toren's left, World War II Nazi broadcast propagandist Mildred "Axis Sally" Gillars convicted of treason in 1949. She was being released at 60 years of age from the Federal Reformatory for Women at Alderson, West Virginia at 6:26 a.m. on June 10, 1961. To her left is Roger Mudd of CBS.
–West Virginia State Archives. Frank Wilken collection

Don Marsh[122] served as a longtime *Gazette* reporter and succeeded Harry Hoffmann as editor where he earned respect with his skilled writing and cerebral column commentary. He is considered to have been an elite writer in the journalism field. Marsh would tell his reporters, "It does matter"—meaning political reforms, elections, and the chronicling of the day-to-day events of life were important to a society and needed to be recorded accurately. Marsh would often quote pioneer feminist Lucy Stone, who said, "Make the world better." Don Marsh certainly did.

Marsh's wry and sometimes-scalding columns were gifted writing that earned him a Distinguished Writing Award from the American Society of Newspaper Editors in 1987. The award he most coveted was being selected as a one-year Nieman Fellowship at Harvard University in 1955. Marsh said it changed his life. *Gazette* editor emeritus Jim Haught said of Marsh, "Don was the most intelligent person I ever knew. He also had vast knowledge... he cared passionately about social injustice, about improving life

---
[122] Formerly Don Seagle.

for the underdogs."

Following retirement Marsh became a radio talk show commentator. He died November 28, 1998, at the age of 72. He was a shining star in West Virginia's journalism history.

JIM HILL

Jim Hill's legacy is one of crime reporting at its best. Hill, whose wife Nancy served Mayor John Shanklin as a skilled receptionist and assistant, was the reporter who resonated those scribes of the 1900s who wore a "Press" card in the band of their hats. Hill never donned a hat, but he was the man who had informants at every level of law enforcement. The readers of the *Charleston Gazette* never overlooked Jim Hill's stories. He was a reporter of whom Dashiell Hammett would have been proud. The man had style.

JACK MAURICE

Pulitzer Prize wining journalist Jack Maurice[123] was born in 1913 in the coal town of Vivian in McDowell County. He grew up there and in the Kentucky coalfields and experienced some hard scrabble years in his youth.

His family moved back to West Virginia, settling in Huntington where he attended Huntington High School and Marshall College, later Marshall University. There, he was editor of the school newspaper, the *Parthenon*, where he sat at the knee of Page Pitt, the storied educator who founded the Marshall School of Journalism. Maurice graduated magna cum laude in 1935.

Jack Maurice.
–Charleston Daily Mail

Upon earning his degree, Maurice began working for the *Huntington Herald Dispatch*. In 1938 he joined the *Charleston Daily Mail*

---

[123] Maurice won the Pulitzer Prize for Journalism in 1975 for his commentaries on the violent Kanawha County textbook controversy.

AFTERWORD

where he covered courts, the West Virginia Statehouse and contributed to general assignment reporting. Then came World War II and Maurice joined the U.S. Naval Reserve, becoming a Lieutenant. He returned to the *Mail* in 1946 as chief editorial writer, becoming editor in 1950, and editor-in-chief in 1969. He remained there until retirement in 1984.

A reporter who worked with Maurice said Jack thought there was nothing defamatory regarding well-known personalities questioned in the Clark murder. The reporter said, "There were attempts to create something scurrilous about Juliet Clark's murder, and I know Jack did not buy into it. He was in a good position to have a judgment on it. He rejected conspiracy theories and said he had never heard anybody come up with credible theories regarding the murder motive or the murderer."

Upon learning of Jack Maurice's death in 1999, *Daily Mail* Publisher Lyell Clay said, "What can you say when a latter–day Moses has completed his time on earth and has come home? He was a great man."

Bob Adams, author of a *Marshall Alumni Magazine* article on Maurice, remarked on Maurice's modesty. He told the *Daily Mail*, "Maurice may well qualify as the most modest newspaperman ever to win a Pulitzer."

CHARLIE CONNOR

In 1981 Charlie Connor, who had moved up from reporter to executive editor of the *Charleston Daily Mail*, became publisher of the Beckley, West Virginia newspapers, a post he held until retirement in 1987. Connor was a native of Huntington and graduate of Marshall University.

He was a World War II veteran of the Army Signal Corps, serving in North Africa. He is unquestionably one of the best journalists West Virginia

Daily Mail reporter Charlie Connor.
–Charleston Daily Mail

has produced. His nature was always joyous and the many men and women he mentored remained eternally grateful to him. Connor died in 2013 at his home in Florida at the age of 89.

BOB MELLACE

Robert Patrick (Bob) Mellace of the *Charleston Daily Mail* moved political reporting to a new level through twenty years of covering statehouse notables and national presidential campaigns in West Virginia. He loved politics, and politicians respected, admired, and at times, feared his reporting and insider's column.

The Parkersburg native was a top-ten receiver at West Virginia University in 1940 and was selected to play in the 1941 College All-Star game against the Cleveland Rams. His first job was sports editor of the *Morgantown Dominion News*. He then wrote sports in New York for the Newspaper Enterprise Association (NEA). Drafted in 1943, he returned from Europe and joined the *Morgantown Post* for seven years before joining the *Daily Mail* from 1953 until retirement in 1980.

Mellace then became district representative for West Virginia Congressman John Slack. After Slack's death, Mellace became director of public relations for Blue Cross Hospital Services of Southern West Virginia.

Mellace died on September 6, 2005, at home, at the age of 87. He was a gifted reporter who never lost his enthusiasm or humor.

DEWEY WILLIAMS

Police Chief Dewey Williams retired in 1963 and died in 1969. He briefly returned to part-time police work after retirement.

Charleston Police Chief
Dewey Williams
–*Charleston Gazette*

AFTERWORD

—II.—
EARLY STAUNTON HISTORY

THOMAS AND JOSEPH STAUNTON

The Stauntons were descendants of landed gentry and yeomen who arrived in England at the time of the Saxon Conquest in the middle of the 5th century. They were described as sturdy, ambitious, strong-minded and shrewd, with prominence in the fields of government, business enterprises, literature, and the arts.[124]

The first of the hardy breed to arrive in America was Thomas Staunton, who took passage to Virginia on January 2, 1635, and recorded himself as twenty years old.[125] A year later he went to Boston, Massachusetts, then to Hartford, Connecticut, where he was married in 1637 to Anne Lord, daughter of Thomas Lord and Dorothy Lord—they would have ten children.

Thomas and Anne then moved from Boston to Stonington, Connecticut, where Thomas was employed by the General Court as

---

[124] Howard Staunton, born in London in 1810, was regarded as the English champion chess player of his time. In 1843 he defeated France's champion in what was at the time the longest chess game in history. His many books on the subject of chess were considered to be the encyclopedia of the game. He edited the *Illustrated London News* and was considered to be an expert on the works of Shakespeare. Howard Staunton died in 1874. Source: *Brewster Buffington King's Journal*.

[125] *Genealogical Sketch of the Staunton Family* by Susan Augusta Staunton.

EARLY STAUNTON HISTORY

an interpreter to negotiate treaties with the native Indian population. He died at 62 on December 2, 1677. His wife Anne died in 1688, at the age of 67.

Six generations later[126], Joseph Marshall Staunton was born September 29, 1819, in Genesee County, New York, the son of John Warren Staunton and Sarah Brewster.[127] His family moved to Ellicottville, New York, about 55 miles south of Buffalo, in 1820 or 1821.[128] On October 10, 1847, in Ellicottville, Joseph Staunton married Mary Elisabeth Wilber[129], daughter of Hannah Sever Gambell and Church Wilber.[130]

At the time of the Staunton-Wilber wedding, Joseph was 28, Elizabeth, 17. Their first child was a baby girl, who died in 1848. Their second child was Sidney Augustus Staunton, born June 7, 1850.[131] During this time, Joseph entered the Geneva Medical College, and upon graduation established a family practice.[132]

Dr. Joseph Marshall Staunton, 1819-1904
–Brewster King's Journal

---

[126] Second generation John Staunton was born in 1641. He married Hannah Thompson. They had six children. John died in 1713. Third generation John Staunton, born in 1665, and his wife (whose name is not recorded) had eleven children. John's death date is not recorded. Fourth generation Daniel, born in 1708, married Dinah Stark in 1737. Dinah died in 1754 and Daniel later married Mary Clark. There were ten children of the first marriage, and one of the second. Daniel died in 1775. Elisha Staunton of the fifth generation was born in 1752 in Connecticut and moved to Vermont before the Revolutionary War and shortly thereafter to Massachusetts. He married Anna Rust in 1781. They had eleven children. Elisha died in 1775 and Anna died in 1808. Source: *Genealogical Sketch of the Staunton Family* by Susan Augustus Staunton.

[127] Thus began the Brewster branch of the Staunton family.

[128] *West Virginia In History, Life, Literature and Industry, Volume III, 1928*, page 2, Morris Purdy Shawkey.

[129] Mary Elisabeth died in 1912. The name "Elisabeth" was also spelled "Elizabeth" in many records.

[130] Joseph's father-in-law Church Wilber would die in Joseph and Mary Elizabeth's home in Charleston, West Virginia on January 21, 1884, at age 89.

[131] *John B. Merrill Address* to the Staunton family reunion November 27, 1980.

[132] *Aunt Kate Staunton's Scrapbook*.

By 1860 there were four little ones in the Staunton household, which eventually would number nine children. The family struggled to survive as Dr. Staunton's medical practice provided few dollars—his patients paid for his services in eggs, pigs, jars of jelly, wild game, and various canned goods.

The family predicament coincided with the discovery that low-grade coal, through a newly-discovered distillation process, could be used to make "Cannel Oil[133]" to light lanterns and lubricate machinery. Prior to that time, oil for lanterns and lubricating processes came from animal fat, whales and fish. Cannel Oil from coal posed an opportunity for entrepreneurs and Dr. Staunton, fascinated by the prospect of a new career, made plans to manufacture the oil.[134]

Coal, however, was required to produce Cannel Oil and coal was not to be found in the state of New York.

It was, however, to be found in distant Virginia[135]—in abundance—in a place called Mill Creek, where a coal oil factory on 100 acres of land was for sale for $9,351.[136] Dr. Staunton asked for financial assistance and received it from from J. Galusha Staunton and Archibald Staunton of Cattaraugus County, New York—the three men purchased the property on May 25, 1860.[137]

In 1860, the Staunton family arrived in Virginia[138], near the town of Charleston that boasted a population of about 1,500 people. It was the county seat of Kanawha County, population 16,500.

---

[133] *West Virginia In History, Life, Literature and Industry,* volume III, page 3, 1928, Morris Purdy Shawkey.

[134] *John B. Merrill Address* to the Staunton family reunion November 27, 1980.

[135] Later, West Virginia.

[136] $293,000 in 2019.

[137] Kanawha County, Virginia Deed Book I of 1860, page 543, as contained in *Aunt Kate's Scrapbook*.

[138] Later, West Virginia.

EARLY STAUNTON HISTORY

Census records of that year reveal 2,124 of the recorded county's citizens were slaves.[139]

The town fronted on the Kanawha River, where Front Street featured a pharmacy, hotel, and a branch of the Bank of Virginia. Methodist, Presbyterian, and Episcopal churches provided places of worship, and a small courthouse recorded deeds and housed legal battles and trials. A jail of "antique design" held the miscreants of the area.[140]

East of the town was an impressive home of Greek Revival architecture known as "Elm Grove[141]". The four-columned residence built by James Craik featured manicured lawns and gardens. Craik was the grandson of Dr. James Craik, personal physician to President George Washington. In 1861 it would become the residence of Colonel George Smith Patton, a hero of the Confederacy and grandfather of World War II General George Patton.

That same year, the Gallipolis, Ohio *Dispatch* would report that Charleston was located on a "beautiful bottom on the northeast bank of the river and is entirely surrounded by lofty hills.[142]" But, the newspaper would leave the impression that the town's architecture left something to be desired—"Here are many pretty residences but they and the public buildings are built after the old style and have not much pretension to magnificence."

Residents of the town sought relief from summer heat and humidity by boarding ferries at the city wharf at the bottom of Summers Street, crossing to the south side of the Kanawha River where carriages drawn by horses transported them to the "South Hills". There, a largely uninhabited forest overlooked the city, with pine, spruce, hemlock and sycamore trees creating canopies

---

[139] *West Virginia Department Of Arts, Culture And History, West Virginia History*, Volume 23, Number 2, (January 1962), p 153, by Roy Bird Cook.

[140] Ibid.

[141] Ibid.

[142] Ibid.

of shade through which cool breezes wafted, nurturing abundant rhododendron and thick foliage.

Horse and carriage transported visitors along a dirt road that trailed upward toward the front of the South Hills. Wherever openings appeared in nature's curtain, the visitors spread picnic lunches on blankets—afternoons were wiled away in a veritable Garden of Eden.

But, in 1860, for Dr. Staunton and his family, Virginia was a world away. He had loaded his family and worldly goods into a wagon and moved them to what could only be thought of as the frontier. The move was fraught with danger and required uprooting his family from the established and populated Ellicottville, New York. It was emotional and unsettling. But, the family forged ahead. On July 4, 1860, they celebrated Independence Day in Mill Creek. The town of Charleston was a ten-mile journey on a dirt road.[143]

With enthusiasm, Dr. Staunton set to work in his new domain. Despite the problem of getting his product to market over coarse roads and treacherous waterways, his business began to prosper. His wife, Mary Elisabeth, proved worthy of tremendous challenges. She cooked, washed, and canned, and gave birth almost every two years.

Productive in parenthood, Dr. Staunton was equally so in producing Cannel Oil, and for 15 years the demand for his offerings was huge. But, the year before the Stauntons made their move to Mill Creek—1859—an

Mary Elisabeth Wilber Staunton, 1830-1912
–*Brewster King's Journal*

---

[143] Prior to the automobile, few folks traveled more than 11 miles from their home in a lifetime–11 miles being the distance that could be covered by a carriage or buckboard in one day's time.

EARLY STAUNTON HISTORY

event in Titusville, Pennsylvania had already begun the process that would bring an end to Staunton's manufacturing career.

Edwin L. Drake had struck "rock oil" and oil wells and refineries began to proliferate. Oil produced kerosene, kerosene was cheaper than Cannel Oil, and it was produced in great supply. The new fuel would become the death knell for Dr. Staunton's business.

Discussions were held, and the decision was made that Dr. Staunton would return to the practice of medicine.[144] Mill Creek offered few prospective patients, so, it was agreed in 1875 that the family would once again load their wagon and head their horses toward Charleston, a growing city that would surely welcome the services of an additional physician.

In Charleston, Joseph quickly began to build a substantial practice—seeing patients in his office and calling on the sick at their homes. On one such visit, on a Friday, traveling home from a long trip to Cabell County, Dr. Staunton encountered more than family illness.

The Cabell County *Citizen* newspaper[145] recorded that Staunton, riding his horse, was accosted by one Phillip C. Russell[146] who emerged from his hiding place in a barn located roadside. Russell aimed a pistol at the doctor, threatening to kill him if he did not give him $150.00.[147] The two argued, and Russell shot Staunton in the chest.

---

[144] No record could be found as to how Staunton paid his backers for the 100 acres of land at Mill Creek and the coal and oil property. Staunton retained ownership of the land, however, and the family used the home on the land for many years as a summer retreat. Staunton's estate at the time of his death in 1904, not counting his home, personal property, medical equipment and books was $2,500, estimated as equivalent to $76,000 in 2019.

[145] *The Citizen,* October 8, 1874.

[146] *Brewster Buffington King's Journal* records that Staunton may have been trying to collect an unpaid bill from Russell or Russell may have been desperate for money owed on his home.

[147] Estimated as equivalent to $4,000 in 2019.

The bullet, the newspaper account said, struck Staunton's sternum and lodged near his shoulder. Upon being shot, Staunton drew his own revolver and shot at Russell. Staunton's horse was spooked and threw Staunton from his saddle, causing Staunton to miss his target. Russell rushed Staunton and the two men fought for each other's pistol.

Staunton was bleeding profusely, causing Russell to fear he had fatally injured his prey. Russell relented, backed off, and offered to assist Staunton, if he would turn over his pistol. Staunton refused, but said he would not shoot Russell. The assailant then ran, catching Staunton's horse, riding away.

Wounded and bleeding, the doctor walked half a mile to the house of N.D. Swear, a justice, and sought assistance while lodging a complaint against the man who had assaulted him. Russell's identity became known when, two hours after fleeing, he surrendered to authorities, admitting his crime. He was held on bail, the *Citizen* reported, but there is no record of any punishment for his assault. Staunton recovered from his wounds and returned to riding horseback to make house calls.

Dr. Staunton continued to work long, hard hours, creating a higher standard of living for his family. In 1902 he built a splendid new home at 1012 Kanawha Street, dying there at age 84. He died in 1904. His wife Mary Elisabeth (Elizabeth) died in 1912.

Dr. Staunton's family church, Kanawha United Presbyterian, commissioned renowned glass artisan Louis Tiffany to create a stained glass window in its sanctuary in memory of him. The Tiffany window, titled *The Good Samaritan,* is representative of the finest ecclesiastical art of any period in American history.

SIDNEY, WILBER & FREDERICK MARSHALL STAUNTON

The children of Joseph and Mary Elisabeth Staunton were exceptional. Sidney Augustus, eldest son of the marriage, was born

EARLY STAUNTON HISTORY

June 7, 1850, in Ellicottville, New York, prior to the family moving to Mill Creek. His life was a prodigious one, and he became a preeminent figure in the Staunton history.

When Sidney, as a ten-year-old boy, set out with his parents for what was at the time an almost unimaginable trek from the Northeast to Virginia, his life was dramatically altered. The family faced the challenges of dirt roads, months aboard a wagon, replacement of supplies to eat and drink for their sustenance, feed for their horses, and the possibility of illness along the way. Atop that was the fear of bodily harm from hostile elements in a largely uninhabited territory. It was a daunting experience for adults, let alone a ten-year-old. But for Sidney, the trip was exciting and memorable, instilling in him a sense of exploration that would affect and drive his adult life.

Life in the wilds of Virginia required arduous labor that nourished and enhanced Sidney's physical prowess. His mother's ability in home-learning provided an education that was perhaps superior to schools of the time. Sidney's intellect and appearance were impressive to all he encountered.

Ambitious, he applied for entrance to the United States Naval Academy in Annapolis, Maryland. He received his congressional appointment from a "close friend of the family" in 1867—the "close friend" was not identified.[148] The appointment was subject to review and weeks passed. One day a letter arrived at Mill Creek that bore the impressive credentials of the United States Government.

The correspondence apprised Sidney and his parents that his application was accepted and that he had been given an appointment to the Naval College. There was jubilation in the Staunton home at the news and, for Sidney, a private apprehension.

Sidney had, on several occasions, visited the town of Charleston,

---

[148] Sydney's life is recorded in the *Address by John Buffington Merrill, Sr. to The Staunton Family Reunion* on November 27, 1980, and various naval records. The "close friend" was in all likelihood a member of Congress in that Congressional nomination to the academy was required.

but he had never ventured farther. Accompanied by his parents, he boarded the family buckboard to travel to Charleston and what would be the start of a new and unfamiliar life. He was a backwoods boy who had been raised in a close and loving family—small wonder that Sidney felt apprehension even as excitement gripped him. The train that would take him north pulled from the station, and he waved goodbye to his mother and father.

Upon arrival in Annapolis he was mustered into the Naval Academy with cadets who were cosmopolitan in nature and of worldly experience, compared to the rough-hewn southerner. His fellow students referred to him as a "hick from the sticks" and Sidney's usually exuberant nature was quickly suppressed.

In a short while the front door at the Staunton house on Mill Creek opened and Sidney, brushing dust from his clothes after a ten-mile walk from Charleston, announced that he was home.

"Sidney! What is wrong with you?" his mother shouted.

"Mother, I can't take the kidding I get," her son answered.

"Sidney," his mother said, in a stern and unforgiving voice, "you are the eldest son and I know you are smart, but I never thought you were a weakling."

The next day Sidney trekked back to Charleston, boarded the train, and returned to Annapolis. There he withstood the barbs aimed at him and persevered. In June 1871, he graduated with honors from the United States Naval Academy as first officer[149] in his class. Sidney was 5' 10" tall and handsome. He was described as having a "kind and open countenance, a natural courtesy and modesty of demeanor, a clear smiling eye, trimmed mustache and beard, and, the rarely failing American alertness of demeanor."

Sidney's military record was extraordinary. He was awarded a

---

[149] Cited in the November 27 John Buffington Merrill, Sr. Address to The Staunton family Reunion. Other sources simply note that Staunton graduated as a midshipman.

EARLY STAUNTON HISTORY

"Master" designation in 1875 and became a Lieutenant in 1881. His service was aboard the USS ships *Iroquois, Congress, Wabash, Plymouth, Sabine, Powhatan, Franklin, Marion, Trenton, Chicago, New York,* and *Tennessee.*

The lad from Mill Creek saw action around the globe. He became a Full Lieutenant in 1898 in Cuban waters during the Spanish-American War. He taught at the US Naval Academy for a time and was assigned to the European theatre four times. He was "instantly recognized by his exuberant personality and the enormous cigar he wielded like a conductor's baton.[150]"

He was dispatched to China and for a time served in the Office of Naval Intelligence. He also was Secretary to the American Delegation to the International Maritime Conference. A motion picture newsreel of the opening of the Panama Canal featured President Teddy Roosevelt dedicating the canal—to his left was Admiral Sidney Staunton.

Staunton was an intellectual, to be certain. In 1884, at 34 years-of-age, he wrote, *The War in Tong-King: Why the French are in Tong-King, and What They are Doing There.*[151] It was selected by scholars as being, "culturally important, and is part of the knowledge base of civilization as we know it.[152]"

Asked about his experiences Staunton said, "I would rather tell you about my squadron than myself.[153]" Sidney was made a Lieu-

---

[150] *A Suitcase From The Titanic,* by Enrique Rodolfo Dick, WIT Press, 2013, page 127.

[151] *The War in Tong-King* was originally published by Cupples, Upham and Company, Cambridge: N.D.C. Hodges, 1884, by Lieut. Sidney A. Staunton, U.S.N. (Staunton may have been bilingual: he cited sources in his book as *Les Francais au Tonkin, La Cochinchine Contemporaine, Reconnaissance du Fleuve do Tonkin.*)

[152] This is a 2019 description on the Amazon website of Staunton's book. Amazon describes the book as its reproduction of a historical artifact. The website says the book is in public domain in the United States and possibly other nations. The citation reads, "This work was reproduced from the original artifact, and remains as true to the original work as possible. Therefore, you will see the original copyright references, library stamps (as most of these works have been housed in our most important libraries around the world), and other notations in the work." WikiTree's website says, "Any student of the conflict(s) in Vietnam should appreciate Staunton's *The War in Tong-King.*"

[153] Sidney's service aboard naval ships is recorded in *The Records Of Living Officers U.S. Navy of 1894.*

tenant Commander in 1899 and a Commander in 1906. In 1910, he was designated a Rear Admiral, the highest rank bestowed and maintained by the Navy during peacetime. It was a long way from Mill Creek, the dirt road, and his mother's admonition that she never considered him a weakling.

Sidney married Emily Duncan Biddle. Two of their children, a boy and a girl, died at birth. They then parented and raised Sidney Smith, born August 2, 1846, and Mary Lucinda, born November 8, 1853. Sidney's wife Emily was killed six years after her marriage, leaving Sidney to raise a son and daughter. Emily died when her horse was frightened and ran away with the buggy in which she was riding. The horse and carriage dragged her to her death. Sidney was at sea at the time of the accident. He never married again. He died at age 88, January 11, 1939, in Washington, D.C.

The man who would rise to the status of Admiral had two brothers, Wilber and Frederick Marshall. Wilber Staunton was born in 1864. He was known as "Will" and was educated at home by his mother, Mary Elisabeth, until the age of eleven. Upon entering public schools, he was popular, a good student, and played the sports of the day. Finances were tight, and Will did not attend college, choosing instead to go into mercantile trade.

Frederick Marshall Staunton, born in 1866 in Elk District, Kanawha County, was the third Staunton child to be schooled at home until he entered public schools in his teens. Frederick Marshall entered Cornell University in the scientific department. Family records differ as to whether he graduated or did not complete his degree.

The brothers, with financial assistance from their older brother Sidney, then founded Charleston's Diamond Ice and Coal Company. Ice-making machinery had been perfected and plants were opening across the United States, but Wilber and Frederick were without means to obtain equipment necessary to begin such a business. Uncle Sidney inquired of financial assistance for his brothers with an associate in Washington, D.C. His presentation was effective, and his friend agreed to back the Charleston entrepreneurs.

Sidney invested in the effort with his own money—it was to be a regular thing. Never asking for recompense, Sidney contributed cash and wisdom so often that his brothers said of his money, "Good old Uncle Sidney, he really doesn't need it."

The Diamond Ice and Coal Company proved to be successful. Ice was sold throughout the year for refrigeration of food and drink, and coal was delivered to businesses and homes for winter heating. Success was not easy, however. The Staunton brothers each toiled 15 hours daily. It was brutal work. Their hands soon became stiff from daily immersion in brine and the handling of coal. The brothers eventually turned management over to employees and branched out to separate entrepreneurial paths that led to even greater success and status in Charleston.

Will went into politics in 1889, at the early age of 26, when he was elected City Sergeant of Charleston, collecting taxes. He then served two terms as Mayor of Charleston, the first in 1892. That same year he married Florence Buffington.[154] He was re-elected Mayor in 1894. Later, as chairman of the Kanawha County Republican Party, he ran for, and was elected, Kanawha County Clerk, winning by 1300 votes against a "fusion" candidate.

A special issue of a Wheeling newspaper said Staunton was "one of the most competent officials in the state and is so regarded at the (state) auditor's office, to which reports of county officials are made." In politics, the newspaper wrote, "Will Staunton is regarded as well-nigh invincible."

Wilber died young in 1904, at age 40. One Charleston newspaper paid him tribute, with a headline reading:

---

[154] Except perhaps he did not–other sources list the marriage as taking place December 15, 1893.

*Kanawha County's Most Famous Politician Died
Shortly after Noon
From an Attack of Pneumonia
Was a Man of Wonderful Force, Though Long Ailing
and a Powerful
Factor in Local Business Affairs as in
County and State Politics*

It was said in the newspaper article that Will, "was followed with a cheerfulness and alacrity that made victories easy."

The *Charleston Gazette* also weighed in with this editorial:

As a newspaper which has frequently taken occasion to criticize him as a politician and as a leader in city and county of the partisan organization to which it opposed, the Gazette pays its modest and deserved tribute to the memory of E.W. Staunton. To the relatives and friends of the deceased, we join the entire community in the expression of sincerest sympathy and regret.

As for Will's brother, Frederick Marshall, he epitomized the term of a business "mover and shaker". In addition to continued oversight of the Diamond Ice and Coal Company, he organized and managed Kelley's Creek Collieries Company, Charleston Interurban Railway Company, Kanawha City Company, Kanawha Land Company, Kanawha Banking & Trust Company, and many others. In November 1892, he married Elsie Quarrier Smith, daughter of the late Isaac N. and Caroline Quarrier Smith.[155] The marriage would be a good one in love and in business.[156]

---

[155] *West Virginia In History, Life, Literature and Industry,* volume III, page 3, 1928, Morris Purdy Shawkey.

[156] Frederick, along with Harrison B. Smith, developed the front side of South Hills off of Louden Heights Road with the lowest road being Bougemont, which would become Smith's magnificent home. Staunton Road, just up from Bougemont, would ultimately become the location for the residences of Frederick's extended family, including the Stauntons, Merrills, Clarks, Clays and Fleesons. Staunton and Smith were more than business partners. They were brothers-in-law. Smith was the "Smith" of *Price, Smith, Spilman & Clay.*

EARLY STAUNTON HISTORY

In June of 1902, Frederick, Wilber, and members of the Isaac Noyes Smith family conceived the idea of a hotel in Charleston. The Stauntons and the Smiths had the means to finance the idea, hire an architect to draw up plans, build the hostelry, and furnish it.

Wilber was cited in a newspaper article[157] as planning the building of the hotel, saying it was done under his personal supervision. His workload must have taken some toll. He died at 40 years of age, just months after the completion of the hotel, the largest hostelry in Charleston at the time.

Frederick Marshall Staunton.
–Morris Purdy Shawkey, *West Virginia In History, Life, Literature and Industry*, 1928, page 158, Bennett, Baltimore.

It was christened the *Hotel Kanawha* and was cited at Will's death as his crowning achievement. A newspaper article said, "The greatest monument to his indomitable energy and capacity is the magnificent new *Hotel Kanawha*, completed and opened April 11, 1904.[158]"

Will's brothers Frederick and Sidney lived on. They honored Will by making certain his family would always be cared for in the manner to which they had become accustomed.

Frederick died 22 years after his brother Will, January 20, 1926, at 7:30 a.m. in his home at 1216 Kanawha Street, at age 60. He had been ill for two years. At his side was Rear Admiral Sidney Staunton, who traveled to Charleston from his home in Washington, D.C. to sit by his brother's bedside for several days. Sidney

---

[157] Found in *Aunt Kate Staunton's Scrapbook*.

[158] Ibid.

lamented that Frederick "gradually sank through the night until the end came quietly this morning."

Frederick Staunton's last appearance in public had been a week prior to his death to preside at a meeting of stockholders at the Kanawha Banking & Trust Company[159], where he remained as president until his death.

Nearly all businesses in Charleston, including the saloons along Front Street, closed to honor the memory of Frederick Marshall Staunton. His last resting place has a gravestone marked, "Strong, Just and Generous".

Admiral Sidney Staunton died at 88 in 1938. He was buried with military salutes and full honors in Arlington National Cemetery.

JULIET BUFFINGTON STAUNTON CLAY CLARK HOME

When originally built, Juliet Clark's home was brick and the garage was stone. Between the house and the garage there was an open porch that was called a breezeway. Laurance and Ann Dick Jones purchased the home after Juliet Clark's death.

Longtime Charlestonian Otis Laury was in the home many times when the Jones' owned the home. He related that the basement was partially finished with knotty pine paneling, popular at the time. Ann Dick, Laury said, built a bomb shelter in the basement. The home changed hands twice after the Jones owned it and was gutted and completely remodeled.

The green rug on which Mrs. Clark was murdered was said to be in the basement of the home for some time after her death. However, Laury said he never saw a rug there and seriously doubted that it would have been placed in the basement.

---

[159] Kanawha Banking & Trust was eventually folded into United Bank.

EARLY STAUNTON HISTORY

Aunt Florence Fleeson lived beyond the Clark house, where Staunton Road ended. Mrs. Fleeson, in elderly years, moved to Long Island and a retirement home. The house was empty for several years prior to its purchase by Lyell Clay. It burned to the ground in 1997.

Lyell Clay's home on Staunton Road burns on November 22, 1997. Florence and Tom Fleeson built the home. Lyell renovated and enlarged the home.
–*Charleston Gazette*

—III.—
NOTES

Research of the Staunton and Buffington families and Charleston Mayor John T. Copenhaver revealed rich and robust stories and background. These notes are included for readers who wish to further explore the Staunton and Buffington legacies, and the life of a unique mayor.

(In Alphabetical Order)

CLINE & SCALES FAMILY

Florence Buffington Merrill was descended from William Buffington of Hampshire County, Virginia, who died in 1799. William's first son, Thomas, was born in 1751. The second son, William, Jr., was born in 1787. As adults, the sons moved to Cabell County, (West) Virginia and settled there. William Jr. was the first surveyor of lands in Cabell County.

Thomas married Ann Cline and William married Nancy Scales. Thomas and Ann had twelve children, only four of whom lived to adulthood. William and Nancy had seven children. Their youngest and fifth son was Jonathon Nathaniel Buffington, born in 1832. He studied medicine in the state of Virginia near Richmond, Virginia.

NOTES

COPENHAVER, SR., JOHN T.

John Thomas Copenhaver died in his home August 13, 1959, at 61 years of age. The "poor boy" from "Up Elk" had been born on a farm near Frame, the fourth of six children of Ulysses Grant and Adaline Copenhaver. He had been elected Charleston's mayor three times, and he campaigned twice for governor in Republican primaries. In 1952 he lost to Rush D. Holt and in 1956 to Cecil H. Underwood. Copenhaver was known statewide and was expected to be, at some point, governor.

The *Charleston Gazette* noted Copenhaver was largely self-educated—he attended Clendenin High School and taught school for several years. His background was multi-faceted, working as a deputy assessor, deputy sheriff, city clerk, insurance salesman, druggist and banker.

Copenhaver said he became interested in law when he worked at the Kanawha County Courthouse:

I enrolled in a correspondence course from Hamilton College of Law and was tutored privately by a lawyer here in town. My goodness, it was hard work. It seems to me that I studied all the time. In the last month before I took the bar examination, my hands were shaking so bad I could hardly hold a book. My wife had to read to me.

Copenhaver was admitted to the Bar in September 1927, when he was 29 years old. He worked 70-hour weeks. "I like to do things right," he said, "the only way I know how is to work on them. In the first four months of my practice, the rent on my office came to $240 and my fees amounted to $148.00." *The Charleston Gazette* complimented him by saying, "Despite his slow start, he became one of the city's most successful lawyers."

"As a matter of fact," he once said, "the size of my practice almost kept me from becoming mayor." Copenhaver told *Gazette* reporter Don Marsh that he was flattered when his candidacy was first suggested. "I sort of led them on," he said. However, when it came time to file, Copenhaver told Marsh he realized he could not stand the financial sacrifice if he were elected.

But, he modestly admitted, so much pressure was put on him that he, "on the most depressing day of my life, said I'd run." It was a theme Copenhaver would use often each time he ran for office, how could he refuse? The populous wanted him!

Don Marsh wrote, "A thorough extrovert, he delighted in the pomp and prestige of his office. He liked seeing his name and his picture in the papers. He liked being pointed to on the street."

"Oh now," Copenhaver protested to Marsh, "that's not always true. I like the job because of the chance I have to help people." He added with a grin, "I always thought I might have made a pretty good publicity man if I'd put my mind to it." He *did* do publicity well, even though it sometimes backfired. He gave the 1958 book *Peyton Place* by author Grace Metalious a great leg up in the capital city by using a city ordinance to ban the book as obscene. Charlestonians then rushed to buy it. Students from Morris Harvey College picketed Copenhaver on the City Hall steps, claiming he was a one-man dictator who censored anything of which he did not approve. Asked if he had read the book himself, Copenhaver maneuvered: "I have not, but someone has read sections of it to me."

"Filth without description!" the mayor fumed on television news broadcasts—and more buyers rushed to Major's Book Store on Hale Street. Floyd Major said he would not order his number one clerk, Tilly, to remove the book from Major's shelves unless ordered to do so by authorities. The bookstore owner said he made $.10 on the $.50 paperback[160], and he did not think the profit was such that he should spend a year in jail and pay a $1,000[161] fine.

---

[160] Estimated as equivalent to $4.50 in 2019.

[161] Estimated as equivalent to $9,000 in 2019.

NOTES

Major, a mild-mannered man whose bookstore was a "must" stop for anyone downtown, did not have to worry. The book sold out before Charleston Police Sergeant George Nunley could process the mayor's order, the obscenity was loose and on the streets before the cops came.

The duties of the mayor were intensive—his war on sin and the more monotonous duties of mayor caused Copenhaver to continue his 70-hour weeks that began when he was a fledgling lawyer. Years later, former Charleston Mayor Danny Jones commented about the never-ending role of the city's chief executive, saying, "You couldn't even have a meal without being face to face with the public."

Mayor Copenhaver was ubiquitous, but had few leisurely interests. He once decided to take up golf but quickly abandoned the game, saying, "A golf club might be handy if you had to kill a snake. I could do that, but I'll be darned if I can hit a ball with one." Tennis? He had no time for that, but he saw that others embraced the game and he built beautiful city courts for devotees to pursue their passion.

From the day he was first elected mayor, surprising the pundits, politicians and public by defeating incumbent Democratic Mayor R. Carl Andrews, Copenhaver seemed indestructible. Both parents had lived until they were 87, and Copenhaver said he planned on beating the record of his grandfather who was in his 90s when he died.

"It looked as though he would do it. He was a young 61, jaunty and irrepressible," Don Marsh wrote in the *Gazette*.

But, a year earlier, complaining of chest pains, he had received a medical warning to slow down. Unfazed, the mayor did not heed his doctor's advice and maintained his exhausting pace.

The day before his death, Sergeant James Gullian chauffeured the mayor to see a new Charleston housing development.

He had a leisurely lunch with friends in South Charleston and visited Hanna Drive, checking on resurfacing along Oakridge Drive.

Sergeant Gullian was at the wheel as he drove the mayor home, arriving a few minutes before 5 p.m. Copenhaver, he said, was in good spirits, sitting in the back seat of his personal car, watching his city glide by, talking about going to the christening of a young son of another police officer.

The mayor bade Sergeant Gullian a good evening and entered his home, greeting his wife, probably grabbing the late edition of the *Daily Mail*. He sat in his favorite easy chair. Then he had a slight dizzy spell, enough to concern Ruth Copenhaver, the former Ruth Cherrington Roberts, devoted wife of John Copenhaver for 39 years, a grand lady. The mayor told her not to worry, waving off his dizziness as nothing but a natural reaction to a busy day in the hot sun.

At 9 the next morning there was a call to police headquarters—send an ambulance to the mayor's home, the new home up Elk that he had built the year before, christening it with a vast homecoming for the "great and little people of Charleston."

Sergeant Mayford Haynes, at the police headquarters desk, received the call. Soon, the police radio network crackled with alarm. Officers in cruisers twice asked for a repeat of a message filled with portent.

Accident Prevention Bureau Sergeant William A. Hammack rushed from the basement offices of City Hall onto Court Street and into the main entrance of the police department. He raced up the short set of steps to Municipal Court and whispered the news to Judge Joe Thomas. Both commandeered Jim Gullian's police cruiser and rushed to the mayor's home.

Sergeant Gullian received a radio message on the way to the mayor's residence—"Pick up city council president pro-tem John

NOTES

Shanklin at his office on Elizabeth Street!" Another cruiser was dispatched to fetch the mayor's son, John T. Copenhaver, Jr., who would later become a distinguished United States Federal Judge.

Charlie Connor wrote, "At the door of the home—strangely quieted by the death—Mrs. Copenhaver met the arrivals."

"We've come to help you," were Shanklin's words of comfort. By that time Big Jim Ireland, council finance committee chairman, had arrived by his own conveyance. Ireland comforted Mrs. Copenhaver by saying, "Don't worry, everything will be taken care of."

Copenhaver's neighbors began moving quietly into the home, extending their arms to Ruth Copenhaver. A cup and saucer, from which the mayor drank his last coffee, and a fruit glass, setting by the mayor's favorite chair, were removed, disappearing into the kitchen. The telephone rang incessantly, friends wanting to know what they could do to help.

Lieutenant Van G. Brown, one of Copenhaver's closest allies in the city administration who often drove the mayor, was next to arrive at the home. Van Brown was visibly shaken. He loved the mayor. "I've not only lost the best boss, but the best friend I ever had," he said.

Then, the *Daily Mail* reported, the mayor's son, John Jr., came through the door, seeking his mother. Reporter Connor wrote, "When the mayor's son arrived he placed a long distance call to Waterbury, Conn. to relate the sad news to his sister, Mrs. Harold W. Smith. An associate of Smith, an executive with the First Federal Savings and Loan Co., told the family she was in Boston. Friends from the bank carried the sad words to the mayor's daughter."

The strange quiet that reporter Connor noted was soon broken as the roadway curving up to the mayor's home became jammed with automobiles; other cars blocked the street in front of the home. A motorcycle policeman received orders not to let further traffic in, "unless it's important." Telegrams began to arrive at the downtown Western Union offices as news bulletins came across the Associated Press and United Press wires.

The entourage that had gathered at the Copenhaver home was silent as the mayor's body was removed. Ruth Copenhaver insisted on standing on the edge of her front porch as her husband's body was carried away. "Every morning I've walked here to see John off to the office," she said.

Connor wrote, "This would be the last time the mayor would ride from his home."

HILL, ARTHUR M. AND CAROLINE STAUNTON

The Georgian home of Arthur M. and Caroline Staunton Hill at 1233 Staunton Road was once the site of a small summer house that was destroyed by fire. The magnificent home that was built on the substantial and lofty site in 1921[162] was a gift from Frederick and Elsie Quarrier Smith Staunton to their daughter Caroline, on the occasion of her marriage to Arthur[163] in 1918.

Caroline and Arthur Hill named the mansion "Killiecrankie" following a visit to Scotland. The river at Killiecrankie was surrounded by mountains on either side, reminding them of their Charleston home, "high on a hill overlooking the Kanawha River."

Hill became president of the Blue and Gray Transit Company in 1925, and vice-president and general manager of the Charleston Interurban Railway Company in 1926. In 1930 the Blue and Gray Transit Company was merged into Atlantic Greyhound Lines, and Hill became president of the iconic Atlantic Greyhound Corporation. President Harry Truman named him to his National Security Council as chairman of the council's resources board.

---

[162] The date was cited by Brooks McCabe, Jr.

[163] *The West Virginia Review,* Volume 8, No. 8, page 223, May, 1933.

NOTES

Hill served with, among others, James Forrestal and George Marshall. Hill died at 80, in 1972, the same year Truman died.

The Hill's daughter and Staunton's granddaughter, Caroline, married Ellsworth Clark, whose grandfather was former Charleston Mayor Colonel Ellsworth Rudesill. The Clarks lived in the house until 1981. At that time, they sold Killiecrankie to Ed Maier and built a more contemporary home, designed by Mr. Clark, at the lower edge of the original tract of land at 1231 Staunton.

Sadly, Killiecrankie has been demolished and an empty lot remains at the site.

JONES, DANNY

Future Charleston Mayor Danny Jones grew up on Staunton Road. Danny's parents, Laurance and Ann Dick Jones, moved back to Charleston from Michigan, purchasing Juliet Clark's home. They did extensive remodeling of the residence and did not think of the house in any negative way, even though they knew of the murder that had taken place there.

Danny has clear memories of the house where Juliet Staunton Clark was brutally bludgeoned:

When we bought the house I was only four years old. I remember the first time I came down the hill. When we moved in I found out shortly thereafter about the murder and I knew the living room area was where it happened. I was rummaging in my dad's den and I found a newspaper article titled, "Murder On The Rumpled Green Rug".

I read about it then, and I talked with Dad about it. He had theories[164], but no one knows. Somebody could have targeted her.

There was an easy way get out of there.[165] You would go past the

---
[164] Regarding who murdered Mrs. Clark.

[165] Staunton Road.

Fleeson house—there was a path that went all the way down the hill to the railroad tracks.[166] I took that road all the time, even rode a horse down that path. It was nothing for a little kid.

When I worked at Shoney's and could not get a ride home one night, I walked from Kanawha Boulevard, all the way down the Southside, in the dark, and all the way up the hill. It was nothing.

Back then there were hoboes that jumped trains. Those trains ran slowly along the tracks where the expressway is—you could literally run alongside the cars and jump on. Anyone could easily get up and down that path to Staunton Road, or they could have gone through the woods. Richard Merrill and I have talked about that. We think some vagrant came along and killed her.

Richard and I were close. I would walk to the Merrill house and he to mine. We played together. It was so dark that when he would get home from my house, or I from his, we would reach the front porch and yell, 'Eeee, awww, key!' It was a way of letting one another know we had gotten home without being killed.

STAUNTON, KATHARINE

Katharine Staunton, in her *Aunt Kate's Scrapbook*, included a newspaper article that chronicled her encounter with a "Mystery Woman".[167] Aunt Kate seemed intent on protecting the woman's reputation, citing her as not a mystery, but an enlightened soul. The newspaper article reported:

Annie Burke, the aged woman who was run down by a taxi cab and killed Sunday night and whose funeral will be held (at) *Sacred Heart Church tomorrow morning at 9 o'clock, was not a "Mystery Woman", according to Katherine Staunton, who said today she had known Miss Burke virtually all her life. She*

---

[166] Along the Southside Expressway.

[167] Aunt Kate did not identify the newspaper or the date of publication.

NOTES

was accustomed to stop up on the bridge to read her newspaper in pleasant weather because "my room is stuffy." She was never married.

Miss Staunton made the following statement concerning Miss Burke:

"I have known Annie Burke since I was a little girl, she was not married nor a widow. She was rather peculiar, but was honest, clean and industrious.

"Her uncle, a man of superior intelligence and education was bank boss (sic) for Col. Edwards, Sr.—at Coalburg for many years, where she and her brother made their home with him, until she came to Charleston.

"Living by herself, poorly and economically, for twenty-eight years, she worked in a laundry and saved several hundred dollars, these savings, so I was told, she gave to the church to buy an altar. She was a devoted Roman Catholic and deeply religious.

"As she grew older she had to give up hard work and support herself by doing odd jobs and was helped a little by friends.

"Living in a room about as poorly as life could be supported, she treasured her belongings and was always cheerful and pleasant.

"She did not sit on the bridge at all times and in all kinds of weather and read newspapers, but she did sit there in pleasant weather and summer evenings, and when I asked her why, she said, 'because my room is so hot and stuffy, and when I get out where the wind blows, and the skies above me, it seems like heaven.'

"With advancing years, she was afraid of falling on uneven sidewalk, and sometime walked in the street, and when I spoke to her about it saying, 'Annie if you don't stop walking in the street a taxi driver will run over and kill you.' Her reply was, 'Honey,

I've always dreaded dying in my room alone, lying several days maybe before anyone found me.' Well, she didn't!"

STAUNTON, SIDNEY AUGUSTUS

The Staunton history is replete with ever-so interesting stories—Sidney Augustus and Sidney S. Staunton led interesting lives. Rear Admiral Sidney Augustus built a house on the corner of Kanawha and Dunbar Streets for his father, mother, Aunt Sue and Aunt Kate—and later Aunt Mary and her husband, Dr. Sidney S. Staunton, a first cousin to her and all the Stauntons.[168]

Brewster King wrote in his *Journal*:

Admiral Sidney was one of Houncie's (Staunton) favorites and we visited at least once, maybe a second time after he had retired. He wintered in Washington and summered on a farm near Warren, PA which is near Oil City, where oil was discovered that put Dr. Joseph Staunton out of business. Derricks are interspersed between the houses. On the farm, the two story house was like a reverse "L" shape, dark colored with a one story vine covered porch on the front. There was no electric. Inside the parlor was across the front of the house (sic).

Brewster King said he once saw Admiral Staunton darning his socks by the light of an oil lamp. He recalled that Staunton had a maid who had one leg:

Lena, his second story maid, had only one leg with a single crutch, she ripped through the rooms, emptying chamber pots, making beds and cleaning as though she had no disability...Maizy, the cook, produces amazing meals on a coal-fired stove. She was a short, round, gray haired, kindly good-natured woman, loved by all. There were lots of cats.

STAUNTON, DR. SIDNEY S.

---

[168] From *Brewster King's Journal*, which attributed this note to Houncie Staunton.

NOTES

In 1912, Dr. Sidney S. Staunton, born June 7, 1850, delivered a lengthy and regal speech to the Kanawha Republican Club about his impressions of seeing Abraham Lincoln on three occasions. It is included here to note the eloquent voice of Dr. Sidney, yet another remarkable Staunton.

On the first occasion I came to jeer, but the tall figure of the angular earnest man was too much, and as he smiled and bowed stiffly, to the right and to the left, none but the most prejudiced, no matter how much he might have differed with him, could doubt his sincerity. One felt that he was straining in the force of a movement that he was beckoning on. "Come on, boys!" might have been his slogan.

Election came and the die was cast and when the result was announced, writhing slave states gnashed their teeth. Sedition was rife; secession came, desertions were frequent, fortresses and munitions of war were misappropriated, guns that should have defended the flag were turned upon it. Trouble was hatching and becoming full fledged and during that round of speech making, which preceded his first inauguration, I saw Mr. Lincoln again.

Well I remember the gray February day chilled by the winds from Lake Erie. Well I remember the great crowd of serious and intent, and as the whistling, singing, locomotives that stood upon the tracks of the lake shore's great yards—his train with the swinging bell slowed down and came to a standstill, bowing to the cheering crowd. I saw this gaunt figure once more.

I now know that in that great earnest, grave face I saw the evidences that in his heart of hearts, he knew that the Lord had spoken to him the great commission for the earthly ratification of which he was going to Washington. That in look, action and word he gave evidence of the good courage that was strong in him based on the knowledge, "I, thy Lord thy God am with thee, withersoever thou goest."

Staunton saw Lincoln for the third time following the Civil War: *The dastard hand was raised. An assassin's stroke fell upon its shining mark, and the great heart was stilled and impotent,* Staunton told the Republican Club members. He then described viewing Lincoln's body as the President's funeral train moved from Washington to Springfield, Illinois, making stops in cities large and small.

Immediately after daylight I was driving about the streets. Already the city awoke and the people were pouring into the streets. Not hurrying in all directions as usual this early, but sedately, all faces were turned to the depot of the New York Central over which he was to come.

Except for the places kept clear by the police, the buildings, the terraces, squares, and streets were packed full: Men, women and children on foot, mounted or in wagons, buggies or carriages, they stood expectant, silent, somber and as the body was tenderly brought and placed upon the beautiful catafalque, drawn by magnificent, draped horses, that were led by grooms in deepest mourning, the level rays of the rising sun, brightening the festooned red, white and blue, the breezes from Lake Erie, stirring the thousands of flags that at half-mast tokened the bereavement and lightened the walls of brick and stone: but despite the brilliant sky they did not relieve the ominous black that was draped everywhere nor dispel the gloom that weighed down the hearts of that concourse.

My mother's younger sister was one of the sweet singers of her day, possessing a voice widely heard and admired. She was a member of the famous St. Cecilia Society that furnished music for the occasion and one of those chosen to sing.

It was my duty and pleasure to escort her from home to the hall in which the body was to lie in state and therefore I was able to secure a favorable position from which to witness the ceremonies... the awe inspiring silence (was) *broken only by the occasional sign and the sweet strains of the requiem "Rest Spirit, Rest" softly*

NOTES

sung by the highly trained voices as the casket was brought in and placed upon the bier.

Staunton ended his speech with these words, *"I stood by the loving heart and looked for the last time into the sad face, still in death, of Abraham Lincoln."*

—IV.—
ACKNOWLEDGMENTS

The authors are greatly indebted to Brewster Buffington King, 90, who provided a voluminous history of the Staunton-Buffington-Merrill family. The admiration of the authors for the historical document he created and shared has no bounds. King's compilation ranged from a genealogy by John B. Merrill to Aunt Kate Staunton's scrapbook and the *Brewster Buffington King Journal*. It is a treasure of historical people and events in Virginia, later West Virginia.

Brooks McCabe, Jr. supplied extensive research papers regarding Staunton Road and the Staunton and Merrill families. Brooks, a historian of note, was always available for fact checking and accuracy of researched material, giving great encouragement to the authors. He read the entire manuscript before the book was sent to the publisher. The authors are honored that Brooks wrote the foreword to the book.

We are grateful to the numerous officials who were considerate of our many requests for records regarding the Clark murder. They include Charleston Mayor Amy Shuler Goodwin and her Assistant, Tina Stinson; Charleston Police Chief Opie Smith and his Office Manager, Samantha Walls; Charleston Police Lieutenant Randy Sampson; and Charleston City Attorney Kevin Baker and his Senior Staff Associate Tiffany Redman.

ACKNOWLEDGMENTS

The Kanawha County Library depository of Charleston newspapers was invaluable as was the assistance of the *Charleston Gazette-Mail.*

The Spilman Thomas & Battle Law firm was generous in supplying both text and photos from *Spilman Thomas & Battle's History of Service, the First 150*. Our thanks to Spilman Managing Member Michael J. Basile and author Elizabeth Jill Wilson for their willingness to share their remarkable publication.

Buffy Merrill Wallace was the first contact the authors made when the idea of a book about the Clark murder was born. She was highly instrumental in suggesting individuals who could add depth to the story. Hearing that a book was planned, her reaction was, "Well, Johnny Merrill and I always said if someone is going to write about the murder of Aunt Juliet they need to interview us!" And then she laughed, a ringing testament to her wonderfully positive outlook on life.

Buffy and John Merrill, 2019, reviewing *Brewster King's Journal.*
–Charlie Ryan

Buffy gave of extensive time to the authors who are grateful for her hours of conversation that painted such a vivid picture of what she calls "that terrible" time of Juliet Staunton Clark's murder. She was asked on many occasions to recheck dates and names in the manuscript and cheerfully did so with alacrity.

Buffy is regarded as the Merrill family historian, and rightly so. Reacting to a "thank you so much," following our interviews with her, she laughingly responded, "Well, I just love history and Wally tells me, 'That's enough family history!', so you've been very patient."

Harry "Wally" Wallace just smiled.

To the dismay of all connected with this writing project, Harry A.

Wallace, known by one and all as "Wally", passed away on March 15, 2020, a few months prior to the publishing of this book. He was a regal man with snow-white hair and a contagious smile that lit up not just a room, but seemingly all of life.

His obituary said, "He loved his life on earth and felt like he was the most blessed man ever to be." He was also said to love all things Scottish–games, bagpipes and Scotch whiskey. His obituary resonated Wally's wonderful outlook on life, with the words, "In lieu of flowers, give your wait staff a big tip, because they are working their way through college."

John and Richard Merrill, Buffy's brothers, also gave generously of their time to articulate recollections of growing up on Staunton Road and the days following Mrs. Clark's murder. They are splendid examples of their rich heritage.

Fanny Staunton Ogilvie was a delight with whom to chat. She continues as a distinguished artist in many art forms.

Betsy Staunton Johnson, Fan's sister, articulated her memories with great clarity and candor. She has a poet's skill in recalling scenes of her family history and observation of personalities. Interviewing her was enjoyable and invaluable.

Lyell Clay's friend Paula Butterfield was gracious in granting a lengthy interview to Mitch Evans. She shared memories of Lyell that were both humorous and poignant—resonating heartfelt admiration and love for Lyell. Her willingness to share her photographs with Lyell added immeasurably to Paula's story.

Beverly Samuelson assisted with many hours of reading and editing. She was especially helpful regarding reviews of the histories of the Staunton and Merrill families. Beverly assisted Charlie Ryan and Pamela Martin Ovens by suggesting the title for their 2018 book—*Deceit, Disappearance & Death on Hilton Head Island*.

ACKNOWLEDGMENTS

Danny Jones was entertaining, as always, in his review of the later days on Staunton Road, following Mrs. Clark's death. The four-term mayor holds the distinction of being Charleston's longest-serving mayor. He says his memoir, when written, will be titled, "Call Me Danny!"

Tom Toliver, age 86, told us he wanted the Stauntons, the Merrills and the Clark relatives to know he holds them in the highest regard and in his remembrance did not want, in any way, to be offensive or cause them discomfort.

Toliver retired from Appalachian Power Company's John Amos Plant and was then employed at Kanawha Presbyterian Church. That's where, in the church's kitchen, he encountered Betsy Staunton Johnson one day and told her of his encounter with the Clark case.

Toliver later founded *Family Youth and Development Services* for incarcerated men and women. He has worked with hundreds of prisoners to assist them to return to society. In his work he has traveled to Africa, Nigeria, Norway, and Germany. He served in the military, and all members of his family have done so. He believes there is no race problem in the United States, but that there is instead, an American problem.

"On my tombstone," he said, I want two words—"I tried."

Toliver is highly regarded in Charleston. Buffy Merrill Wallace calls him, "a wonderful man."

Detective Rick Westfall assisted us in verifying that the Clark case files could not have been destroyed by a flood in the 1980s. Westfall said that he personally reviewed the Clark files several times during his 17-year career as a Charleston police department detective. The case file, he confirmed, was on the fourth floor of Charleston City Hall, high above the reach of any flood.

We extend our thanks to Dave Dickens, an eight-year Charleston detective, who was, in the mid 90s, the Charleston Police Department Information Services Division Commander. Dickens was in charge of information services and criminal warrants during that time, with supervision of the police department computer system. Dickens said the Department would never have checked out the Clark file and "we would never get rid of a murder case."

Jim Reader, a former television journalist in the Charleston and Cleveland markets, gave us significant background information regarding his wife Kay's effort to chronicle the Clark murder questions while she was a reporter for both the *Charleston Gazette* and *Charleston Daily Mail*. Kay was ordered at both newspapers, Reader told us, to cease her research efforts on the case—causing her great frustration.

Thanks also to former *Daily Mail* business editor George Hohmann for his recollections of his time at the Clay-owned newspaper, and to *The Charleston Gazette-Mail* Editor Emeritus, James Haught for his memories of *The Charleston Gazette* regular reminders of an unsolved case that so upset Detective Red Fisher.

Pam Steelhammer was of great assistance in obtaining a critical interview, and offered valuable support in the research effort. Many thanks to her for the encouragement she gave the authors.

Our thanks also to Kathy Becker, Judge John T. Copenhaver, Bill Davis, Otis Laury, and David Rollins for graciously talking with us by phone.

Becky Ryan, Charlie Ryan's wife, edited in her usual eagle-eyed manner and generously allowed her husband to spend 1,000+ hours in research and writing of this book. Charlie conveys his everlasting love to her for her support and 26 years of a wonderful marriage.

Mitch Evans, who co-authored with Charlie, was indefatigable in his research. He filed numerous Freedom of Information Act

ACKNOWLEDGMENTS

(FOIA) requests, made many visits to law enforcement agencies in search of the Juliet Clark file, followed up with emails and correspondence, and exhibited unbridled enthusiasm throughout the two-year research and writing journey.

Charlie thanks Mitch for his massive effort and his original suggestion that they join forces and write this book. Mitch is grateful to Charlie for providing him with the opportunity to share in this project and his thoughtful leadership and encouragement.

The authors were greaty assisted by Rinck Heule of M.J. Jacobs, LLC. in the design of this book. Rinck's patience and expertise are of the highest standards.

Cara Flanery, an intern in Mitch Evans' office, trained an eagle eye on the finished manuscript and was simply terrific in adding the final edits and conformity in style and consistency. We cannot thank her enough for her attention to detail and dedication to perfection.

Finally, our thanks to Pamela Martin Ovens for her timely suggestions regarding marketing and distribution strategies.

—V—
BIBLIOGRAPHY

LITERATURE
-*A Suitcase From The Titanic,* Enrique Rodolfo Dick, WIT Press, 2013, page 127.
-*Col. Benjamin Harrison Smith, His Family and Its Impact on Charleston, West Virginia*: Brooks McCabe, Jr.
-*History of the Great Kanawha Valley*: Volumes I and II, Brant, Fuller & Co., 1891.
-*History of Kanawha County*: George Atkins, 1876.
-*Legendary Locals of Wheeling, West Virginia*: Sean Duffy and Brent Carney; page 62, 2013.
-*Lie Detection and Criminal Interrogation:* Fred Edward Inbau; The Williams and Wilkin Co., 1942.
-*Spilman Thomas & Battle's History of Service, The First 150*: Elizabeth Jill Wilson, Spilman Thomas & Battle, PLLC, 2014.
-*The West Virginia Encyclopedia:* West Virginia Humanities Council, January 31, 2006.
-*The Records of Living Officers U.S. Navy of 1894*
-*The War in Tong-King,* Boston: Cupples, Upham And Company, Cambridge, N.D.C. Hodges, 1884.
-*The West Virginia Review:* Vol. 8, No. 8; page 223; May 1933.
Chicago and New York, Lewis Publishing Company, 1928.
-*West Virginia In History, Life, Literature and Industry:* Morris Purdy Shawkey.
- *YOU, Selected Poems and KNOT: A Life:* Fanny Staunton Ogilvie, 2008.

BIBLIOGRAPHY

BROADCAST
-WSAZ-TV
-WCHS-Radio
-WCHS-TV

FAMILY ARCHIVES
-*Aunt Kate Staunton's Scrapbook*
-*Brewster Buffington King Journal*
-*Brewster Buffington King Booklet*
-*Brewster Buffington King Letter*, January 28, 2019
-*Descendants of Joseph Marshall Staunton*, Mary Elisabeth Wilber Staunton
-*Genealogical Sketch of the Staunton Family*, Susan Augustus Staunton
-*John Buffington Merrill Address to Family Reunion*, Nov. 27, 1980
-*Staunton-Buffington-Merrill Genealogy*, Brewster Buffington King

INTERVIEWS
-Becker, Kathy, October 9, 2019
-Butterfield, Paula, January 24, 2020
-Copenhaver, John Thomas, Jr., April 11, 2019
-Davis, Bill, October 10, 2019
-Dickens, David, November 6, 2019
-Goodwin, Amy, April 30, 2019, October 19, 2019 (voicemail)
-Haught, James, April, 17-2019
-Johnson, Betsy Staunton, February 20, 2019
-Jones, Danny, January 27, 2019, November 3, 2019
-King, Brewster, January 24, 2019
-McCabe, Brooks, February 10, 2019, March 17, 2019
-Merrill, John Buffington, Jr., February 23, 2019
-Merrill, Richard, February 21, 2019
-Ogilvie, Fanny Staunton, February 11, 2019
-Rollins, David, January 21, 2019
-Toliver, Tom, March 4, 2019, March 5, 2019
-Wallace, Buffy Merrill, January 18, 2019, January 25, 2019, February 12, 2019, February 23, 2012, March 12, 2019
-Westfall, Rick, April 1, 2019, November 4, 2019

LETTERS
-*Fred Staunton Letter to Robert Hannah*, January 23, 1959
-*Robert Hannah Letter to Fred Staunton*, January 26, 1959
-*Merrill Family History-A Brief History of Staunton Road*
-*"Q" Giltinan Letter To Her Daughter in Pittsburgh, Pennsylvania*

NEWSPAPERS
The Bluefield Daily Telegraph
<u>1953</u>
-Associated Press story of September 4;
  Son-In-Law (Arch Alexander, Sr.) of Murdered Charleston Socialite Undergoes Lie Detector Test; Lyell Clay mention

The Citizen (Cabell County, West Virginia)
<u>Circa 1875</u>
-Phillip C. Russell attacks Dr. Joseph Staunton on his way home from a house call

The Charleston Daily Mail
<u>1950</u>
-February 5-"Walter E. Clark, Publisher, Succumbs"
-October 1-"Miss Juliet Clark Married to Mr. Arch Alexander, Jr."

<u>1951</u>
-April 17-"Copenhaver Wins as GOP Sweeps Major Offices In City Election"

<u>1952</u>
-December 18-"Court Charges Recount Cost To Lyell Clay"
-December 18-"Court Speeds Vote Recount"
-December 26-"Vote Recount, Heydrick Leading Lyell Clay By 79"

<u>1953</u>
-August 22-"Mrs. W.E. Clark Discovered Dead"
-August 23-"Intruder Slays Mrs. W. E. Clark; *Daily Mail's* Owner Bludgeoned"
-August 23-Editorial, "Mrs. Walter Clark, 1894-1953"

BIBLIOGRAPHY

-August 28-"Police Quiz Mrs. Clark's Son-In-Law"
-August 28-"Estate of Mrs. Clark Left Equally To Three Children"
-August 29-"Famed Crime Ace May Sift Bludgeoning"
-August 30-"Hammer Not Mrs. Clark's Death Cudgel"
-August 31-"Clark Probe in 10th Day"
-September 2-"Lie Detector Operator Due"
-September 3-"Crime Expert Arrives Here In Death Quiz"
-September 4-"Alexander's Lie Detector Test At End"
-September 5/7-"Take Test In Death Quiz"
-September 6-"Clark Inquiry 'Progressing'"
-September 7-"Lie Detector Expert Back"
-September 10-"Inbau Ending Probe Today"
-September 13-"Police Widen River Search"
-September 23-"Police Deny Clark Killer Confession"
-October 27-"A Statement In Review"

1954
-February 9-"Award Raised to $15,000"
-April 9-Editorial, "Way Out On A Limb"
-April 22-"Mystery Cloaks Clark Murder After Year"
-April 22-"Record Costs City $12,000"
-August 22-"Mrs. Lyell Clay Has Natural Pride In Husband"
-July 6-"*Gazette* Editor Frank Knight Dies At Age 48"
-October 31-"Lawyer-Candidate Meets The People"

1955
-March 9-Notice Of *Daily Mail* "Withdrawal of Offer To Pay Award"
-March 13-Bob Mellace column, "How To Twist A Solemn Truth"
-April 19-"Copenhaver Wins Second Mayor Term"

1956
-June 29-"Clay Quits City Office; Joins *Mail*"

1958
-January 1-"*Mail, Gazette* Form Business Consolidation"
-November 14-Harry Hoffmann Column-"Democratic '58 Sweep Spurred Talk of Party Switch"

1959
-August 13-"Children, Animals Great Favorites Of Mayor"
-August 13-"Old Town Won't Be The Same Without Copenhaver"
-August 14-"City Mourns Mayor's Death, Funeral Will Be Saturday"
-August 14-"Body of Copenhaver Viewed By Hundreds"

1976
-November-*Daily Mail* Editorial, "Fred Staunton, 1903-1976"

2014
-April 4-*Daily Mails*, "Goals for 100 Years"
-April 4-*Daily Mail* Editorial, "*Daily Mail* Founder Was Committed to Fairness"
-April 4-"Pulitzer Winning Journalist Continues To Influence *Daily Mail* Philosophy"

1966
-July 20-"Fan White Staunton Married To Donald G. Ogilvie Saturday"

The Charleston Gazette
1953
-August 23-"Police Scour Area For Clark Slayer"
-August 24-Editorial, "The Clark Murder"
-August 26-"Man Is Held On Suspicion In Clark Case"
-August 29-"Hammer May Be Weapon Used To Slay Mrs. Clark"
-August 30-"Probe Pressed In Clark Killing"
-August 30-Frank Knight "Today" column, "In Its Lead Editorial The *Gazette* Took This Position On The Juliet Staunton Clark Murder"
-September 6-"Police Hint Hammer Still Vital Clue in Clark Death"
-September 6-"Strange Parallel of the Two Cousins"
-September 21-"Inbau and Reed meet with Clark relatives"
-October 25-Editorial, "Has Justice Failed?"
-October 26-"Mayor Rips *Gazette* Stand in Clark Case"
-October 27-Editorial, "Time For Action"

BIBLIOGRAPHY

-October 27-"Clark Probe 'Bungled,' Parkersburg Newspaper Says"
-October 27-Editorial, "Time For Action"

1954
-February 14-"No Closer To Solution Than At Start"
-February 14-"Six Months Work Fails to Find Answer to Question 'Who Killed Mrs. Clark?'"
-March 13-"Thomas To Reopen Clark Investigation, Judge Declares Probe "Stinks"
-March 13-"Today" column-"Mayor Has Controlled Police"
-March 24-"City Police Grill Suspect In Murder of Juliet Clark"
-April 7-"Mayor Says Killer Is 'Known'"
-April 8-"*Gazette* 'Unfair' In Clark Story, Mayor Charges"
-April 10-"Mayor says he has formed opinion and so has Fred Staunton"
-July 16-Editorial. "Has Justice Failed?"
-August 8-"Clark Case Figures Plan Unheralded Divorce Action"
-December 12-Harry Hoffmann column, "Life and Slander On The Lay-Away Plan"

1955
-March 13, "Thomas to Reopen Clark Investigation; Judge Declares Probe 'Stinks'; Rips Copenhaver"
-April 19-"Copenhaver Wins Second Mayor Term"
-July 11-"Wrench Clark Case Weapon?"
-July 17-"Today" column, "It Was A Busy Week for Police Reporter Jim Hill"

1959
-March 27-Harry Hoffmann column, "Stability Is Democratic Key In Opposing Mayor"
-August 18-"Democratic '58 Sweep Spurred Talk of Party Switch"
-August 14-"City Mourns Mayor's Death, Funeral Will Be Saturday"
-August 14-"Copenhaver Story Is Told"
-August 14-"Shanklin Likely To Finish Term"
-August 14-"Overworked Heart Fails"
-August 15-Editorial, "John T. Copenhaver: He Was THE MAYOR"

The Charleston Gazette-Mail
2014
-April 4-"Lyell Clay Editor, Publisher and Dad"

The Cincinnati Enquirer
1953
-August 24-"Trio Quizzed In Brutal Killing"
-August 25-"No Clues"
-August 27-"'Suspicious' Man Freed In Murder of Mrs. Clark"

The Courier-Journal (Louisville, Kentucky)
1953
-August 23-"Society Leader, Major Owner of Paper, Is Murdered"

The Dominion News (Morgantown, West Virginia)
1958
-February 13-"Mayor Of Charleston Hits Book"

The Gallipolis, Ohio Dispatch
1861
-The *Dispatch* reports on colonial Charleston, Virginia

The Huntington Herald Dispatch
2018
-March 13-"*Charleston Gazette-Mail* purchased *by* HD Media"

The Illustrated London News
1843
-"Howard Staunton defeats French champion chess player in longest chess match on record"

The Indiana Gazette (Indiana, Pennsylvania)
1955
-July 16-"Doubt Story Of Man Over Old Murder"

The Lubbock Evening Journal (Lubbock, Texas)
1953
-"Brutal Slaying Of Paper Owner"

BIBLIOGRAPHY

The Morning Call (Allentown, Pennsylvania)
1953
-August 23-"Beaten To Death"

1958
-March 9-"The Body on the Rumpled Green Rug"

The Morning Herald (Hagerstown, Maryland)
1953
-August 24-"Police Sift Clues in Baffling Slaying"

The New York Sunday News
1958
-March 9-"The Body on the Rumpled Green Rug"

The New York Times
1977
-Harry Hoffmann death

Ogden Newspapers
1953
-October 28-*Charleston Gazette* and *Daily Mail* reference

The Parkersburg News
1953
-October 28-Editorial regarding Clark investigation

The Pittsburgh Post Gazette
1956
-May 31-"Socialite's '53 Murder In W.Va. Solved"

The Pittsburgh Press
1954
-August 8-"Mystery Death Talk Revived By Divorce Suit"

The Philadelphia Inquirer
1953
-August 28, "Son-In-Law Is Grilled In Socialite Slaying"

The Raleigh Register (Beckley, West Virginia)
1954
-February 9, "Clark Murder Reward Increased To $15,000"

West Virginia Record
2017
-May 9-"Former *Daily Mail* Owners Say Domain Name Was Sold Without Permission"

ONLINE
-Amazon
- Ancestry.com
-*Charleston Daily Mail* History
-Clay Center Website
-Juliet Staunton Clark Death Certificate, State of West Virginia
-Kanawha County Public Library
-Lawrenceville Academy Website
-Major League Baseball
-Newspapers.com
-*The Herald Dispatch* "herald-dispatch.com" site
-Wikipedia
-WikiTree

PERIODICALS
-*Air Progress*-September 20, 1953
-*Marshall Alumni Magazine*-Jack Maurice remembrance

PHOTOGRAPHS
-*Charleston Gazette*
-*Charleston Daily Mail*
-*Charleston Sunday Gazette-Mail*
-Charlie Ryan
-Brewster Buffington King
-Kanawha County Public Library
-Merrill-Wallace Families
-Mitch Evans
-West Virginia State Archives - Frank Wilken Collection

BIBLIOGRAPHY

WIRE SERVICES
Associated Press
-1956, July-AP Bureau Chief Harry Ball eulogizes Frank Knight
-Various stories in state, national newspapers

United Press
-Various stories in state, national newspapers

—VI.—
ABOUT THE AUTHORS

Charlie Ryan's writing career began in 1962 and spanned eighteen years of reporting in radio, television, wire service, and newspaper venues. His focus on politics brought him into contact with prominent names of the sixties and seventies where he interviewed such notables as Lyndon Johnson, Richard Nixon, Eleanor Roosevelt, Hubert Humphrey, Robert Kennedy, Sargent Shriver, John Connally, George Wallace, and Jimmy Hoffa. Charlie was voted into the West Virginia Broadcasting Hall of Fame.

Photo by Peter Ovens

In 1974 Charlie founded *Charles Ryan Associates*, an integrated marketing firm with services of public relations, advertising and social media, in West Virginia, Virginia and Washington, D.C. His advertising and public relations career spanned 33 years and created four business entities. He sold those firms in 2007 and became the Founding Dean of the Graduate School of Business at the University of Charleston. He retired from the University in 2009 and returned to his writing career.

His books include *Dead Men's Clubs—A Story of Golf, Death and Redemption*, the fictional account of a high handicap golfer from Hilton Head Island who suddenly begins to play like a champ when he buys used golf clubs; *The Pullman Hilton—A Christmas*

ABOUT THE AUTHORS

Mystery for young adults; *My Life with Charles Fraser*, a history of the men and women who worked with Charles Fraser as he dreamed of and developed Hilton Head Island, South Carolina; *Deceit, Disappearance & Death*— written with co-author Pamela Martin Ovens—the story of the 10th anniversary of the disappearance of Hilton Head entrepreneurs John and Elizabeth Calvert and the death of their accountant, Dennis Gerwing; and *Alacrity*, a memoir—75 years of recollections that recount Charlie's early years, broadcast career, agency ownership, academic role, and writing career.

Charlie is a native of Keyser, West Virginia and a graduate of Potomac State College and West Virginia University. He and his wife Becky live in South Carolina—they have three daughters, four grandchildren and one completely spoiled Maltese.

Charles M. "Mitch" Evans, CFP®, CFS®, CRPC® is a native of Clarksburg, West Virginia. He is a 1979 graduate of Clarksburg Washington Irving High School, and a 1983 graduate of West Virginia Wesleyan (BA, Sociology) where he studied Sociology, Psychology, Criminology, Religion, and Business Administration.

While always maintaining a keen eye toward the study of history and criminology, he followed his entrepreneurial and pastoral instincts and began his career in 1983 as a third generation financial planner practitioner in Charleston, WV (CERTIFIED FINANCIAL PLANNER™ 11/22/1993) with IDS Financial Services Inc. and it successors (American Express Financial Advisors Inc. and Ameriprise Financial, Inc.) where he celebrated his 35th anniversary on October 12, 2018.

Mitch is one of six members of his family to serve in a financial planner capacity which accounts for over 192 years in collective experience.

Mitch splits time between his beloved West Virginia and his

home on Hilton Head Island.

In *Murder on Staunton Road,* Mitch returns to his interest in History, Sociology, and Criminology. A review of the information surrounding the sale of the *Charleston Daily Mail's* web domain name to the *Daily Mail* (UK) drew him into further study of the history of the *Charleston Daily Mail*, thus his engagement in this project.

Whether in West Virginia or on Hilton Head Island, you will find Mitch with his wife, Ann, as well as their two "West Virginia Brown Dogs" - "Sasha" and "Winston".

ABOUT THE AUTHORS

Also By Charlie Ryan
~
Dead Men's Clubs

The Pullman Hilton

My Life With Charles Fraser

Deceit, Disappearance & Death
With Pamela Martin Ovens

Alacrity
A Memoir

—VII.—
INDEX

A

Adams, Bob 318
Alcock, Thomas 238
Alexander, Arch ix, xi, xii, 80, 86, 97, 98, 99, 101, 106, 107, 125, *126*,127, 128, 131, 132, 133, 135, 137, 142, 145, 147, 159, 161, 207, 208, 209, 210, 258, 262, 295, 304, 305, 359
Alexander, Arch Johnson 208
Alexander, Guy J. 305
Alexander, Helena 305
Alexander III, Arch xi, 68, 86
Alexander, Juliet Clark xi, 305
Alexander, J.W. 209
Alexander, Lucille F. 305
American Rose Society 45
Andrews, Carl 117, 118, 340
Andrus, Oren 35
Atkinson, George 29, 282
Augustus, Sidney 309, 322, 327, 347

B

Bailey, Pamela Jane 305
Bailey, Steven 305
Baker, Kevin 274, 276, 277, 278
Baldwin, Charles xii, 204, 205
Ball, Harry 314, 366
Ballinger, Richard 36
Baranet, Robert 310
Barber, Sadie 32
Becker, Kathy 358
Benson, Clarence J. 240
Bias, Dallas 166, 185
Biddle, Emily Duncan 331
Bond, Phil 79
Bonham, Joe 246
Bowe, Jesse 138
Bower, Bob 159
Brewster, Sarah 322
Brightwell, Elisabeth 309
Brightwell, Elizabeth (Dip) xii, 191
Brightwell, Fanny White 309
Brightwell, Henry Platt 309
Brightwell, H.P. 191
Brooks, Gilbert 159
Brown, J.V. 138
Brown, Van G. 342
Bryan, Herbert W. xii, 68
Buffington, Florence Garland xi, xii, 13, 23, 24, 29, 46, 309
Buffington, Jonathon Nathaniel 337
Buffington, Peter Cline xii, 203
Buffington, William 337

INDEX

Burke, Annie 345, 346
Burke, Southall 54
Butterfield, Paula 294, 296, 298, 302

C

Calloway, Franklin 152
Calvert, Elizabeth 368
Calvert, John 368
Carney, Brent 152, 357
Caron, Leslie 159
Case, Mary 250
Chilton III, W.E. "Ned" 289
Clark, Caroline Hill 13, 15, 16, 17, 18, 19, 20, 21, 22
Clark, Ellsworth 344
Clark, Jeanette (Jones) 35
Clark, Juliet and Clark, Juliet Staunton vii, xi, 2, 7, 8, 10, 13, 16, 17,18, 19, 20, 22, 23, 47, 48, 50, 51, 54, 56, 62, 65, 66, 69, 73, 76, 79, 80, 81, 87, 89, 90, 91, 93, 94, 97, 101, 103, 104, 106, 107, 109, 112, 125,135, 136, 142, 143, 147, 153, 157, 159, 161, 162, 163, 166, 169, 170, 173, 174, 179, 181, 183, 184, 185, 187, 190, 195, 203, 204, 207, 210, 213, 221, 222, 223, 224, 228, 234, 253, 258, 261, 262, 263, 264, 266, 272, 274, 277, 279, 281, 282, 286, 290, 296, 307, 318, 335, 344, 352, 365
Clark, Mary 322
Clark, Mrs. Juliet Staunton 10, 73, 74, 159, 190, 215, 221, 231, 238, 269
Clark, Mrs. Walter E. 59, 70, 74, 75, 83, 88, 147, 188, 208, 221, 305, 353, 359, 362
Clark, Walter Eli xi, 2, 10, 13, 17, 18, 19, 20, 21, 35, 36, 37, 38, 39, 40, 41, 42, 43, 45, 46, 47, 50, 51, 52, 53, 54, 55, 56, 59, 70, 73, 87, 88, 101, 105, 147, 188, 208, 221, 282, 286, 292, 301, 304, 305, 359
Clay, Ashton deLashmet 292
Clay, Brutus J. 281
Clay, Courtney 292
Clay, Green 281
Clay, Henry 286

Clay, Juliet Staunton 46
Clay, Jr., Buckner Woodford xi, 20, 21, 47, 48, 49, 56, 86, 98, 99, 147, 193, 195, 208, 216, 217, 282, 289, 291, 292, 297, 298, 306
Clay, Leslie Staunton 159, 292
Clay, Lyell Buffington xi, 20, 47, 48, 49, 73, 78, 79, 88, 97, 99, 108, 126, 129 130, 135, 137, 147, 148, 149, 150, 193, 194, 195, 197, 217, 219, 258, 262, 282, 283, 284, 285, 286, 287, 288, 289, 290, 291, 292, 294, 295, 296, 297, 298, 299, 300, 301, 302, 303, 304, 312, 336, 353
Clay, Patricia 292
Clay, Sr., Buckner Woodford xi, 31, 46, 49, 282
Clay, Toni 49, 195, 292, 306
Clay, Whitney 292
Cline, Ann 337
Conlin, Renee 298
Conlin, Thomas 298
Connally, John 367
Connor, Charlie xiii, 110, 112, 153, 158, 194, 217, 229, 230, 250, 251, 292, 318, 342
Copenhaver, Adaline 338
Copenhaver, John T. xii, 3, 7, 68, 84, 88, 93, 109, 110, 111, 112, 117, 118, 119, 120, 121, 122, 125, 127, 129, 131, 135, 136, 137, 139, 149, 151, 152, 153, 154, 155, 157, 158, 159, 160, 166, 169, 172, 173, 174, 177, 179, 180, 182, 183, 186, 187, 188, 190, 211, 212, 213, 217, 218, 219, 220, 222, 223, 224, 225, 226, 227, 228, 229, 231, 232, 234, 237, 238, 239, 240, 241, 242, 243, 245, 246, 247, 248, 249, 250, 251, 257, 258, 261, 262, 286, 313, 337, 338, 339, 340, 341, 342, 343, 358, 359, 360, 361, 362
Copenhaver, Jr., John T. 342
Copenhaver, Ruth 341, 342, 343
Copenhaver, Ulysses Grant 117, 338
Cox, A.W. 142
Coyle, Julia 87
Craft, Joe xii, 68, 71, 74, 84, 112, 127, 128
Craik, Dr. James 324

Craik, James 324
Crouse, Bob 122
Cuisset, Ginette Wery 306
Cuisset, Jr., Michael Scott 306
Cuisset, Michael 306
Cuisset, Nicholas 306
Cuisset, Phillipe 306
Cuisset, Shelley xi, 305, 306
Cuisset, Virginia 306
Cuisset, Zion 306
Curry, Hugh 142

D

Damron, Grady 41
Davis II, Mrs. J. Horner 94
Davis, Jack 316
Dawson, Daniel Boone 157
Dick, Enrique Rodolfo 330, 357
Dickens, David 358
Dickinson, John 142
Diller, Whitney Clay 292
Dirksen, Everett 287
Donnally, Moses 39
Drake, Edwin L. 326
Duffy, Sean 152, 357

E

Early, Carl 142
Edwards, Ross 136, 159
Rudesill, Ellsworth 344
Enslow, Andrew Jackson 203
Enslow, Frank 24, 203
Enslow, Juliette Buffington xii, 204, 206
Erwin Shipley 238
Evans, Mitch i, ii, iii, 1, 4, 20, 264, 267, 269, 271, 273, 276, 277, 278, 302, 355

F

Ferguson, Milton xii
Ferguson, Mr. and Mrs. Lucian B. 209
Fisher, W.W. "Red" xii
Fleeson, Florence xii, 107, 297, 336
Fleeson, Neville 311

Fleeson, Tom xii, 66, 195, 311, 312, 336
Floyd, John B. 38
FOIA 253, 254, 263, 264, 265, 269, 270, 272, 274, 356
Ford, Richard E. 304, 305
Forrestal, James 344
Fraser, Charles 368, 370
Freedom Of Information Act 253, 269
F.R. Swann 38

G

Gambell, Hannah Sever 322
Garland, Julia Lyell 23
Geary, Wehrle 142
Gerwing, Dennis 368
Gill, Mr. B. Stanley 208
Giltinan, David 87
Giltinan, "Q" 87, 88, 359
Giltinan, Zon 87, 88
Goldman, M.B. 141
Goodwin, Amy Shuler 253, 263, 276
Gorman, LaRoy 10
Goshorn, John Lynn 240
Graham, Katharine 80
Graney, Pat 199
Grosscup, Ben 34
Gullian, James 340
Gwinn, Adrian 42, 43
Gypsy Club 26

H

Hall, Cullen 240
Hallanan, Walter S. 117
Hammack, William A. 341
Hammett, Dashiell 317
Hannah, Robert 200, 201, 359
Harold, Zach 38, 43
Stansbury, Harry 142
Harry Truman 343
Hatfield, Zeke 141
Hawkins, Bob 310
Hawkins, Jenny 310
Haynes, Mayford 111, 341

INDEX

Hepburn, Kathryn 48
Heydrick, Paul 284
Hildreth, Willie 201
Hildreth, Willy 200
Hill, Arthur M. 343
Hill, Jim xii, 68, 71, 77, 87, 160, 161, 166, 185, 230, 234, 317, 362
Hill, Nancy 317, 337
Hindman, Sam 292
Hodges, N.D.C. 330, 357
Hoffa, Jimmy 367
Hoffman, Helen 301, 302
Hoffmann, Harry xii, 9, 119, 151, 154, 239, 315, 316, 360, 362, 364
Hohmann, George 10
Holt, Rush D. 338
Horan, Bob 230
Howard Staunton 321, 363
Hudson, Dick 54
Huffman, Mrs. D.H. 49
Hughes, Howard 48
Humphrey, Hubert 367

I

Inbau, Fred E. ix, xiii, 92, 109, 110, 111, 112, 113, 129, 130, 131, 135, 136, 137, 174, 175, 181, 217, 219, 262, 263, 357, 360, 361
Ireland, Jim 342
Isaac Noyes Smith 334

J

Jarrett, George 255
Jarrett, John W. 38
Jenkins, Clyde 54
Jennings, Vint 54
Johnson, Betsy Staunton xii, 5, 103, 105, 106, 107, 113, 114, 132, 193, 195, 197, 214, 309, 310, 353, 354, 358
Johnson, Caroline Staunton 343
Johnson, Lyndon 367
Johnson, Owen 283
Jones, Ann Dick 335
Jones, Danny 283, 340

Jones, Herbert 283
Jones, Laurance 335, 344

K

Kay, Robert H.C. xiii, 117, 131, 210
Kennedy, John F. 286
Kennedy, Patricia 288
King, Brewster 347
King, Brewster Buffington 31, 32, 321, 326, 351, 358, 365
King, Gordon Coltart 32, 311
Knight, Frank 9, 151, 169, 174, 179, 213, 224, 234, 312, 313, 314, 360, 361, 366
Knox, Philander C. 36

L

Ladd, Alan 159
Lafollette, "Tell" 141
Laidley, W. Sydney 23
Laury, Otis 335
Leroy, Frank 26
Lewis, Abbot 186, 187, 188
Lias, Bill 152
Lilly, Goff P. 68, 70, 85, 98
Lincoln, Abraham 348, 350
Lord, Anne 321
Lord, Thomas 321
Love, Thomas 21
Loveless, Melvin 176
Lowe, Rev. C. Oral 186
Lucy Stone 316

M

MacCorkle, Sam 117
Maier, Ed 344
Major, Floyd 339
Marsh, Don 77, 245, 247, 316, 338, 339, 340
Marshall, George 344
Marshall, Jr., Frederick (Freddy) 309
Martin, J.B. 54
Martin, Jimmy 194
Maurice, Jack xiii, 42, 54, 55, 56, 57, 83,

194, 197, 314, 315, 317, 318, 365
McCabe, Barbara Given 27
McCabe, Brooks 1, 4, 24, 25, 290, 343, 351, 357, 358
McCabe, Dorothy 28
McCabe, Jr., Brooks Fleming 27, 28
McCabe, Robert E. 27, 28, 33
McCarthy, Joe 152
McCorkle III, Alvin 240
McDavid, Bill 298
McGhee, Chuck 150
McGuffin, Harold xiii
McGuffin, Thomas xiii
McGuffin, Tom xiii, 166, 167, 219
McLaughlin, James Kemp 240
McQueen, Arthur 54
McWhorter, Julius 241
Meade, Jeff xiii, 166, 219
Meador, P.G. 141
Mellace, Bob xiii, 225, 228, 319, 360
Mellett, Donald "Ring" 313
Melton, Kemp 263
Merrill Wallace, Buffy xi, 28, 32, 33, 50, 77, 78, 79, 81, 87 91, 106, 107, 131 132, 165, 195, 282, 306, 307, 311, 312, 352, 354, 358
Merrill, Florence Buffington 337 50, 78, 106, 195, 308
Merrill, Jr., John Buffington xi, 33, 34, 50,78,106,194,195,307,308
Merrill. Mary Louise 28, 106, 195
Merrill, Mrs. John Buffington 208
Merrill, Rhuel ix, 29, 32, 33, 191
Merrill, Richard xi, 79, 93, 106, 195, 306, 308, 345, 353
Merrill, Sr., John Buffington xi, 32, 51, 328, 329
Metalious, Grace 339
Miller, Robert 229, 236
Monnier, Pierre xi, 305
Monnier-Thuret, Antoinette 305
Moore, John T. 240
Morgan, Denver 141
Morgan, George 129

Morris, Lawrence 138
Moses, Faze 158
Mudd, Roger 316

N

Newton, Mrs. L. Thomas 99
Nixon, Richard 367
Norvell, Lucy Harrison 36
Nunley, George 166, 340

O

Ogilvie, Donald Gordon 80
Ogilvie, Fanny Staunton v, xii, 80, 310, 353, 357, 358
Ogilvie, John Black 80
Olmsted, Frederick Law 283
Ovens, Pamela Martin 353, 368, 370

P

Patton, George 324
Patton, George Smith 324
Patton, Jack 141
Payne, Charles K. 20
Peck, Joe 106
Peraza, Courtney Clay 292
Peyton, Angus 131
Picklesimer, Hayes 142
Pitt, Page 317
Poffenbarger, Nathan 142
Polk, Frank 54
Putschar, Walter 70, 85

Q

R

Reader, Jim 10
Reader, Kay 11
Redman, Tiffany D. 253
Reed, Sarah 175, 176
Reeves, Sr, George W. 240
Reid, John 136, 219
Reynolds, Ruth xiii, 98, 126, 129, 207, 262

INDEX

Rice, Marie 233
Rice, Thurman 229, 230, 231, 234
Roberts, Ruth Cherrington 341
Rollins, David 92
Roosevelt, Eleanor 367
Roosevelt, Theodore 36, 330
Rudesill, Ellsworth 344
Runyon, Damon 151
Rust, Anna 322
Ryan, Charlie i, ii, iii, 1, 4, 352, 353, 355, 365, 367, 370

S

Sampson, Randy 253, 266
Samuelson, Beverly 353
Savage, D.J. "Jack" 210
Scales, Nancy 337
Seagle (Marsh), Don 159, 160
Shanholtzer, K.V. 68
Shanklin, John 117, 246, 317, 341
Shawkey, Morris Purdy 322, 323, 333, 334, 357
Shipley, Erwin 238
Shriver, Sargent 367
Sidney Augustus 309, 322, 327, 347
Simms, Bernard 121
Skeen, Oral 230
Slack, John 319
Slade, Helen 47
Smith, Bessie xii, 15, 17, 21, 22, 59, 60, 61, 62, 63, 64, 65, 66, 68, 70, 71, 74, 98, 312
Smith, Caroline Quarrier 333
Smith, E.D. 138
Smith, Elsie Quarrier 333
Smith, Harrison B. 88, 333
Smith, Isaac Noyes 334
Smith, Mrs. Harold W. 342
Smith, Ned 314
Smith, Opie 269
Smith, Sr., Robert L. 257
Spillane, Frank Morrison "Mickey" 179
Spilman, R.S. 20
Stansbury, Harry 142

Stark, Dinah 322
Staunton, Archibald 323
Staunton, Daniel 322
Staunton, Edward Wilber xi, 24, 27, 46, 80, 208
Staunton, Elisha 322
Staunton, Fanny White Brightwell (Fan) 309
Staunton, Florence Brightwell 29, 30, 32, 33, 106, 292, 332, 337
Staunton, Fred xi, xii, 5, 20, 22, 56, 62, 80, 98, 99, 103, 113, 132, 137, 150, 181, 182, 183, 190, 191, 193, 195, 197, 198, 199, 213, 217, 224, 262, 263, 279, 289, 307, 309, 310, 359, 361, 362
Staunton, Frederick Marshall, Jr., (Freddy) 309
Staunton, Galusha 323
Staunton, Henry Platt Brightwell 309
Staunton, Houncie 347
Staunton, Howard 321
Staunton, John Warren 32, 322
Staunton, Joseph Marshall xi, 32, 322, 358
Staunton, Katharine 195, 345
Staunton, Mary Elizabeth (or Elisabeth) xi, 32, 322, 325, 327, 358
Staunton, Sidney Augustus 309, 322, 327, 347
Staunton, Sidney S. 347, 348
Staunton, Thomas xi, 321
Steele, R.R. 206
Steelhammer, Pam 355
Stephens, Mrs. Elmer R. 80
Stinson, Tina 264, 272
Stone, Lucy 316
Stover, Delbert 231
Stover, Dink 283
Summerfield, Fred 142
Staunton, Susan Augusta 47
Sutton, Walt 159
Swann, F.R. 38
Swear, N.D. 327

T

Taft, William 36, 37
Thomas, Joseph 222
Thomas, Katharine Staunton 195
Thomas, Lewis Newton 31
Thomas, Nancy 317, 337
Thomas, Ruth 195
Thompson, A. Garnett 240
Thompson, Hannah 322
Thompson, Maria 23
Thompson, Robert 54
Tiffany, Louis 327
Toliver, Tom xii, 92, 114, 115, 256, 261, 354
Toren, Dick 316
Tracy, Dick 224
Truman, Harry 343
Twichell, Mrs. Charles 49

U

Underwood, Cecil 199, 202

V

Venderbeek, Rev. Bernard E. 54
Vintroux, Kendall 225

W

Walker, Charles xii, 127, 131
Wallace, George 367
Walls, Samantha 269
Ward, Charles Edwin 27
Ward, Charles Edwin (Ed) 27
Warne, H. Russ 27
Warren, George 38
Watson, Carrie 24
Welch, Ed 299
Westfall, Dr. Bedford 142
Westfall, Rick xii, 254, 270, 273, 354
White, I.C. 191
White, William A. 210
Wilber, Church 322
Wilber, Edward xi, 24, 27, 29, 30, 32, 46, 80, 208, 309
Wilber, Jr., Edward 29
Wilber, Mary Elizabeth xi, 32, 325
Wilber, Jr., Edward 29, 30
Wilken, Frank 316, 365
Wilkerson, Garland 141
William A. White xiii, 210, 211
Williams, Dewey xii, 68, 70, 73, 74, 84, 93, 94, 98, 112, 127, 128, 138, 159, 183, 213, 217, 231, 319
Wilson, Elizabeth Jill 31, 47, 281
Wilson, P.P. 141
Wilson, President Woodrow 37
Wolfe, Howard 54
Woodford, Rex 292, 293
Woodson, John xii, 17, 21, 22, 50, 62, 63, 65, 70, 74, 77, 78, 79, 85, 98, 312
Wrath, Clay 206

X

Y

Young, Houston 142
Young, Tommy 166

Z